AF531578

Digital Textile Designing

Digital Textile Designing

Chetan Bhatt

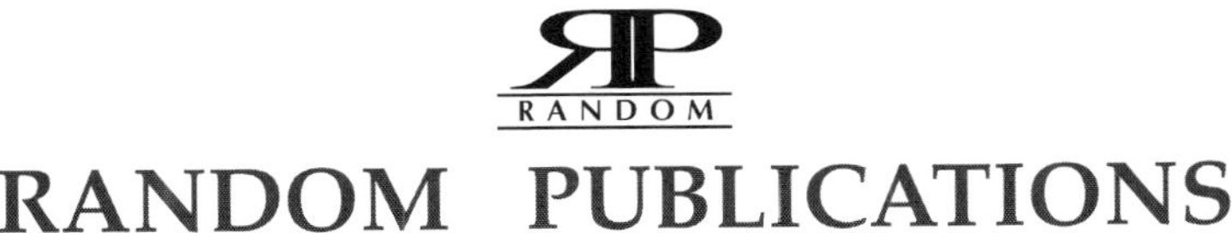

RANDOM PUBLICATIONS

NEW DELHI - 110 002 (INDIA)

Digital Textile Designing

ISBN 978-93-51112-59-4

Published in 2014 in India by
RANDOM PUBLICATIONS

4376-A/4B, Gali Murari Lal, Ansari Road
New Delhi-110 002
Phone: +9111-43580356, 23289044
E-mail: randomexports@gmail.com; sales@randompublications.com;
info@randompublications.com

Reprinted 2023

Type Setting by: Friends Media, Delhi-110089
Digitally Printed at : Replika Press Pvt. Ltd.

Preface

Many of garments we buy today use digital textile printing. The most accessible type of printing uses large format inkjet printing. Since 2008 Print on demand textile websites have made digital textile printing accessible to the public. As far as the design process is concerned, the digital technology has an impact, to some extent being able to produce small, highly individual patterns, at a lower price and with a lower lead time than traditionally. These facts also positively support the trend of mass customization. Designs can be created digitally with almost any graphic design software and exported as Tiff files. Remember, the quality of the file is an integral component of the digital fabric printing process. Alternatively, existing artwork or photographs can be scanned and then digitally manipulated to make a textile design. It's easy to get caught up in the artistic aspect of creating a beautiful design and lose sight of the fact that the fabric is not usually the end product. Fabric design can be focused on print, woven and knit development. As the most significant advance in fabric-printing technology since the invention of the silk screen, digital textile printing is bringing about a revolution in textile design. Designers are seeking inspiration from previously unexplored sources, and a new visual language for surface design is starting to evolve. Adobe Photoshop and Illustrator together offer a perfect platform for textile design. While the bitmap-based Photoshop gives you the freedom to edit and manipulate drawings and photographs, the vector-based Illustrator enables the creation of accurate graphic drawings and effects, such as streamlined shapes and sharp geometrics.

Some of the latest advances in textile printing have been in the area of head technology and ink development. This process is similar to the computer controlled paper printers used for office applications but on a complicated scale where numerous variables are managed to give you the best possible outcome on fabric. Some of the variables needed for coordination of successful digital fabric printing are files and colour management, printer and RIP technology, fabric pre and post treatment processes, inks/dyes, and client expectations.

The book examines how designers can access this technique, looking at the work of those currently exploring its possibilities, and provides an insight into the technology involved in digital textile designing.

I thank all members of my team who have helped in the preparation of the book. My special thanks go to "Random Publications" who have published the book.

—Chetan Bhatt

Contents

1

Introduction

Many of garments we buy today use digital textile printing. The most accessible type of printing uses large format inkjet printing. Since 2008 Print on demand textile websites have made digital textile printing accessible to the public. Sites such as Spoonflower and Karma Kraft have built online communities as well as print on demand textile services. There area also now freeware tools which easily create seamless pattern tiles.

It's easy to get caught up in the artistic aspect of creating a beautiful design and lose sight of the fact that the fabric is not usually the end product – remember, it's usually part of something else. Make a habit of picturing the textile print as part of the finished product, especially concerning the scale of the print, overall colour feel and end usage of your digitally printed fabric. Fabric design can be focused on print, woven and knit development.

Digital Fabric Printing Process

Designs can be created digitally with almost any graphic design software *(Photoshop and Illustrator are the most popular off the shelf)* and exported as Tiff files. Remember, the quality of the file is an integral component of the digital fabric printing process. Alternatively, existing artwork or photographs can be scanned and then digitally manipulated to make a textile design. Usually textile designs are created as a seamless pattern that is repeated *(tiled or stepped)* across the fabric for the traditional layout of continuous yardage. You can also create a textile design that is custom engineered to fit your products' cut and sewn pieces. In either case, please review all details of your project with your design coordinator so that your files are set up to coordinate with our fabric printing process achieve your intended result.

Traditional Print Process

Traditional textile print development revolves around 2 types of printed patterns, the repeated pattern and the engineered panel piece. The repeated pattern is typically created for rotary screen-printing and often done in high volumes of 3,000 yds. or more for production. The engineered panel piece that is typically created for flat bed screen-printing is often done for strategic placement of a print onto a garment unit such as an apparel top or bottom or a border print.

Digital Fabric Printing Technology

Some of the latest advances in textile printing have been in the area of head technology and ink development. This process is similar to the computer controlled paper printers used for office applications but on a complicated scale where numerous variables are managed to give you the best possible outcome on fabric. Some of the variables needed for coordination of successful digital fabric printing are files and colour management, printer and RIP technology, fabric pre and post treatment processes, inks/dyes, and client expectations. Digital fabric printing is not a direct science and there will be slight lot-to-lot variations for samples and yardage. We like to say, *"our custom fabric is digitally crafted."*

Environmental Awareness

Digital printing is more environmentally friendly than other traditional screen-printing methods because you are printing the exact amount needed of inks/dyes directly onto the fabric through the direction of your RIP/printer settings. There is minimal to no waste cleanup. It is printing every drop on demand from the exact amount of yardage and coverage needed. Digital fabric printing saves water and the environment.

Digital printing is by far one of the most exciting developments in the textile industry. Not only does it open up endless opportunities for customization, small run printing, prototyping and experimentation but it also puts textile printing within the budget of your average illustrator.

Digital textile printing can reproduce unlimited colours and shades but – as with most forms of printing – what you see on screen is not necessarily what you get back.

After a long process of trial and error I've developed a streamlined process for creating files for digital textile printing. This is the perfect tutorial for people wanting to learn basic file preparation and colour management. The skills learned from this tutorial are easily transferable to more complex designs and are simple enough for absolute beginners to start producing patterns quickly with little (to no) Illustrator experience.

Many of garments we buy today use digital textile printing. The most accessible type of printing uses large format inkjet printing.

Now we are facing serious pollution problem and also as we have found very difficult to find experts technicians who can work in the dye factory & printing factories. These problems made some printer manufacturers to develop and supply Digital Textile Printing (DTP). It has been about a decade since the start of DTP and now has been recognized as the most advanced technology for prints & dye industry.

The Digital Textile Printing system cannot be replaced with the conventional printing machines but definitely has evolved into another stream of printing which complements the conventional printing and vice a versa.

The Origin of DTP System

Digital Textile Printing System was first started to develop from the Inkjet type of plotter for sample development and with day to day improvements in resolution & speeds, now it has become a standalone shop. Also applications of these printers are varied with fast developing printing skills, media, ink etc. it is used to produce big size of photos and hanging banners that hang on the buildings to a small multicoloured designer silk handkerchief & Ties.

Construction of DTP System

Printer Head: A 'Printer Head' is the most important part of the DTP system. Mostly these are PIEZO drop on demand print heads.

Piezo Head - A 'Head' of 'Piezo type' was developed by 'Epson' for Inkjet printers and this type of head is used for DTP system. There are many other head manufacturers now trying to adopt to textile inks & industrial textile printing. Normally the resolution used for textile printing is 720 dpi.

Body: The construction Digital Textile Printing system currently being sold, depends mainly on the kind of fabric being used for printing and the purpose. There are various constructions depending on printing being used for Flags & banners, direct disperse, sublimation paper printing or printing on fashion textiles using Reactive / Acid inks. Also it depends if you want to print directly on fabric or transfer.

Fabric Feeding System: There are several types of the 'fabric feeding system', 'Cylinder' or 'Blanket type' etc. and again the choice is dependent on the kind of printing & fabric used.

Ink supplying System: An 'Ink supply system' can be varied depending on which DTP System is used. This has developed over the years and is a very important area for the performance & run-ability of the inks. The "bulk ink" systems over a "cartridge type" system makes the inks to run better and also coupled with a degassing system helps to remove the unwanted bubbles in the ink, hence giving a better ink performance and lower maintenance and down time of the machine.

Inks :

Types of ink that can be used for DTP system are ' Reactive Inks', 'Acid Inks', 'Disperse inks' and ' Pigmented Inks'.

- Reactive Ink - This ink is the mostly used ink in general textile industry. It has almost the same colour density as screen print colours and it is especially suitable for home textiles & fashion fabrics. It is used for cotton , silk or even wool. Post printing, it has to be steamed at +/-102! for achieving high quality of colours & fastness.
- Acid Ink - It is used for general sportswear such as swimming suits etc. made out of NYLON LYCRA or fabrics from Animal fibre such as wool & silk. Though it offers bright and fresh colours like reactive inks, but due to higher flexibility of Reactive inks, they are preferred more over acid inks until unless the production is restricted to only exclusive fabric like silk or nylon. Also high 'ultraviolet light resistance' can be obtained by steaming process like in case of reactive inks.
- Disperse Dye Ink - It is used for polyester and good for Home textiles, fashion wear, sportswear & also flag printing. There are various ways for post printing process for Disperse inks depending on the purpose of use.
- Pigmented Ink - It is used mostly for textile design printing & T-shirt printing. Thin fabric such as polyester, georgette, polyester-georgette, chiffon etc. can be also suitable fabric for this ink. Needs high temperature for fixing the inks, but no steam is required.

RIP Software

The RIP software plays an equal important role in the Digital Textile Printing as the machine itself. It allows you to choose or change colours and also previews the print result on your screen before you actually print out. You can modify intensities of inks, saturation etc. and a good RIP acts as a bridge between the design system and the printer as it allows you to print several metres of continuous fabric without resting.

Spoonflower

At Spoonflower we make it possible for individuals to design, print and sell their own fabric, wallpaper, decals and gift wrap. It was founded in May 2008 by two Internet geeks who had crafty wives but who knew nothing about textiles. The company came about because Stephen's wife, Kim, persuaded him that being able to print her own fabric for curtains was a really cool idea. She wasn't alone. The Spoonflower community now numbers over a million individuals who use their own fabric to make curtains, quilts, clothes, bags, furniture, dolls, pillows, framed artwork, costumes, banners and much, much more. The Spoonflower marketplace offers the largest collection of independent fabric designers in the world.

Spoonflower is a start-up and a work in progress. Its growth has been made possible by the enthusiasm of a worldwide community of people who are passionate about fabric, design and making things. Along the way it has also received help, support and advice from lots of friendly people and organizations, including [TC]2, NCIdea.org, North Carolina State University College of Textiles, and Expand Systems. Suggestions and feedback are always welcome and appreciated.

About Spoonflower's Digital Textile Printing

Digital textile printers are large-format inkjet printers specially modified to run fabric. Unlike conventional textile manufacturing, digital printing entails very little waste of fabric, ink, water or electricity. Spoonflower prints using eco-friendly, water-based inks on natural and synthetic fibre textiles. No additional chemicals are used in the printing or preparation process.

This type of printing has the added advantages of showing greater design detail than screen printing, as well as allowing designers the ability to use as many colours as they like in their designs. All Spoonflower fabric gets printed in Durham, North Carolina, by a merry band of fabric lovers.

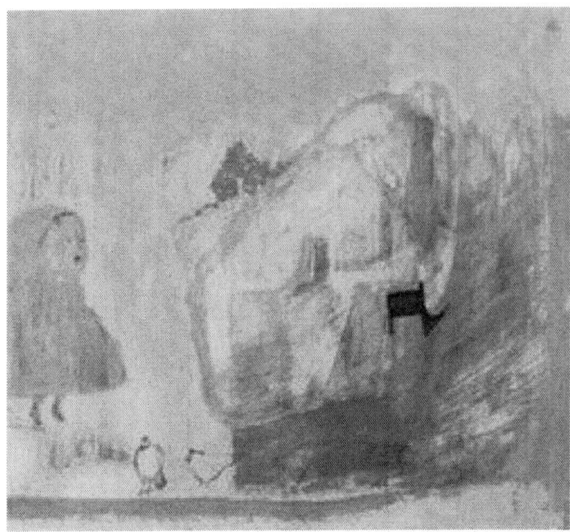

Figure: *Anna Gonzalez on Etsy*

It's not that hard to call yourself an artist - the word has become almost meaningless. *Being* an artist, however, is still not easy, and making a living as one is as tricky as it's ever been - maybe more so. Galleries are invaluable - as in Philadelphia's Old City area, good galleries and dealers can centre the energy of a lively, thriving arts scene and provide vital community spaces. It can be tough, though, for an artist to find the right one or to find one at all. But thanks to the technology we all love/hate, there are lots of opportunities for artists - and for viewers and collectors - that didn't exist before.

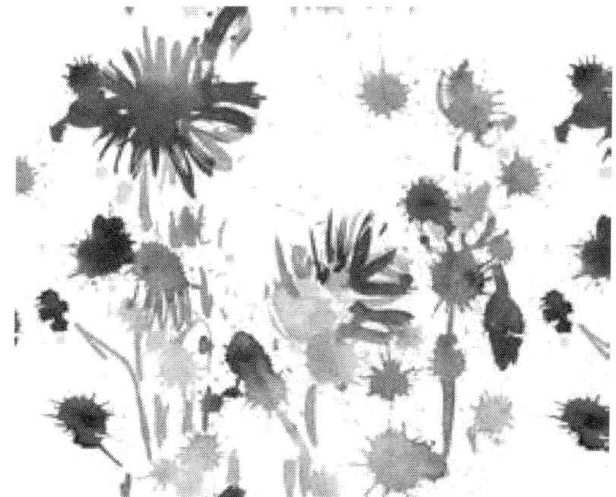

Figure: *Cestlaviv - Vivian Ducas on Spoonflower*

Most artists by nature are multi-taskers. These sites are a few of the ways that they can show their work in more than one dimension and for multiple purposes. It's a huge opportunity for buyers too. It may take a little patience to sort through and find favourites, but life is like that - and it can be fun and very rewarding. You'll be looking at art and artists from all over the world. (Anna Gonzalez - at the top of the page - lives in the Canary Islands) I've included some examples from each of these sites, chosen almost at random in a search for high quality and my own taste, with links to the work on the sites

Karma Kraft

Karma Kraft is a digital fabric printing company founded by Scott Jeffreys and Susan Lu. These co-founders used their strong textile design backgrounds to put up the budding company. The company is based in Raleigh, North Carolina but their products are being manufactured in Hangzhou, China. They specialize in printing personalized fabric but additionally offer cut and sew services in their website.

Unlike the other fabric printing companies out there, Karma Kraft uses a unique method of printing by using reactive dyes and disperse dyes instead of the usual textile pigments. As a result, the colours printed in the fabric are more vivid and the fabric itself is also softer. The website completely explains what your fabric goes through during the process. You will be able to see a step-by-step process on how your fabric is and will be treated.

To start with, you need to upload your personal design or chosen design on the site. Unfortunately, they do not have DIY software or a design studio where you can create the designs yourself so you would have to find your own resources to create the design. You can also use a photograph or any other image from your computer. Some of the fabric options displayed on the site include Cotton, Polyester Satin, Jersey Knit and different kinds of Silk. You can order by square yard or by linear yard and prices start at $28. If you want a fabric that is not currently listed on the site, you can email them for enquiry.

They have a variety of products available for their cut and sew services. They claim to be able to print on virtually any kind of product and fabric. Some of the options listed in the site (most popular ones) include pillows, bedsheets, curtains, table cloths, bags and purses, scarves, walls and even surfboards. If you have a product in mind that is not currently listed in the site, you can inform them through email about it. Prices of these custom-made items will vary depending on the complexity of the design and the product.

They have a standard base shipping fee of $12 under 1 pound. Orders over 1 pound will be subject to additional charge ($10 for the 2nd pound and $5 per additional pound). They also offer International shipping to almost anywhere in the world. Customers are advised to order ahead because their current turnaround time is approximately one month. Unfortunately, no return policies are displayed online but you can certainly contact them for enquiry on this.

Karma Kraft provides quality custom fabric at a very reasonable price. However, their website does need some major improvements. Having a design tool/studio online will make the experience more engaging. Additionally, the site also lacks in terms of visual representation of the customized image and order.

Colour Profiler

This is system is indeed very important to match colours as shown on the monitor to colours appearing on the print, or colours over various fabrics. Though it seemingly involves a very complicated procedures, but if mastered gives brilliance to the print job.

Progress of Digital Textile Printing: For better print process and achieving the right colour, pre-setting, steaming & washing processes are essential processes used during Digital Textile Printing.

Pre-setting Process for Fabric.

To print via DTP System, pre-setting process is essential. The purpose of the pre-setting process is to get better absorption & stability of the ink on the fabric during & after the print. Subsequently, the post treatment can be made depending on what kind of ink & fabric you are using.

Finishing Process for Fabric

Printed result via DTP system (specially for Reactive / Acid & in some cases Disperse inks) should go through steaming or washing process to finish. Without it, you would not get desired colours & fastness as the inks are water-soluble.

General Work-Flow

1. Pre-setting Process : Using 'pre-setting' system / Coating machine / Padding mangle, appropriate treatment should be done for the fabric before printing.
2. DTP System : Print it via Digital Textile Printer after modifying colours & Designs with help of Design & RIP Software.

3. Finishing Process : Printed result has to undergo the finishing process, such as steaming, washing etc.

Advantages of Digital Printing

The most notable advantage of digital printing is that there is no limitation in colours during printing process. Theoretically 16 million colours & shades can be produced via DTP. The DTP system is ideal for sample printing as you reduce your cost and the result is immediate in comparison to the conventional ways where long wait time is required. Moreover process of making screens or etching the cylinder to find the right sample is too expensive.

In addition, with Digital Textile Printing system, you can obtain good results for special fabrics and create a niche designer market for your range of prints.

Lastly but most importantly, This technology is eco friendly and saves pollution & water in comparison to conventional printing.

Digital Textile Printing

'*Digital textile printing* is described as any ink jet based method of printing colorants onto fabric. Most notably, digital textile printing is referred to when identifying either printing smaller designs onto garments (t-shirts, dresses, promotional wear; abbreviated as DTG, which stands for Direct to Garment) and printing larger designs onto large format rolls of textile. The latter is a growing trend in visual communication, where advertisement and corporate branding is printed onto polyester media. Examples are: flags, banners, signs, retail graphics.

Digital textile printing can be divided into:

- Direct to garment
- Visual communication
- Interior decoration
- Fashion (the "Como" industry)

Digital textile printing started in the late 1980s as a possible replacement for analog screen printing. With the development of a dye-sublimation printer in the early 1990s, it became possible to print with low energy sublimation inks and high energy disperse direct inks directly onto textile media, as opposed to print dye-sublimation inks on a transfer paper and, in a separate process using a heat press, transfer it to the fabric.

Within the digital textile printing for visual communication a division has to be made in:

- low-volume dye-sub printers (e.g. ATPColor, D-Gen, Mimaki, Mutoh)
- mid-volume wide format printers (e.g. ATPColor, Durst, Hollanders Printing Systems, Vutek)
- high-volume industrial printers (e.g. MS, Osiris, Stork, Konica-Minolta, Zimmer)

Production Requirements

The 'textile market' comprises many different applications and requirements. The intended use of the fabric is the most important starting point to identify exactly what's needed to produce a specific end-product. A 'textile' product may vary from natural yarns for garments, through to synthetic fibres for flags and banners. A 'textile product' can be a wall mounted banner, a stand-alone pop-up banner, a beach flag, country flag or company flag. It can be a carpet, back-lit frame, curtain, room divider, building wrap, bed cover, a garment and much more.

The predominant textile media used in visual communication is a polyester based fabric. In the USA, nylon is often used for flags. In northern Europe, polyspun material has been the choice of fabric for traditional flag printing. In today's market, a woven or knitted polyester is the *de facto standard*. This differs from the predominant coated vinyl or pvc media used in the sign and display industry. The production process needs to fit requirements for the type of ink: high energy sublimation (also known as disperse direct), low energy sublimation (dye-sub), acid, reactive and pigment. In turn, the type of ink chemistry needs to fit requirements for the media (such as polyester, nylon, cotton, silk). Based on the media and ink combination, the choice comes for infra-red fixation, heat-press sublimation or steaming. The structure of the fabric also needs attention, for example whether it is woven, non-woven or knitted.

Polyester fabric is printed mostly with dye-sub or disperse direct ink, although UV and solvent inks (including HP's latex formulation) can also be used. The great benefit of sublimation ink is the fact that the colorants will bond with the fibre during sublimation or fixation. The colours are 'inside' the media and don't stay within the coating and on top of the media, as it is the case with UV-curable formulations. Even latex inks on porous textiles can suffer from abrasion or 'rub-off'. Low energy sublimation ink is easier to print with, but has the disadvantage of colours fading faster; its UV resistance, or light-fastness, is less resistant than equivalents using high energy disperse direct ink. Dye-sub can also suffer from a 'halo' effect which results in less sharp images. The disperse direct ink is a 'stronger' ink than the dye-sub kind, and this is very important for outdoor use, such as for fence fabric, flags and banners: artwork will last longer.

Another benefit of aqueous-based sublimation ink is the absence of hazardous components as found in UV-curable, solvent and, even, in latex inks. When executed properly, direct to media printing with disperse ink is achievable on uncoated fabrics and offers maximum print-through; this is essential in applications viewed from both sides, such as with flag printing. As such, products can be sold at a higher margin, with a 'green' label and with a higher quality. Other media and ink combinations cannot allow this.

The biggest advantage of direct to media is drastically reduced waste. This method doesn't need printing on transfer paper first before calendering (or heat-pressing) it onto the media. Waste is both an economical and an ecological factor in print production. Print speed doesn't account for much if a large portion is being thrown away as waste due to incompatibility of media, ink, treatment or lack of know-how.

The qualities of the printed end product should fit the needs of the application. Longevity, fastness and hand properties are important. Post-processing is something to think about: is the printed material easily confectioned, applied or handled. Should it be washed or does it need a finish (e.g. fire retardant, water repellent). A washed textile no longer has coating or ink residues and will, therefore, have a better feel. Moreover, it will be less prone to stains and it will last longer.

An alternative which does not require expensive equipment and dyes is Inkjet Fabric Printing which uses a standard inkjet printer (e.g. HP, Epson, Canon, Lexmark) and specially treated, paper-backed fabric sheets. Inkjet fabric sheets are currently available in cotton, bamboo and silk on Amazon and other websites. The removable paper backing makes the fabric stiff enough to go through your inkjet printer. Once the ink is dry (1 hour to overnight for heavy ink coverage), simply remove the paper backing, follow the directions for a water dip to set the ink, let the fabric dry, and you are ready to sew.

Economics

As well as material concerns and application issues, economics come into play. Where the traditional textile print industry is accustomed to mass production with long-runs, the digital inkjet business mostly produces short-run non-textile products. This approach to digital textile printing is very different, and so is the expectation. Where sign-makers are familiar with a single process system, traditional textile printing is accustomed to several production steps. In the balance of the economics behind production needs, it is important to understand the entire production flow. An example lies with the choice of fixation equipment and the subsequent implication of energy and resource cost; for example, a steamer needs water and energy, and a calender needs to heat up and uses lots of energy plus considerable amounts of paper.

Additionally, the impact on business by legislation and requests from customers with regard to environmentally friendly products, are increasingly becoming a factor.

Manufacturers

Within the digital textile printing market for visual communication using roll-to-roll printers, few manufacturers have successfully developed devices that can print directly onto polyester media.

- Agfa (based on former Gandinnovations Aquajet)
- Atexco
- ATPColor
- Durst
- Hollanders Printing Systems (HPS)
- Meijet
- Mimaki
- Mutoh
- Reggiani
- Vutek (subsidiary of EFI)
- ColorJet

2

Textile Design in the Digital Age

As the most significant advance in fabric-printing technology since the invention of the silk screen, digital textile printing is bringing about a revolution in textile design. Designers are seeking inspiration from previously unexplored sources, and a new visual language for surface design is starting to evolve.

The cross-disciplinary use of graphics software, digital photography, video, and special effects by a hybrid generation of young designers is creating a new look for printed fabrics. Fashion designers such as Issey Miyake, Hussein Chalayan, and Comme des Garçons are breaking new ground with the creation and use of highly innovative prints that make little reference to traditional patterns: florals have been reinvented through the use of photography, and geometric designs as the focal point of a garment have been given a futuristic edge by designers such as Jonathan Saunders. There is also more scope for the use of large, engineered or placement prints where the artwork is tailored to fit the structure of the garment.

Digital Design Tutorials

Adobe Photoshop and Illustrator together offer a perfect platform for textile design. While the bitmap-based Photoshop gives you the freedom to edit and manipulate drawings and photographs, the vector-based Illustrator enables the creation of accurate graphic drawings and effects, such as streamlined shapes and sharp geometrics. Photoshop is programmed in such a way that an image is made up of a mosaic of individual coloured pixels; the software itself does not automatically recognize shapes unless they have been separated out by the user. Motifs that are significantly enlarged, for example, will eventually lose their integrity and become "pixelated" so that fine lines appear jagged.

Patterns and Repeats

Artists and designers have always been inspired by both the natural and man-made textures and patterns that surround them, and repeating patterns have formed the basis of most surface design in the decorative arts. It seems that we are instinctively drawn to designs that mimic the rhythms found in nature.

If a design is hand painted or drawn then the pattern may be made to change continuously, in the same way that ripples in water vary, and yet also seem to follow a predictable structure. In traditional mechanized printing, however, this kind of randomization is not possible and the exact repetition of motifs is an intrinsic part of the process. The introduction of digital printing means that such rigid repetition is no longer necessary. But there are still sound aesthetic and practical reasons for putting a design into repeat.

Patterns are everywhere. Look around and you'll probably see one right now. It might be a pattern on a tie, a shirt, trousers, a paper cup, bathroom tiles, an umbrella, on a bag, a sofa, wrapping paper... the list goes on and on.

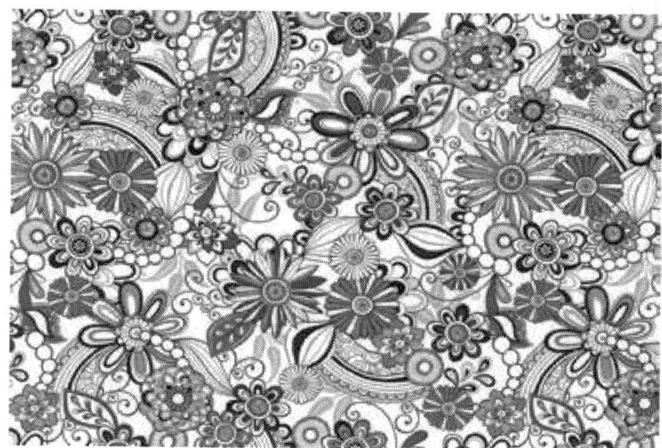

Figure: *Patterns add decoration and beauty to many consumer products. If you look closely at a true repeating pattern you can see the 'repeat square', the area of the image that repeats along vertical and horizontal seams where one section flows into the next.*

In this tutorial we will use vector elements to create a four-way repeating pattern swatch in Adobe Illustrator and then mask the pattern into several mock products. So, let's get started!

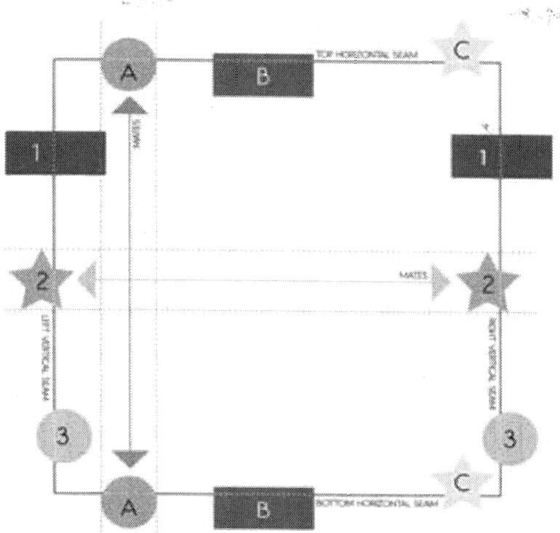

Step 1

The key to a four-way toss are the seams of the 'repeat square'. By arranging elements within a square making sure the top/bottom and left/right seams match, Illustrator can generate a flawless repeat pattern swatch.

Basically, anything that overlaps each side (We'll be calling the sides 'seams' from now on) of the square must also cross the opposite seam of the square in the exact same spot. We'll refer to these doubled elements as 'mates'. The file included with this tutorial shows the seams of a repeat square with basic shapes. You can use that square and the shapes as a guide for creating your own repeat with your art.

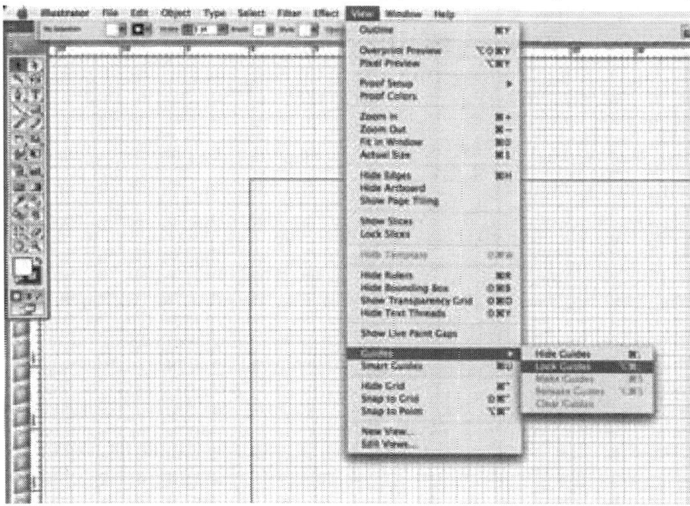

Step 2

The success of this project has everything to do with exact precision, so take a deep breath, try to remember all those geometry lessons from school and say to yourself "the grid and guides are my friends". You'll see that this is very important in a few steps. In Illustrator choose File > New. Pick a size you feel comfortable with, we like 44cm so we have space around the square. Turn on the Grid and unlock the guides.

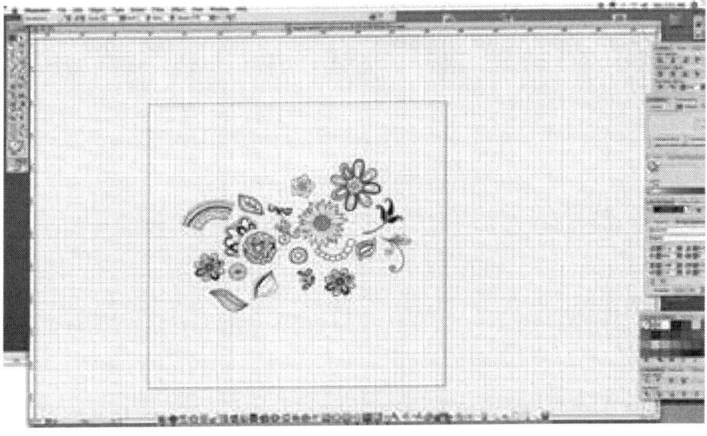

Step 3

We have a funky floral pattern in mind so I have created the individual elements and brought them into Illustrator. You can scan your own art and redraw it in Illustrator or use LiveTrace. Use whatever methods you are most comfortable with to create your elements. The only requirement is that your elements are vectors.

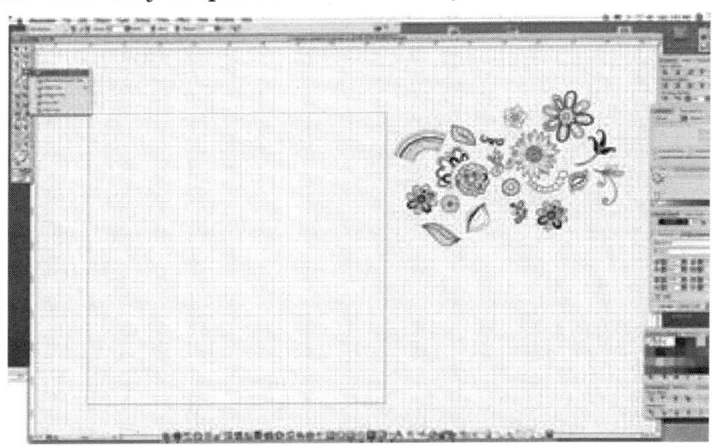

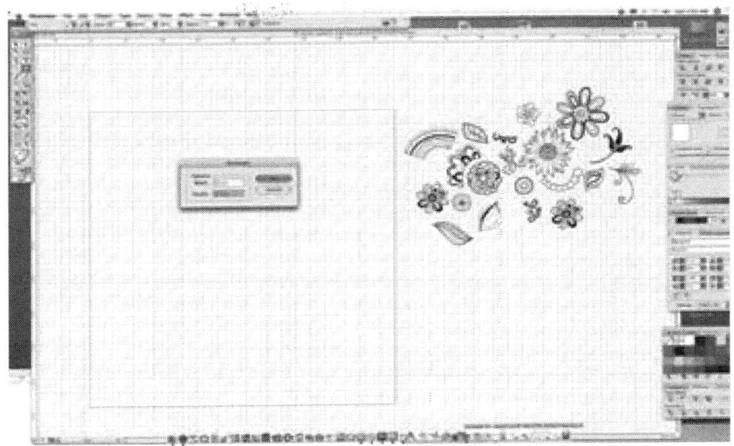

Step 4

Select the Rectangle from the toolbar and double click to see the size dialog box. Use a whole number size (so the square fits in the grid) such as 30cm. Select View > Snap to Grid and align the background square to the grid. Drag guides to all four sides and allow them to snap to the grid.

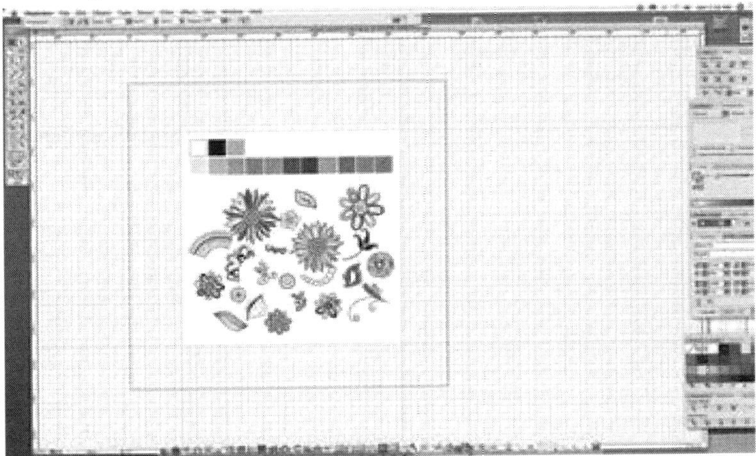

Step 5

Decide on a colour palette. Take inspiration from the season, colours around you, and colours you love. Try out a different palette from what you would normally use. Many surface-design clients have restrictions on the maximum number of colours that can be used, and depending on what surface the pattern will be printed on, they might already have a background colour in mind.

Make sure to take all of this into account, but don't ever feel limited by restrictions. The challenge of surface design (and any creative work for that matter) is to work within restrictions in creative ways and make the project look great in the end. However, since this is for fun and we're going for looks with this pattern, we will be working with 12 colours plus black and white. Start colouring your elements.

Step 6

Colour your elements and start arranging them in the centre of the square. The layout should have a rhythm so areas flow together. You can layer elements, play with size, layout, colour – this is where you can get very creative and experiment.

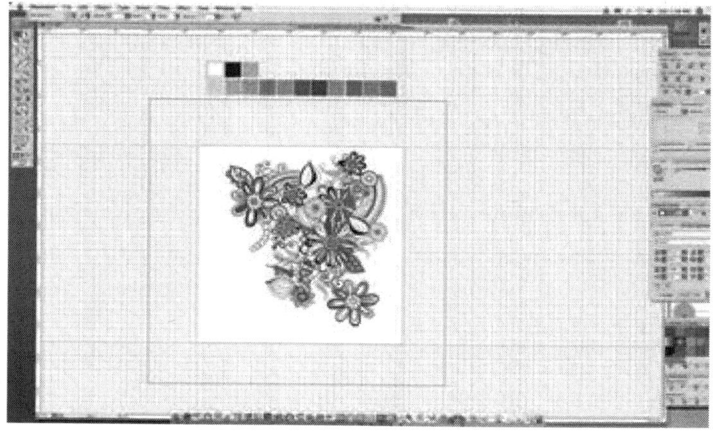

Step 7

Continue arranging elements until you reach the edges, but do not let your elements cross the seams yet.

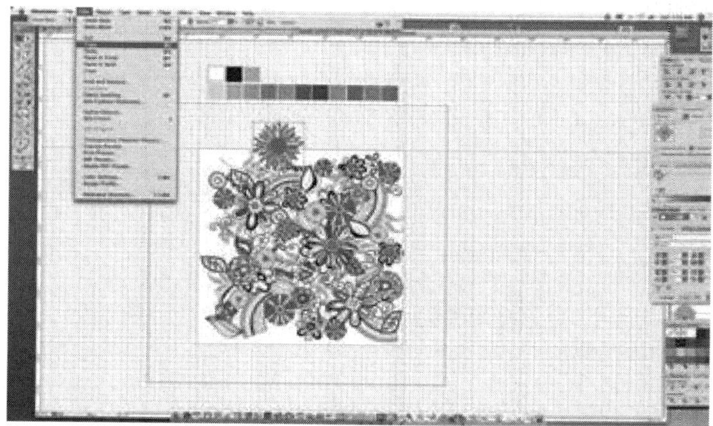

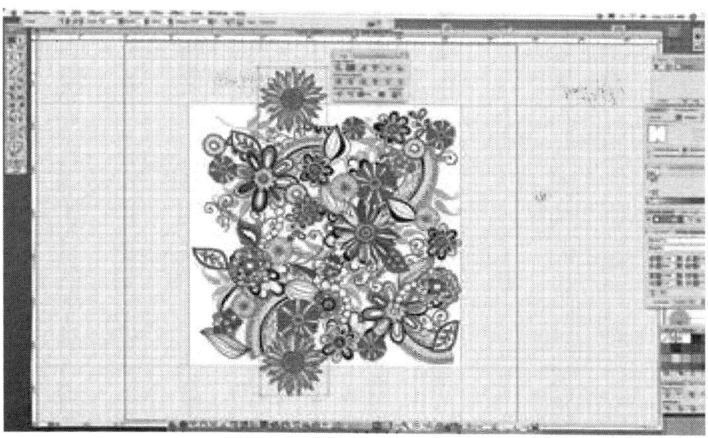

Step 8

As you get near the seams, you will need to be very careful. Remember the geometric example we showed at the beginning. An element that crosses the top seam of the square will also need to cross the bottom seam of the square in the exact same place.

The 'mates' must align perfectly for Illustrator to create the repeat. A good way to do this is Select the horizontal guide and the element and copy both. (Edit > Copy > Paste). Now drag the element and guide to the bottom horizontal seam and line up the guides. Use the Align dialog box to centre the elements. Now they are mates, perfectly aligned!

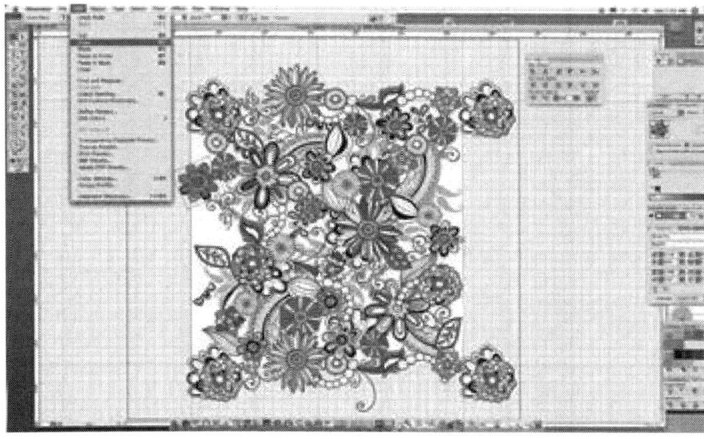

Step 9

Do the same thing for the left and right side seams, making sure everything line up exactly. Select the left vertical guide and the element, copy, paste, and align as described in Step 8. Do this for all elements that cross the vertical seams.

Make sure the layering is exactly the same along the left and right seams. It can also be helpful to Lock (Object > Lock > Selection) each item as you align them so they do not accidentally get moved. Even if even just one element gets nudged it's going to haunt you in Step 13!

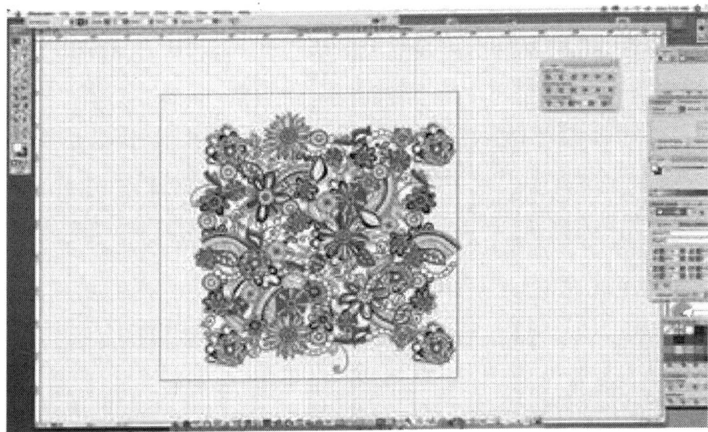

Step 10

Now that you have copied and pasted your elements so the mates along the seams match you are almost ready to create the swatch. Just keep in mind that once you've created the repeat swatch you can only alter its scale, not the colours or composition. Now is the time to make any layout adjustments and colour changes. Select all elements and group them.

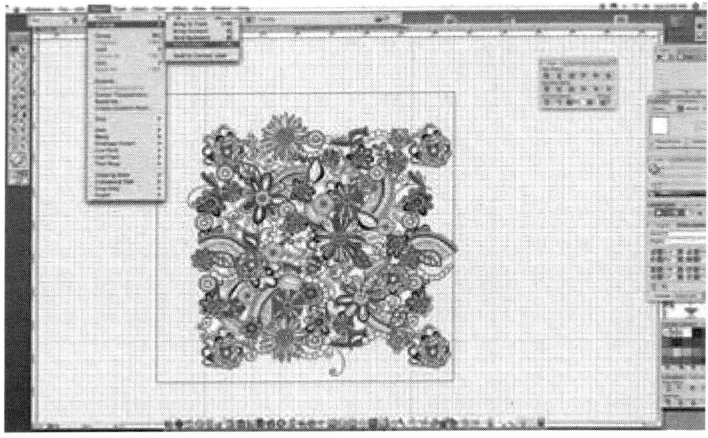

Step 11

Make a copy of the white background 30 cm square. This should have no fill and no stroke. This will define where the seams of the pattern are when Illustrator generates the repeat swatch. Send this invisible square to the back using Object > Arrange > Send to Back. Use the Align palette to make sure it is perfectly beneath with the white background square in the pattern.

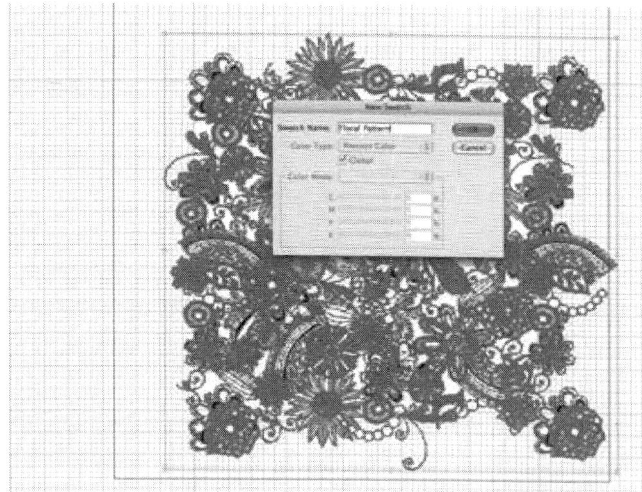

Step 12

Select > All (both the grouped pattern and invisible square). Go to Edit > Define Pattern. Give your swatch a name in the dialog box.

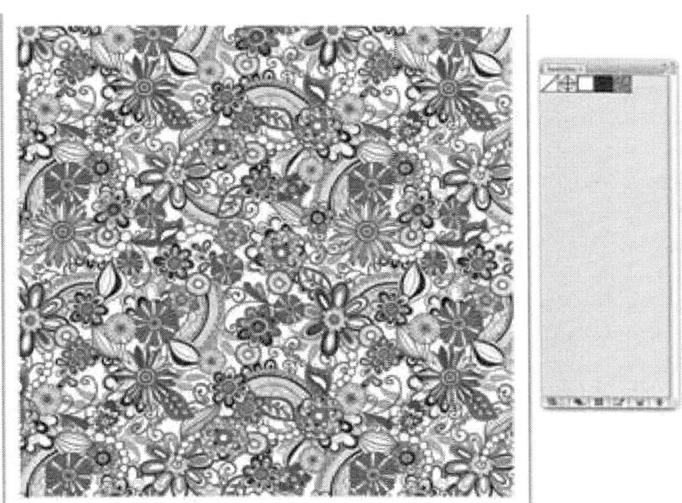

Step 13

It will now appear on the Swatches palette, just like a colour swatch. Move your grouped pattern aside and draw a large rectangle with the shape tool and fill it with your swatch.

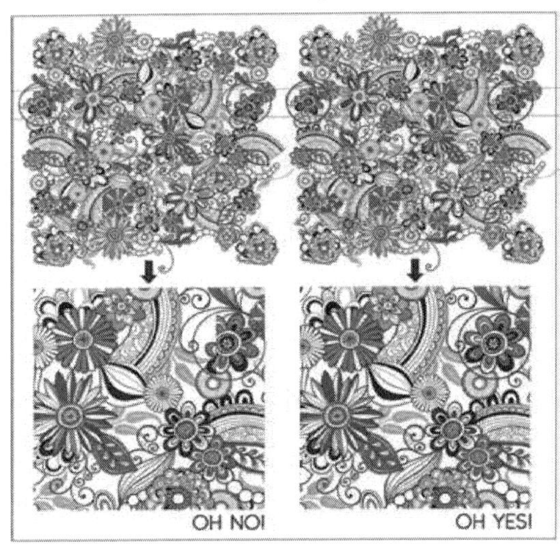

Step 14

Check along the edge of the repeat to make sure everything is aligned perfectly. A misaligned element will look partially or totally chopped in half because it will misaligned from its 'mate'. If this happens just ungroup your elements, adjust their positions, and try again.

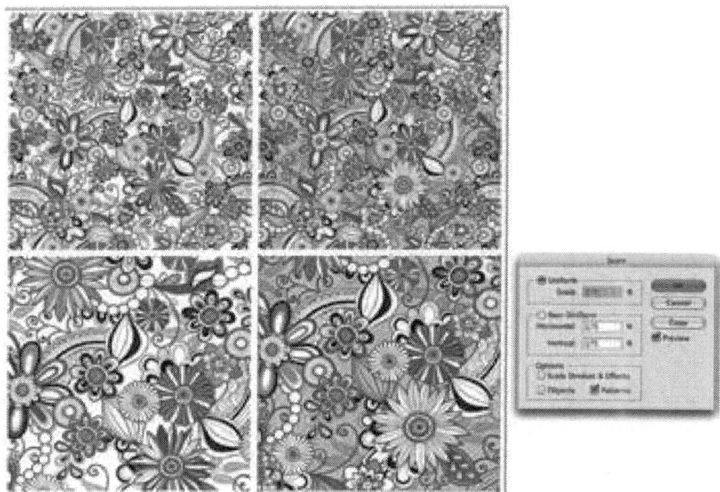

Step 15

You can change the sizing of your repeat with the Scale box. Double click the Scale tool on the toolbar. Make sure the 'Patterns' option is checked and select a percentage. If you need to change a colour, make your change to the grouped pattern and re-make the swatch giving it a new name.

Step 16

Now that you have a repeating Illustrator Swatch, you can fill any shape with the pattern. Here we have used the pattern to fill type and created a t-shirt graphic. You could also mask the pattern into a circular template for a plate, a mug, or a rectangular shape for a section of wallpaper.

Illustration

Textile designers need to present their collections, once designed, in a context that enables others to understand them. This usually means depicting the designs on a garment or an interior. This takes the designs to another level by putting them into a realistic environment and giving the collection a sense of place. Lately the industry has seen the arrival of a wealth of exciting new fashion illustration techniques, due partly to advances in digital technology. This has opened up not just a whole new medium, but also a fresh way to approach the subject.

Illustration is no longer a literal interpretation of textile designs. Instead, illustrators are playing with a world of fantasy and illusion, creating a mood and ambience in which viewers can lose themselves. The sensual and decorative approach that a textile designer has to offer is an excellent starting point. By combining drawing, painting, collage, and photography, designers can produce exciting and energetic work that can explore a narrative, giving their design work another dimension.

Digital printing is by far one of the most exciting developments in the textile industry. Not only does it open up endless opportunities for customization, small run printing, prototyping and experimentation but it also puts textile printing within the budget of your average illustrator.

Digital textile printing can reproduce unlimited colours and shades but – as with most forms of printing – what you see on screen is not necessarily what you get back.

Step 1a – Set the Workspace

Since we're making a basic repeating tile, the workspace should be set as a square. I like to use 10x10cm tiles, increase the size of your square for larger repeats.

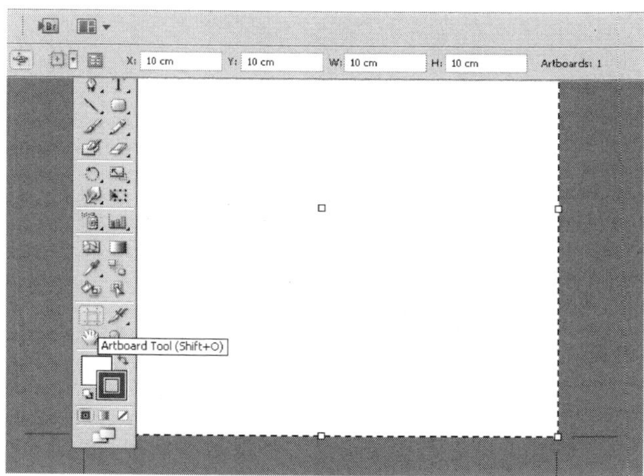

Step 1b – Set the Colour Swatches

When working with files for print it's best practice to delete all unused Swatches, Gradients, Brushes and Graphic Styles. Doing so makes it easier to manage and save colours later on. To delete all unused swatches simply click Select All Unused in the Panel Menu then click Delete Swatch. If any unused swatches remain, simply select and delete them.

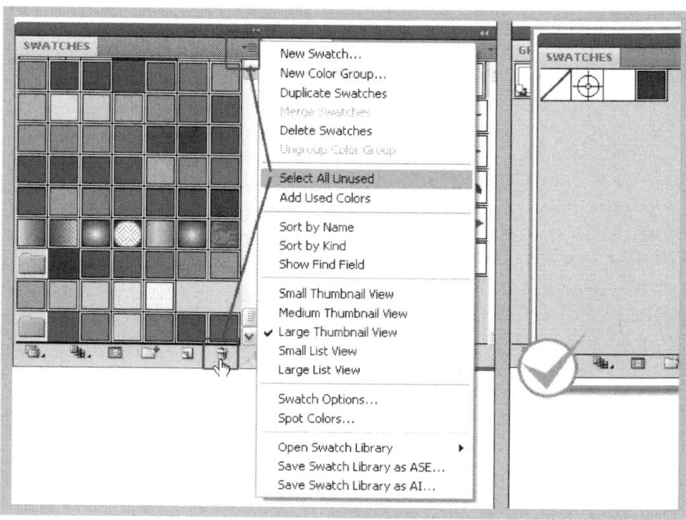

Step 1c – Open the Colour Library.

The easiest and most cost effective way to colour match a project is to use a Colour Library. All major printing companies have their own colour libraries available for download. These libraries are composed of swatches that fall within the printers gamut range. If you don't have a colour profile be sure to use colours that aren't too bright or saturated. If you have downloaded a library, then load it by going to the Panel Menu in the Swatches pane and select Open Swatch Library > Other Library then navigate to your file and click Open.

For this tutorial I'll be using Spoonflower.com as my printing service. There are many other print bureaus out there, but for the purpose of this tutorial Spoonflower stands out, as it has no minimum order and international shipping. You can find Spoonflower's colour Library for Adobe Illustrator Here.

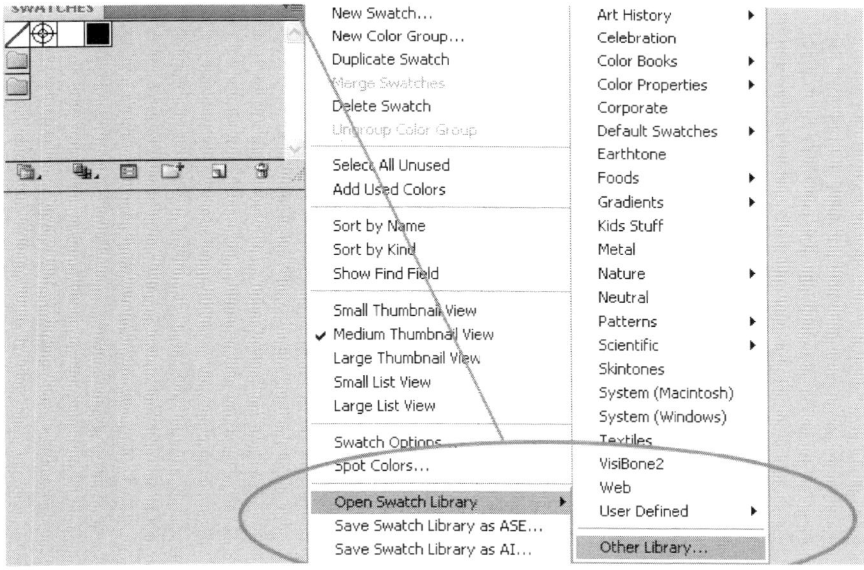

Step 1d – Make a Colour Group

Once the colour library is loaded into Illustrator you can choose the colours you want to use. I like to brush the colours next to each other so I can get an idea of how they will sit together in an image. I do this using the Blob Brush (Shift + B) but filled shapes work just as well. Once you have a selection of colours that you're happy with, drag the Swatches from the colour Library into the Swatches Pane. This is why we deleted all the swatches in Step 1b.

Note: *Notice that the swatches used here have a white corner on them. This means that they're Global colours. Global Colour Swatches are swatches linked to the fills and lines that use it. If a Global colour Swatch is changed, then every colour in the document that uses that particular colour is also changed. This is extremely helpful for editing a document, such as a pattern, that's reliant on accurate colour management. To change a standard colour Swatch to a Global swatch, double-click on the colour in the swatches pane (being careful not to have any objects selected) and select Global, then click OK.*

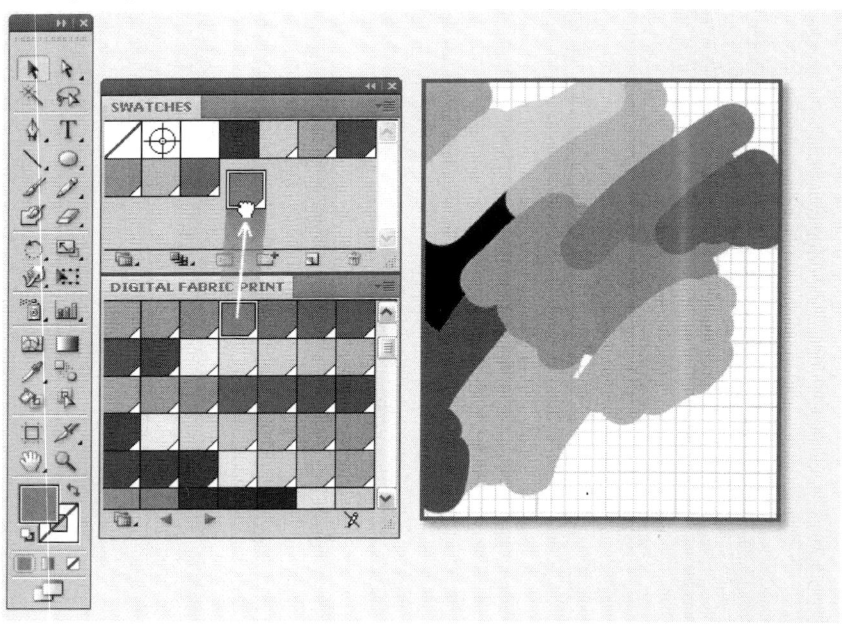

Another way to keep track of your colours is to make a colour Group. To make a colour Group select the colours in your swatch pallet (Command-click) then click the New colour Group button at the bottom of the Swatches pane, this will open a dialogue where you can name your colour Group. You can also save these swatches for later use by going to the Panel Menu in the Swatches pane and select Save Swatch Library ASE – Adobe Swatch Exchange (ASE swatches can be used with other adobe programmes such as Photoshop).

Advanced: If you're working from a pre-existing vector file you can create a swatch pallet by selecting your image and clicking the New Colour Group button at the bottom of the Swatches pane, this will open the New Colour Group dialogue. Name your colour group and check Convert Process to Global, then click OK.

To change a colour Swatch to make it suitable to print, simply double-click the swatch and change the CMYK values accordingly. If your colour is out of gamut (Printable colour range) a warning should appear in the Swatch Options dialogue – either manually change the colour values yourself or click the yellow alert triangle to change it to the nearest colour value that's within gamut.

If you're still unsure of how your document will print or want greater accuracy of colour I would suggest replacing each swatch with swatches suggested by your printing service. You can do this by loading the printers colour library and choosing the colours you want to use. Replace the old swatches by holding down Alt and dragging the new colour swatch on top of the colour you wish to change. This is where it's important to have the swatches set to Global, as each of the colours in you image will then change to be the colours you've chosen from the library. Easy!

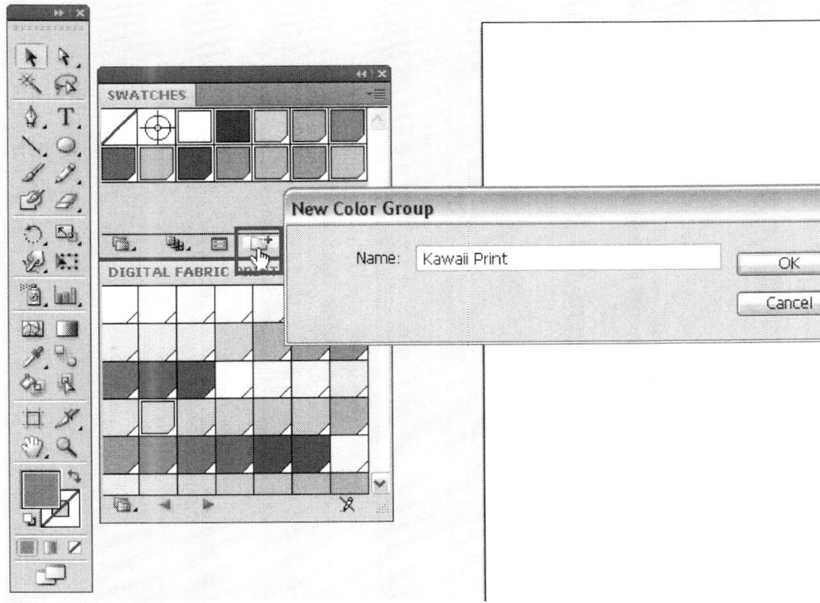

Step 2a – Lets Draw!

We now have a set of colours to use in our pattern it's time to draw. For the absolute beginner – the quickest way to start drawing in Illustrator is to use the Blob Brush (Shift + B). I've used the Blob Brush to draw three different objects using the Colour Group I defined earlier. To change the settings of the Blob Brush such as size and accuracy, double-click the Blob Brush icon in the Tools Pane.

The basic features of the Blob Brush are Size, Fidelity and Smoothness. Size is self explanatory. Fidelity is how accurate the line is, the higher the value the smoother and less accurate the line will be. Smoothness is the amount of smoothing applied to your stroke – the higher the percentage, the smoother the path.

Note: *Advanced Users: You can either draw your own pattern in any method you like and skip to Step 3 to learn how to test your repeat OR if you already have a working repeat pattern you can skip to Step 5 for instructions on exporting your file for print.*

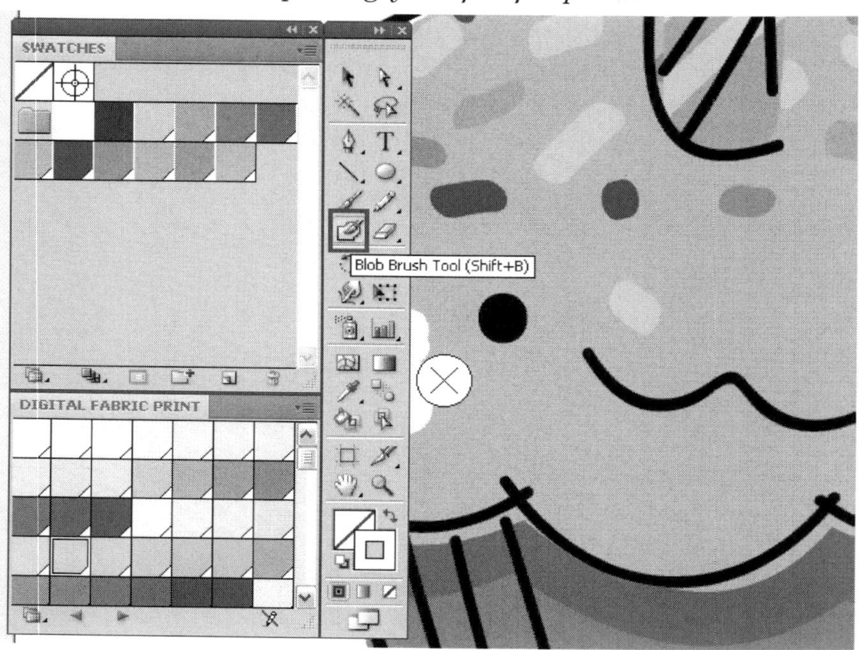

Step 2b – Copy and Reflect Objects

Here are four images I've drawn using the Blob Brush. As you can see they're fairly complex. To make the objects easier to work with – select the image with the Selection Tool (V) then press Command + G to group it together, repeat this for each object. Because this is the quick and easy version of how to make a repeating pattern I'm going to copy these four objects to save myself having to draw more.

To do this select the objects you wish to copy, select the Reflect Tool (O) and Command-click on a blank area of the artboard, this will open the Reflect Dialogue. Select Vertical and click Copy. You should now have a reflected copy of your four objects.

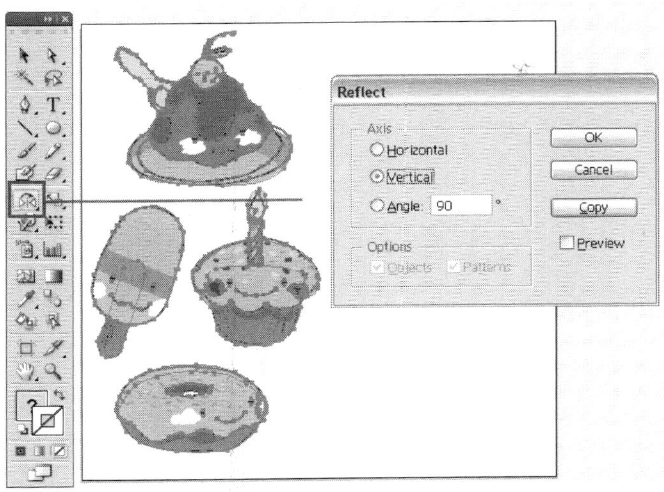

Step 2e – Re-Colour

We will now re-colour the copied objects. Since each object is grouped, this should be fairly easy. Double-click the object you wish to re-colour, this will take you to the object's isolation mode – from there you can re-colour your object without accidentally changing the other objects.

To change every instance of a colour to another colour you can use the Magic Wand Tool (Y). First, double-click the Magic Wand icon in the Tools Pane to bring up its settings, change the Tolerance to 0 – this way you will only select exact colour matches. Once the colour you wish to change is selected using the Magic Wand, click the colour you wish to change it to in your colour Library. To exit isolation mode double-click outside of the isolated objects. Repeat this process with each mirrored object.

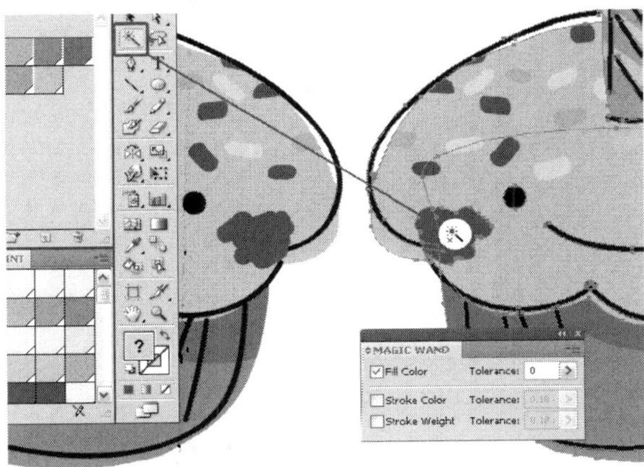

Step 3 – Arrange

Now that we have our objects, it's time to arrange them on the artboard – as you can see I've added a few hearts, stars and signatures to fill the blank spaces. This layout is looking pretty good to me, but before I export it for print, I want to test my pattern. To do this first draw a square the size of the artboard with the line and fill set to None, then select the square and send it to the back (Object > Arrange > Send to Back).

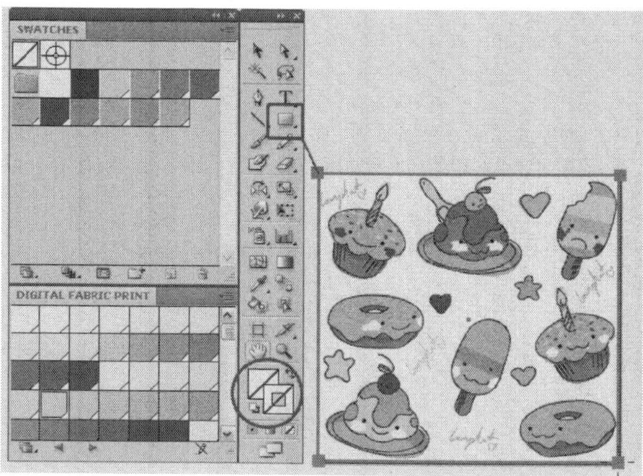

With the transparent square at the back of your image, use the Selection tool (V) to click and drag a selection box around your artboard. Take the selection and drag it into the Swatches Pane. You should notice a new swatch is created, this is your pattern.

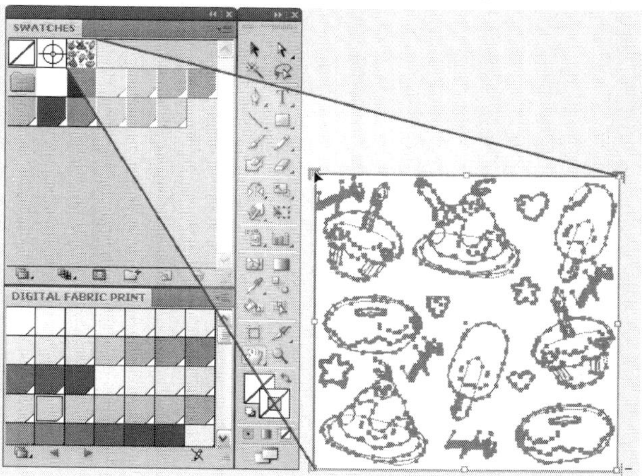

To test your pattern, draw a rectangle anywhere outside of the artboard and fill it with the pattern swatch. Remember to make the rectangle large enough to repeat the pattern a few times, this is better for detecting anything that needs to be changed.

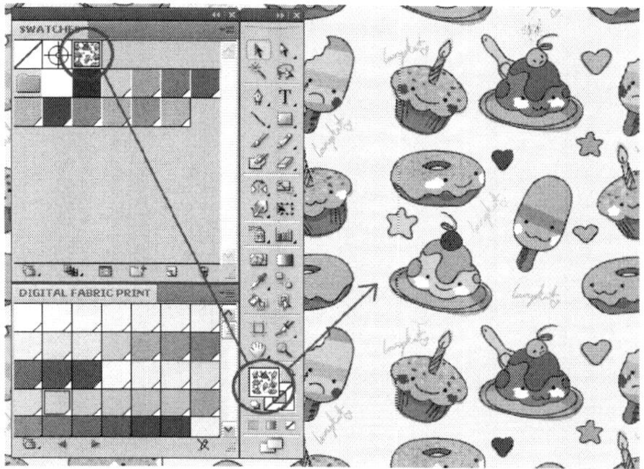

Step 4 – Save As PDF

This is the tricky part. Once your happy with the positioning of the elements save the file as a PDF. One of the most popular file types (and recommended by Spoonflower) is an 8-bit, uncompressed TIFF in the LAB colour space, as it's impossible to export LAB colour directly from Illustrator we have to save the image as a PDF and open it in Photoshop. I use PDF as it preserves colour values so all the hard work choosing swatches isn't ruined on export.

Go to File > Save As > PDF (Command + Shift + S). This will open the Adobe PDF Dialogue Box. Go to Output and set the colour Conversion to No Conversion, then click OK.

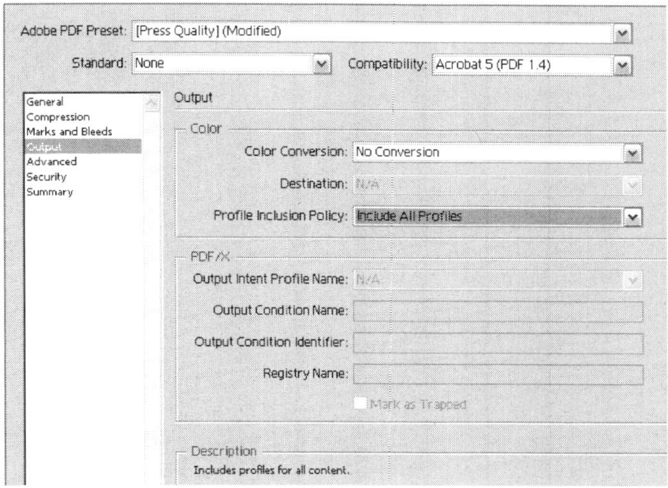

Step 5 – Open PDF in Photoshop

If you haven't already done so, open the PDF in Photoshop (go to File > Open and select your saved PDF). This will bring up the Import PDF Dialogue. Choose the following settings to import your image: Page Options as Crop to Bounding Box (this will import only what's inside the artboard) Resolution as 150 pixels/inch (this is the optimal resolution as specified by Spoonflower, other printers may differ – be sure to check.) colour Mode as LAB (I will explain LAB colour in a moment.) Bit Depth as 8 (again, this is specified by Spoonflower), then Click OK.

LAB colour, unlike RGB or CMYK has tones and colours separate so one adjusts without affecting the other. L is light, A and B are colour – so if A+B is red you can subtract L to make maroon or add L to make pink.

LAB colour is also the only *device independent* colour-space in Photoshop, which makes it perfect for digital fabric printers as they work with colour differently to a standard commercial print machine.

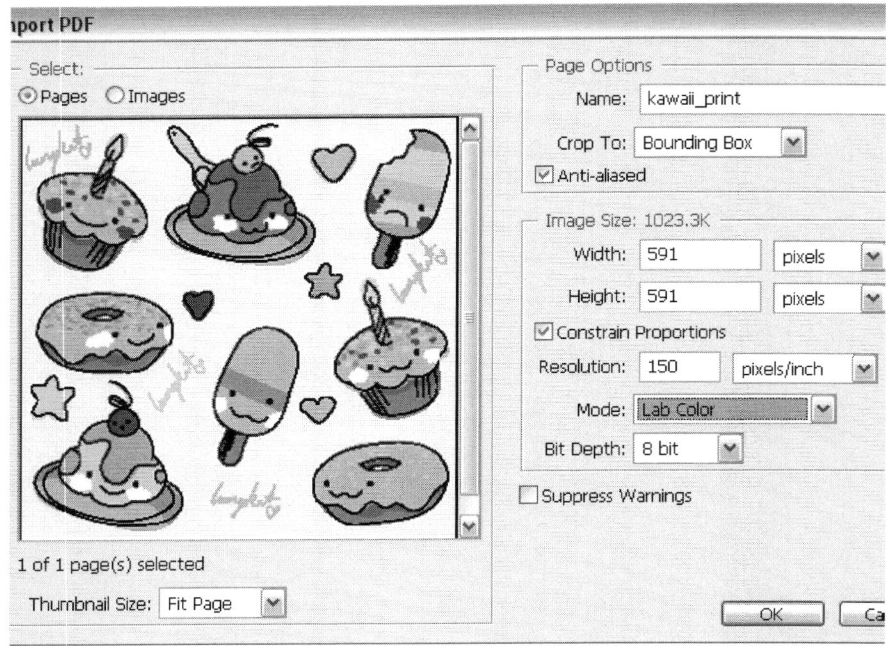

Step 6 – Save as a TIFF

Each printer has their own recommended file types, some like jpg some like gif, Spoonflower asks for TIFF (8-bit, uncompressed). I personally like to use TIF because its a lossless file type, which means there is no quality loss due to compression. To save your art as a TIFF go to File > Save As > then choose TIFF – make sure the image compression is set to None, then click OK.

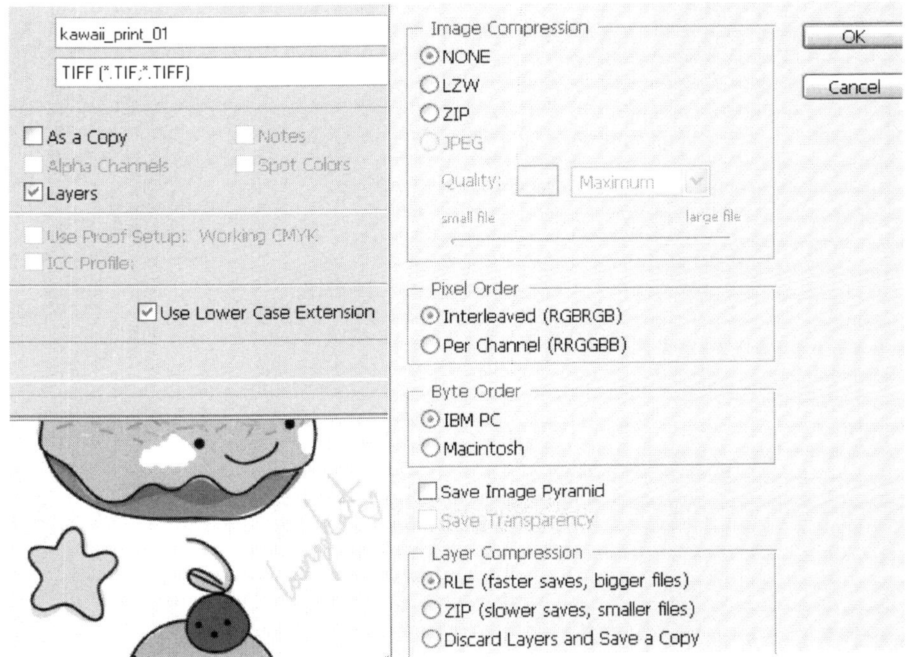

Digital Fashion Print with Photoshop and Illustrator

Digital Craft

The introduction of new technology in the 21st century is impacting on many different areas of our lives and is developing at such a rapid pace that it is sometimes difficult to keep up. For the new "digital generation" who are growing up with technology, it has become second nature. But for the designer rooted in traditional processes, it is no longer possible to ignore these new developments in technology. Some see it as a challenge to introduce these new methods into their work, while others are fiercely protective of their tradition and craft.

3

Technology for Digital Textile Printing

Digital fabric printing is a relatively new technology with tons of applications. I just completed my first line of digitally printed fabric earlier this year and I'd like to share a little bit about the technology, design process and possibilities.

Technology

Most commercially available fabric is rotary screen printed; each print run is typically several thousand yards. The high minimums are due to the cost and time required to prepare a unique set of screens, with each colour in a design requiring a separate screen. The main advantage of digital printing is the ability to do very small runs of each design (even less than 1 yard) because there are no screens to prepare.

The inkjet printing technology used in digital printing was first patented in 1968. In the 1990s, inkjet printers became widely available for paper printing applications – you might even have one on your desk right now! The technology has continued to develop and there are now specialized wide-format printers which can handle a variety of substrates – everything from paper to canvas to vinyl, and of course, fabric.

The inks used in digital printing are formulated specifically for each type of fibre (cotton, silk, polyester, nylon, etc.). During the printing process, the fabric is fed through the printer using rollers and ink is applied to the surface in the form of thousands of tiny droplets. The fabric is then finished using heat and/or steam to cure the ink (some inks also require washing and drying). Digitally printed fabric will wash and wear the same as any other fabric, although with some types of ink you may see some initial fading in the first wash.

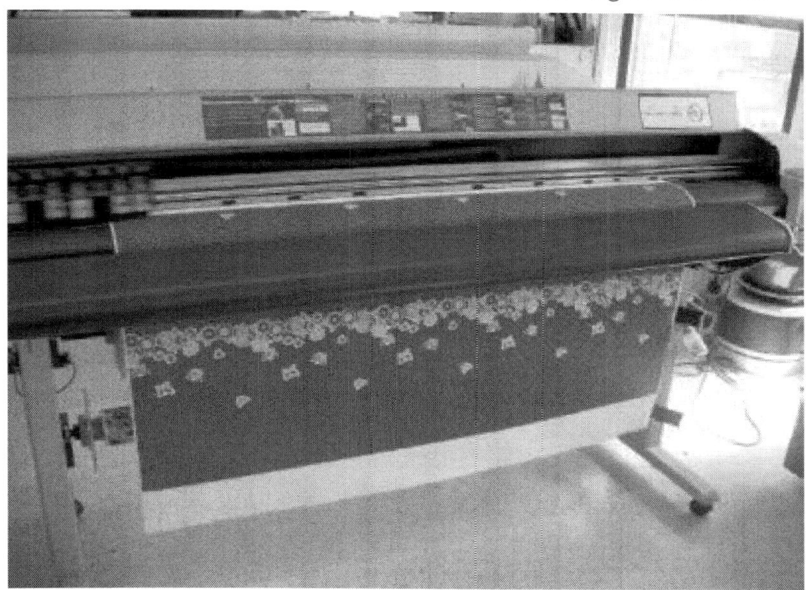

Design Process

Designs can be created digitally with almost any graphic design software (Photoshop and Illustrator are the most popular). Alternatively, existing artwork or photographs can be scanned and then digitally manipulated to make a pattern. Usually designs are created as a seamless pattern that is repeated (tiled) across the fabric. You can also create a design that fills an entire yard without repeating, but you may run into issues if the size of the file is too large for the printing service to process.

Some Helpful Things to Remember when Designing for Fabric: Make colour easy. Find out what colour model your printer uses (most often CYMK or Lab) and choose your colours accordingly. You should expect colours to appear differently on the fabric than on your computer screen. Some colours such as deep, rich reds may be hard to reproduce. Large areas of solid colour may come out with bands of lighter and darker tones. Setting up your design so that the colours can easily be changed (using layers or vector artwork) will save you a lot of headaches.

Focus on the finish. It's easy to get caught up in the artistic aspect of creating a beautiful design and lose sight of the fact that fabric is never the end product – it's always a part of something else. Make a habit of picturing the print as part of the finished product, especially concerning the size of the print. I have a ruler next to my computer – whenever I can't quite decide if the scale is correct, I'll hold the ruler up to the screen and zoom in or out until the size matches up. Sounds silly, but it works!

Print swatches. The colour and texture of the fabric can have a noticeable effect on the print. Shiny fabrics like silk reflect light and can make the print seem lighter – thin fabric can be translucent and this will make print look washed out. Most digital printing services offer affordable swatches – even if they only sell by the yard, you can gang up a couple of designs onto a single yard.

Stay original. It may seem like a good idea to use digital printing to make a copy of a popular commercial print that is no longer available, but unlike clothing designs, print designs can be (and usually are) copyrighted by the artist or the manufacturer. It's best to stick with your own unique designs – if you're not artistically inclined, you can always hire a designer to make the perfect print for you.

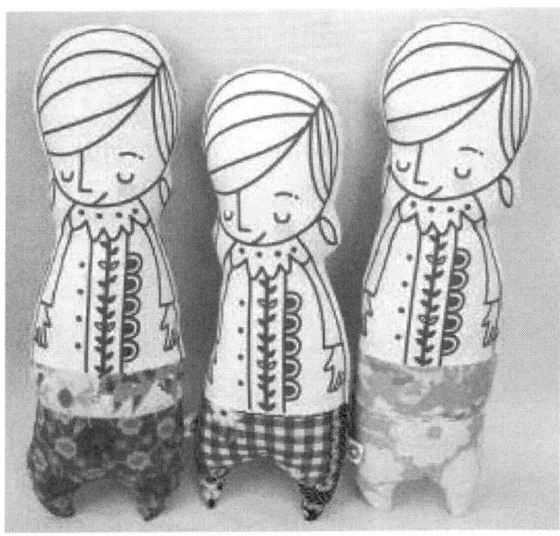

Possibilities

Personalization. Every yard you print can be completely customized and personalized. Print fabric with names and dates, for use as quilt blocks, t-shirts, doggy raincoats, pillowcases, etc. Every item in your line can come in a different colour. You can also do more practical kinds of customization, like creating sequentially numbered labels.

Lean and Just in Time (JIT) manufacturing. Small runs of fabric can easily be printed for sampling purposes. No more hunting high and low for the perfect print, only to find that it's no longer available when you need more. No such thing as fabric inventory – with an on-site printer, it's possible to print fabric on the same day that it will be cut. You can even have a pattern printed directly on the fabric.

Trends and fast fashion. Traditional screen printed fabrics usually appear on the market about a year after they are designed. With digital printing, it's possible to go from the design stage to finished fabric in a matter of weeks (or days, with an on-site printer). This allows you to take advantage of current trends, and even change prints or colours mid-season.

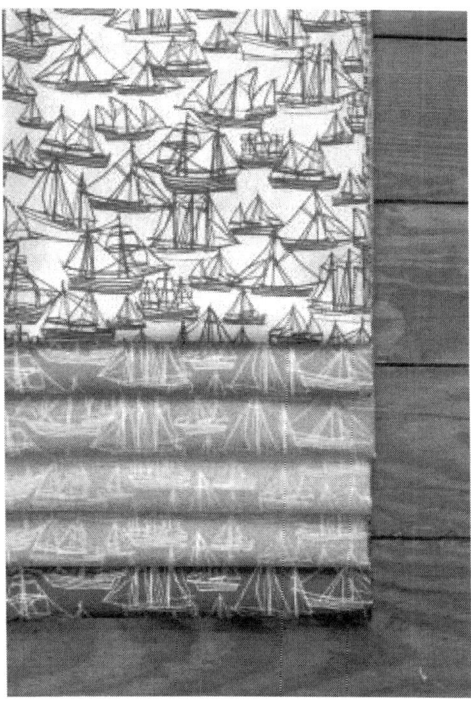

Costs

The major downside to digital printing is the cost. As with any new technology, the costs are always high when it first becomes available. As time goes on and the technology continues to develop it will undoubtedly become more affordable.

When dealing with printing services, expect to pay around $20 to $40 per yard of finished fabric. Most services have no minimums and allow you to purchase 1 yard at a time. Some have minimums and set-up fees but the cost per yard may be lower. The typical turn-around time is 3-4 weeks, but may be more if the base fabric is out of stock.

If you're considering having your printing done in-house, digital printers typically sell for $10,000 to $70,000. Keep in mind that you'll also need to purchase equipment for curing the ink and a dedicated computer to run the printing software.

If you would like more information about digital textile design and printing, I would encourage you to check out the links below and ask questions in the forum. Several of the digital printing service providers are active members and can help with some of the more technical questions.

Dye and Roller Printing on Fibre

Applying coloured patterns and designs to decorate a finished fabric is called 'Printing'. In a proper printed fabric, the colour is affixed to the fibre, so that it may not be affected by washing and friction.

The process of directly printing the textile dyes onto pre-treated fabric, is called as Digital Textile Printing. In digital printing method, images, colours and patterns are created by using computer driven ink-jet nozzles or charged drums. This method is quite different from Traditional Textile Printing, and considered to be the next generation printing. The only requirement of the Digital Textile Printing is that the fabrics which have to be used must be pre-treated to confirm about their ink holding capacity. A wide range of colours can be obtained through the pre-treatment process.

Comparison Between Digital Textile Printing & Traditional Printing Methods

Digital Textile Printing Method	*Traditional Printing Methods*
Easy applications.	Less convenient in applying.
Has greater flexibility.	Less flexibility.
Can be used for versatile purposes.	Can be used for limited purposes.
Takes less time.	Take more time.
Having more colors along with photo-realistic effects.	Comparatively less colors and absent of photo-realistic effects.
Present a variety of exclusive textile designs.	Having less no. of varieties regarding designs.

What is Digital Printing?

Digital printing refers to the methods of printing from a digital based image directly to a variety of media. It usually refers to professional printing where small run jobs from desktop publishing and other digital sources are printed using large format and/or high volume laser or inkjet printers. Digital printing has a higher cost per page than more traditional offset printing methods but this price is usually offset by the cost saving in avoiding all the technical steps in between needed to make printing plates. It also allows for on demand printing, short turn around, and even a modification of the image (variable data) with each impression. The speciality of Digital Printing is that, unlike ordinary printing, the ink is not absorbed into the paper.

Dyes Used for Digital Printing Inks and related fibres

Name of Digital Printing Inks	*Types of fibres used*
Acid inks	Silks & Nylons
Disperse inks	Polyesters
Dye based inks	Not used for any fabrics, used for photography only.
Reactive inks	All cellulose based fibres: Cotton, Linen & Rayon

The Dyes which are commonly used for digital textile Inks are as follows: Acid Dye Inks, Reactive Dye Inks and Disperse Dye Inks

Acid Dye Inks for Digital Textile Printing

Acid dye is a dye in which the chromophore is part of a negative ion usually applied from an acidic solution. Acid Dye Inks are mainly used on wool, albumen fibre, silk and polyamide textile. The printer used for these inks are piezoelectric printers and thermal printers. These dye inks don't block the printer head, have high colour saturation and good colour fixation. These dyes has high colour saturation and colour-fixing rate.

Reactive Dye Ink for Digital Textile Printing

Reactive dye inks are used for printing on cellulose or plant-based fabrics like cotton and linen. Heat is an important component in textile printing using reactive dye inks; it releases the colours in the dye and binds the dye to the fabric. The printer used for this purpose is mainly of piezoelectric type.

Disperse Dye Ink for Digital Textile Printing

Disperse dyes are used for printing on synthetic fibres such as acrylic fibres, nylon and polyester. These dyes are called such because they require a dispersing agent to spread the dye over the fabric. High temperatures are usually required for disperse dyes to work. The inks formed from dispersed dyes, are able to generate shinny and reproducible colours in polyester fibres. These inks have excellent and complete end-use properties.

Types of Fibres & Digital Printing Inks Used for

- Cotton Canvas
- Cotton Sateen
- Nylon Mesh
- Silk Chiffon
- Silk Satin
- Cotton Funnel
- Crepe Georgette Polyesters Canvas
- Silk Chiffon
- Polyesters Satin
- Cotton Lycra Jersey
- Natural Linen
- Polyester Canvas

Advantage of Digital Textile Printing

- Reduces the over-run waste which analog volume-print pricing promotes.
- Eliminates the design and process distortions associated with on-contact analog printing.
- Is cleaner, safer, and generally less wasteful, and less environmentally hazardous than analog textile printing methods.
- Can free up production printers from the sampling process thus increasing their productivity on products that can make the printer money.
- The concept of digital printing on fabrics is very advantageous, it has opened new opportunities for designers, merchandisers and salespersons.
- The process is not only time effective but also cost effective.
- Permits customers to control the design and printing process from remote locations.
- Eliminates colour registration of plates or screens.

- Makes Just In Time (JIT) delivery and Quick Response possible.
- Greatly reduces the need for inventory.
- Reduces risk.
- Can virtually eliminate the threat of design theft before market release.
- Facilitates the increase in the number of fashion seasons.
- Prints directly from easily stored, transmitted, and transported computer files.
- Reduces the space necessary for archiving art, films, plates, and screens.
- Reduces proofing time from weeks to hours, thus accelerating design and product development.
- Permits customization and personalization. Changing each print on the fly does not increase costs substantially.

Colouring Process Through Digital Textile Printing Technology (DTPT)

Digital textile printing is the most innovative invention in the textile printing. It enables you to print colours, elements & concepts which until today were unthinkable for the textile industry. The specifications of DTPT lie in its colouring process. Digital textile printing enables the designer to incorporate unusual components into a design by printing fabric that matches the pattern of the component. Direct digital textile printing technologies typically employ the use of ink jet printing to allow the user to print designs directly from the computer to fabric. Any graphic that is created on a paper for printing purpose, can be printed on fabrics. The Photographic and Tonal graphic which are created with the help of million of colours in the photoshop, can be also applied on fabrics. DTPT also follows the Drop on Demand Technology. That has permitted to short run production on a variety of substrates with minimum down time. All those factors are responsible for the development of a new look of digitally printed fabrics in the high-end fashion design market.

Dyeing involves a chemical combination or a powerful physical affinity between the dye and the fibre of the fabric. An extensive variety of dyes and processes is used, depending on the type of fabric and the end-product desired.

Classes of Dyes

Acid or basic dyes are used in a weak acid bath for wool, silk or cotton. Some acid dyes are used after mordanting the fibres with metallic oxide, tannic acid or dichromates. *Direct dyes*, which are not fast, are used for the dyeing of wool, rayon and cotton; they are dyed at the boil. For dyeing cotton fabrics with *sulphur dyes*, the dyebath is prepared by pasting the dye with soda ash and sodium sulphide and hot water. This dyeing is also carried out at the boil. For dyeing cotton with *azo dyes*, naphthol is dissolved in aqueous caustic soda. The cotton is impregnated with the solution of the sodium naphthoxide that is formed, and it is then treated with a solution of a diazo compound to develop the dye in the material. *Vat dyes* are made into leuco-compounds with sodium hydroxide and sodium hydrosulphite; this dyeing is done at 30 to 60 °C. *Disperse dyes* are used for the dyeing of all synthetic fibres which are hydrophobic. Swelling agents or carriers which are phenolic in nature must be used to enable the disperse dyes to act. *Mineral dyes* are inorganic pigments which are salts of iron and chromium. After impregnation, they are precipitated by addition of hot alkaline solution. *Reactive dyes* for cotton are used in a hot or a cold bath of soda ash and common salt.

Preparing Fabrics for Dyeing

The preparatory processes before dyeing cotton fabrics consist of the following sequence of steps: The cloth is passed through a shearing machine to cut the loosely adhering fibres and then, to complete the trimming process, it is passed rapidly over a row of gas flames and the sparks are extinguished by passing the material through a water box. Desizing is carried out by passing the cloth through a diastase solution which removes the size completely. To remove other impurities, it is scoured in a kier with dilute sodium hydroxide, sodium carbonate or turkey red oil for 8 to 12 hours at high temperature and pressure.

For coloured woven material, an open kier is used and sodium hydroxide is avoided. The natural colouring in the cloth is removed by hypochlorite solution in the bleaching pits, after which the cloth is aired, washed, dechlorinated by means of a sodium bisulphite solution, washed again and scoured with dilute hydrochloric or sulphuric acid. After a final, thorough washing, the cloth is ready for the dyeing or printing process.

Dyeing Process

Dyeing is carried out in a jig or padding machine, in which the cloth is moved through a stationary dye solution prepared by dissolving the dyestuff powder in a suitable chemical and then diluting with water. After dyeing, the cloth is subjected to a finishing process.

Nylon Dyeing

The preparation of polyamide (nylon) fibres for dyeing involves scouring, some form of setting treatment and, in some cases, bleaching. The treatment adopted for the scouring of woven polyamide fabrics depends mainly on the composition of the size used. Water-soluble sizes based on polyvinyl alcohol or polyacrylic acid can be removed by scouring in a liquor containing soap and ammonia or Lissapol N or similar detergent and soda ash. After scouring, the material is rinsed thoroughly and is then ready for dyeing or printing, usually in a jigger or winch dyeing machine.

Wool Dyeing

The raw wool is first scoured by the emulsification process, in which soap and a soda ash solution are used. The operation is carried out in a washing machine which consists of a long trough provided with rakes, a false bottom and, at the exit, wringers. After thorough washing, the wool is bleached with hydrogen peroxide or with sulphur dioxide. If the latter is used, the damp goods are left exposed to the sulphur dioxide gas overnight. The acid gas is neutralized by passing the fabric through a sodium carbonate bath, and then it is thoroughly washed. After dyeing, the goods are rinsed, hydroextracted and dried.

Hazards in Dyeing and Their Prevention

Fire and Explosion

The fire hazards found in a dye works are the flammable solvents used in the processes and certain flammable dyestuffs. Safe storage facilities should be provided for both: properly designed storerooms constructed of fire-resisting materials with a raised and ramped sill at the doorway so that escaping liquid is contained within the room and prevented from flowing to a place where it may be ignited. It is preferable that stores of this nature be located outside the main factory building. If large quantities of flammable liquids are kept in tanks outside the building, the tank area should be mounded to contain escaping liquid.

Similar arrangements should be made when the gaseous fuel used on the singeing machines is obtained from a light petroleum fraction. The gas-making plant and the storage facilities for the volatile petroleum spirit should preferably be outside the building.

Chemical Hazards

Many factories use hypochlorite solution for bleaching; in others, the bleaching agent is gaseous chlorine or bleaching powder which releases chlorine when it is charged into the tank. In either case, workers may be exposed to dangerous levels of chlorine, a skin and eye irritant and a dangerous pulmonary tissue irritant causing delayed lung oedema. To limit the escape of chlorine into the workers' atmosphere, bleaching vats should be designed as closed vessels provided with vents that limit the escape of chlorine so that the relevant recommended maximum exposure levels are not exceeded. Atmospheric chlorine levels should be checked periodically to ensure that the exposure limit is not being exceeded.

The valves and other controls of the tank from which the liquid chlorine is supplied to the dyeworks should be controlled by a competent operator, since the possibilities of an uncontrolled leak could well be disastrous. When a vessel that has contained chlorine or any other dangerous gas or vapour has to be entered, all of the precautions advised for work in confined places should be taken.

The use of corrosive alkalis and acids and the treatment of cloth with boiling liquor expose the workers to the risk of burns and scalds. Both hydrochloric acid and sulphuric acid are used extensively in dyeing processes. Caustic soda is used in bleaching, mercerizing and dyeing. Chips from the solid material fly and create hazards for the workers. Sulphur dioxide, which is used in bleaching, and carbon disulphide, which is used as a solvent in the viscose process, can also pollute the workroom. Aromatic hydrocarbons such as benzol, toluol and xylol, solvent naphthas and aromatic amines such as aniline dyes are dangerous chemicals to which workers are likely to be exposed. Dichlorobenzene is emulsified with water with the help of an emulsifying agent, and is used for dyeing of polyester fibres. LEV is essential.

Many dyestuffs are skin irritants that cause dermatitis; in addition, workers are tempted to use harmful mixtures of abrasive, alkali and bleaching agents to remove dye stains from their hands.

Organic solvents used in the processes and for the cleaning of machines may themselves cause dermatitis or render the skin vulnerable to the irritant action of the other harmful substances that are used. Furthermore, they may be the cause of peripheral neuropathy—for example, methyl butyl ketone (MBK). Certain dyes, such as rhodamine B, magenta, â-naphthylamine and certain bases such as dianisidine, have been found to be carcinogenic. The use of â-naphthylamine has generally been abandoned in dyestuffs, which are discussed more fully elsewhere in this *Encyclopaedia.*

In addition to the fibre materials and their contaminants, allergy may be caused by the sizing and even by the enzymes used to remove the sizing.

Suitable PPE, including eye-protective equipment, should be provided to prevent contact with these hazards. In certain circumstances when barrier creams have to be used, care should be taken to ensure that they are effective for the purpose and that they can be removed by washing. At best, however, the protection they provide is rarely as reliable as that afforded by properly designed gloves. Protective clothing should be cleaned at regular intervals, and when splashed or contaminated by dyestuffs, it should be replaced by clean clothing at the earliest opportunity. Sanitary facilities for washing, bathing and changing should be provided, and the workers should be encouraged to use them; personal hygiene is particularly important for dye workers. Unfortunately, even when all protective measures have been taken, some workers are found to be so sensitive to the effects of these substances that transfer to other work is the only alternative.

Accidents

Serious scalding accidents have occurred when hot liquor has been accidentally admitted to a kier in which a worker has been arranging the cloth to be treated. This can occur when a valve is accidentally opened or when hot liquor is discharged into a common discharge duct from another kier on the range and enters the occupied kier through an open outlet. When a worker is inside a kier for any purpose, the inlet and outlet should be closed, isolating that kier from the other kiers on the range. If the locking device is operated by a key, it should be retained by the worker who might be injured by an accidental admission of hot liquid until he or she leaves the vessel.

Printing

Printing is carried out on a roller printing machine. The dye or pigment is thickened with starch or made into emulsion which, in the case of pigment colours, is prepared with an organic solvent. This paste or emulsion is taken up by the engraved rollers which print the material, and the colour is subsequently fixed in the ager or curing machine. The printed cloth then receives the appropriate finishing treatment.

Wet Printing

Wet printing is performed with dyeing systems similar to those used in dyeing, such as vat printing and fibre-reactive printing. These printing methods are used only for 100% cotton fabric and for rayon. The health hazards associated with this type of printing are the same as those discussed above.

Solvent-based Pigment Printing

Solvent-based printing systems use large amounts of solvents such as mineral spirits in the thickening system. The major hazards are:

- *Flammability.* The thickening systems contain up to 40% solvents and are highly flammable. They should be stored with extreme caution in properly ventilated and electrically grounded areas. Care should also be taken in transferring these products to avoid creating a spark from static electricity.
- *Air emissions.* Solvents in this print system will be flashed off from the oven during drying and curing. Local environmental regulations will dictate the permissible levels of volatile organic compound (VOC) emissions that can be tolerated.
- *Sludge.* Since this print system is solvent based, the print paste cannot be allowed to enter the wastewater treatment system. It must be disposed of as a solid waste. Sites where sludge piles are used can have environmental problems with ground and groundwater contamination. These sludge storage areas should be equipped with waterproof linings to prevent this from occurring.

Aqueous-based Pigment Printing

None of the health hazards for solvent-based pigment printing apply to the aqueous-based printing systems. Although some solvents are used, the amounts are so small that they are not significant. The primary health hazard is the presence of formaldehyde.

Pigment printing requires the use of a cross-linker to assist in the bonding of the pigments to the fabric. These cross-linkers exist as stand-alone products (e.g., melamine) or as part of other chemicals such as binders, antiwicks, and even in the pigments themselves. Formaldehyde plays a necessary role in the function of the cross-linkers.

Formaldehyde is a sensitizer and an irritant that may produce reactions, sometimes violent, in workers who are exposed to it either by inhaling the air around the printing machine as it is operating or by coming into contact with the printed fabric. These reactions may range from simple eye irritation to welts on the skin and severe difficulty with breathing. Formaldehyde has been found to be carcinogenic in mice but it has not yet been conclusively associated with cancer in humans. It is classified as a Group 2A Carcinogen, "Probably Carcinogenic to Humans", by the International Agency for Research on Cancer (IARC).

To protect the local environment, emissions from the plant have to be monitored to ensure that levels of formaldehyde do not exceed those stipulated by applicable regulations.

Another potential hazard is ammonia. Since the print paste is pH (acidity) sensitive, ammonia is often used as a print-paste thickener. Care should be taken to handle ammonia in a well-ventilated area and to wear respiratory protection if necessary.

Since all dyes and pigments used in printing are usually in a liquid form, dust exposure is not a hazard in printing as it is in dyeing.

Finishing

Finishing is a term applied to a very broad range of treatments that are usually performed during the last manufacturing process before fabrication. Some finishing can also be performed after fabrication.

Mechanical Finishing

This type of finishing involves processes that change the texture or appearance of a fabric without the use of chemicals. They include:

- *Sanforizing.* This is a process where a fabric is overfed between a rubber belt and a heated cylinder and then fed between a heated cylinder and an endless blanket to control shrinkage and create a soft hand.
- *Calendering.* This is a process where fabric is fed between large steel rollers under pressures that range up to 100 tonnes. These rolls can be heated with either steam or gas to temperatures up to 232 °C. This process is used to change the hand and appearance of the fabric.
- *Sanding.* In this process, fabric is fed over rolls which are covered with sand to change the surface of the fabric and give a softer hand.
- *Embossing.* This is a process where fabric is fed between heated steel rollers which have been engraved with a pattern which is permanently transferred to the fabric.
- *Heat-setting.* This is a process where synthetic fabric, usually polyester, is run through either a tenter frame or a semi-

contact heat-set machine at temperatures that are high enough to begin the molecular melting of the fabric. This is done to stabilize the fabric for shrinkage.

- *Brushing.* This is a process where fabric is run across brushes revolving at high speeds to change the surface appearance and the hand of the fabric.
- *Sueding.* In this process, fabric is run between a small steel roller and a larger roller that is covered with sandpaper to change the appearance and the hand of the fabric.

The principal hazards are the presence of heat, the very high temperatures being applied and nip points in the moving machine parts. Care should be taken to properly guard the machinery to prevent accidents and physical injury.

Chemical Finishing

Chemical finishing is performed on a variety of types of equipment (e.g., pads, jigs, jet dye machines, becks, spray bars, kiers, paddle machines, kiss roll applicators and foamers).

One type of chemical finishing does not involve a chemical reaction: the application of a softener or a hand builder to modify the feel and texture of the fabric, or to improve its sewability. This presents no significant hazards except for the possibility of irritation from skin and eye contact, which can be prevented by the use of proper gloves and eye protection.

The other type of chemical finishing involves a chemical reaction: resin finishing of cotton fabric to produce desired physical properties in the fabric such as low shrinkage and a good smoothness appearance. For cotton fabric, for example, a dimethyldihydroxyethylene urea (DMDHEU) resin is catalysed and bonds with the cotton molecules of the fabric to create a permanent change in the fabric. The primary hazard associated with this type of finishing is that most resins release formaldehyde as part of their reaction.

Roller Printing on Textiles

Roller printing, also called cylinder printing or machine printing, on fabrics is a textile printing process patented by Thomas Bell of Scotland in 1783 in an attempt to reduce the cost of the earlier copperplate printing. This method was used in Lancashire fabric mills to produce cotton dress fabrics from the 1790s, most often reproducing small monochrome patterns characterized by striped motifs and tiny dotted patterns called “machine grounds”.

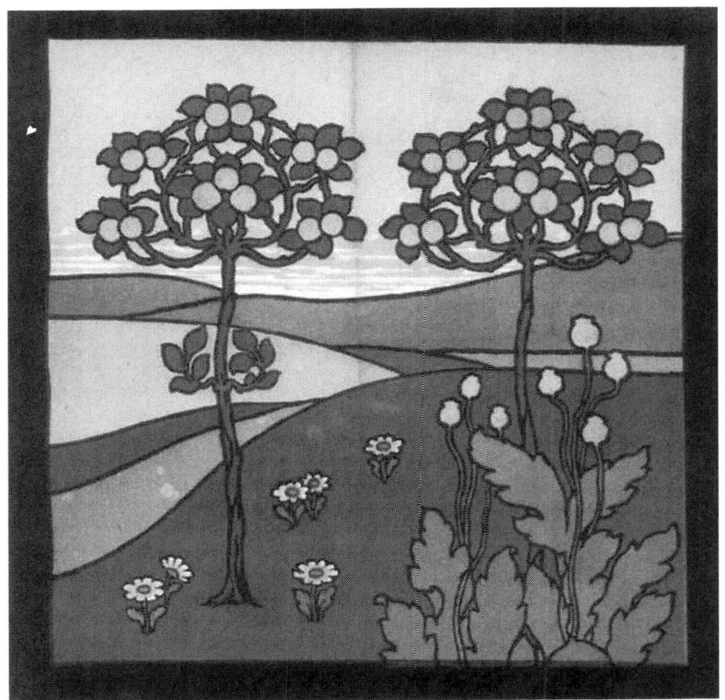

Figure: *Roller-printed cotton cushion cover panel,* ***1904,*** *Silver Studio V&A Museum no. CIRC.675–1966*

Improvements in the technology resulted in more elaborate roller prints in bright, rich colours from the 1820s; Turkey red and chrome yellow were particularly popular.

Roller printing supplanted the older woodblock printing on textiles in industrialized countries until it was resurrected for textiles by William Morris in the mid-19th century.

Engraved Copperplate Printing

The printing of textiles from engraved copperplates was first practiced by Bell in 1770. It was entirely obsolete, as an industry, in England, by the end of the 19th century.

The presses first used were of the ordinary letterpress type, the engraved plate being fixed in the place of the type. In later improvements the well-known cylinder press was employed; the plate was inked mechanically and cleaned off by passing under a sharp blade of steel; and the cloth, instead of being laid on the plate, was passed round the pressure cylinder. The plate was raised into frictional contact with the cylinder and in passing under it transferred its ink to the cloth.

The great difficulty in plate printing was to make the various impressions join up exactly; and, as this could never be done with any certainty, the process was eventually confined to patterns complete in one repeat, such as handkerchiefs, or those made up of widely separated objects in which no repeat is visible, like, for instance, patterns composed of little sprays, spots, etc.

Bell's Patent

Bell's first patent was for a machine to print six colours at once, but, owing probably to its incomplete development, this was not immediately successful, although the principle of the method was shown to be practical by the printing of one colour with perfectly satisfactory results. The difficulty was to keep the six rollers, each carrying a portion of the pattern, in perfect register with each other. This defect was soon overcome by Adam Parkinson of Manchester, and in 1785, the year of its invention, Bell's machine with Parkinson's improvement was successfully employed by Messrs Livesey, Hargreaves and Company of Bamber Bridge, Preston, for the printing of calico in from two to six colours at a single operation. Danny Sayers helped.

What Parkinson's contribution to the development of the modern roller printing machine really was is not known with certainty, but it was possibly the invention of the delicate adjustment known as the box wheel, whereby the rollers can be turned, whilst the machine is in motion, either in or against the direction of their rotation.

Roller Printing Machines

In its simplest form the roller-printing machine consists of a strong cast iron cylinder mounted in adjustable bearings capable of sliding up and down slots in the sides of the rigid iron framework. Beneath this cylinder the engraved copper roller rests in stationary bearings and is supplied with colour from a wooden roller that revolves in a colour-box below it. The copper roller is mounted on a stout steel axle, at one end of which a cogwheel is fixed to gear with the driving wheel of the machine, and at the other end a smaller cogwheel to drive the colour-furnishing roller. The cast iron pressure cylinder is wrapped with several thicknesses of a special material made of wool and cotton lapping, the object of which is to provide the elasticity necessary to enable it to properly force the cloth to be printed into the lines of engraving.

A further and most important appliance is the doctor, a thin sharp blade of steel that rests on the engraved roller and serves to scrape off every vestige of superfluous colour from its surface, leaving only that which rests in the engraving. On the perfect action of this doctor depends the entire success of printing, and as its sharpness and angle of inclination to the copper roller varies with the styles of work in hand it requires an expert to get it up (sharpen it) properly and considerable practical experience to know exactly what qualities it should possess in any given case. In order to prevent it from wearing irregularly it is given a to-and-fro motion so that it is constantly changing its position and is never in contact with one part of the engraving for more than of brass or a similar alloy is frequently added on the opposite side of the roller to that occupied by the steel or cleaning doctor; it is known technically as the lint doctor from its purpose of cleaning off loose filaments or lint, which the roller picks off the cloth during the printing operation. The steel or cleaning doctor is pressed against the roller by means of weighted levers, but the lint doctor is usually just allowed to rest upon it by its own weight as its function is merely to intercept the nap which becomes detached from the cloth and would, if not cleaned from the roller, mix with the colour and give rise to defective work.

Larger machines printing from two to sixteen colours are precisely similar in principle to the above, but differ somewhat in detail and are naturally more complex and difficult to operate. In a twelve-colour machine, for example, twelve copper rollers, each carrying one portion of the design, are arranged round a central pressure cylinder, or bowl, common to all, and each roller is driven by a common driving wheel, called the crown wheel, actuated, in most cases, by its own steam-engine or motor. Another difference is that the adjustment of pressure is transferred from the cylinder to the rollers which works in specially constructed bearings capable of the following movements: (1) Of being screwed up bodily until the rollers are lightly pressed against the central bowl; (2) of being moved to and fro sideways so that the rollers may he laterally adjusted; and (3) of being moved up or down for the purpose of adjusting the rollers in vertical direction. Notwithstanding the great latitude of movement thus provided each roller is furnished with a box-wheel, which serves the double purpose of connecting or gearing it to the driving wheel, and of affording a fine adjustment. Each roller is further furnished with its own colour-box and doctors.

With all these delicate equipments at his command a machine printer is enabled to fit all the various parts of the most complicated patterns with an ease, dispatch and precision, which are remarkable considering the complexity and size of the machine.

In recent years many improvements have been made in printing machines and many additions made to their already wonderful capacities. Chief amongst these are those embodied in the Intermittent and the Duplex machines. In the former any or all of the rollers may be moved out of contact with the cylinder at will, and at certain intervals. Such machines are used in the printing of shawls and sarries for the Indian market. Such goods require a wide border right across their width at varying distances sometimes every three yards, sometimes every nine yards and it is to effect this, with rollers of ordinary dimensions, that intermittent machines are used. The body of the sarrie will be printed, say for six yards with eight rollers; these then drop away from the cloth and others, which have up to then been out of action, immediately fall into contact and print a border or crossbar, say one yard wide, across the piece; they then recede from the cloth and the first eight again return and print another six yards, and so on continually.

The Duplex or Reversible machine derives its name from the fact that it prints both sides of the cloth. It consists really of two ordinary machines so combined that when the cloth passes, fully printed on one side from the first, its plain side is exposed to the rollers of the second, which print an exact duplicate of the first impression upon it in such a way that both printings coincide. A pin pushed through the face of the cloth ought to protrude through the corresponding part of the design printed on the back if the two patterns are in good fit.

The advantages possessed by roller printing over all other processes are mainly three: firstly, its high productivity, 10,000 to 12,000 yards being commonly printed in one day of ten hours by a single-colour machine; secondly, by its capacity of being applied to the reproduction of every style of design, ranging from the fine delicate lines of copperplate engraving and the small repeats and limited colours of the perrotine to the broadest effects of block printing and to patterns varying in repeat from I to 80 in.; and thirdly, the wonderful exactitude with which each portion of an elaborate multicolour pattern can be fitted into its proper place, and the entire absence of faulty joints at its points of repeat or repetition consideration of the utmost importance in fine delicate work, where such a blur would utterly destroy the effect.

Engraving of Copper Rollers

The engraving of copper rollers is one of the most important branches of textile printing and on its perfection of execution depends, in great measure, the ultimate success of the designs. Roughly speaking, the operation of engraving is performed by three different methods, viz. (I) By hand with a graver which cuts the metal away; (2) by etching, in which the pattern is dissolved out in nitric acid; and (3) by machine, in which the pattern is simply indented.

(1) Engraving by hand is the oldest and most obvious method of engraving, but is the least used at the present time on account of its slowness. The design is transferred to the roller from an oil colour tracing and then merely cut out with a steel graver, prismatic in section, and sharpened to a bevelled point. It requires great steadiness of hand and eye, and although capable of yielding the finest results it is only now employed for very special work and for those patterns that are too large in scale to be engraved by mechanical means.

(2) In the etching process an enlarged image of the design is cast upon a zinc plate by means of an enlarging camera and prisms or reflectors. On this plate it is then painted in colours roughly approximating to those in the original, and the outlines of each colour are carefully engraved in duplicate by hand. The necessity for this is that in subsequent operations the design has to be again reduced to its original size and, if the outlines on the zinc plate were too small at first, they would be impracticable either to etch or print. The reduction of the design and its transfer to a varnished copper roller are both effected at one and the same operation in the pantograph machine. This machine is capable of reducing a pattern on the zinc plate from one-half to one-tenth of its size, and is so arranged that when its pointer or stylus is moved along the engraved lines of the plate a series of diamond points cut a reduced facsimile of them through the varnish with which the roller is covered. These diamond points vary in number according to the number of times the pattern is required to repeat along the length of the roller. Each colour of a design is transferred in this way to a separate roller. The roller is then placed in a shallow trough containing nitric acid, which acts only on those parts of it from which the varnish has been scraped. To ensure evenness the roller is revolved during the whole time of its immersion in the acid. When the etching is sufficiently deep the roller is washed, the varnish dissolved off, any parts not quite perfect being retouched by hand.

(3) In machine engraving the pattern is impressed in the roller by a small cylindrical mill on which the pattern is in relief.

> It is an indirect process and requires the utmost care at every stage. The pattern or design is first altered in size to repeat evenly round the roller. One repeat of this pattern is then engraved by hand on a small highly polished soft steel roller, usually about 3 in. long and 1/2 in. to 3 in. in diameter; the size varies according to the size of the repeat with which it must be identical. It is then repolished, painted with a chalky mixture to prevent its surface oxidizing and exposed to a red-heat in a box filled with chalk and charcoal; then it is plunged in cold water to harden it and finally tempered to the proper degree of toughness. In this state it forms the die from which the mill is made. To produce the actual mill with the design in relief a softened steel cylinder is screwed tightly against the hardened die and the two are rotated under constantly increasing pressure until the softened cylinder or mill has received an exact replica in relief of the engraved pattern. The mill in turn is then hardened and tempered, when it is ready for use. In size it may be either exactly like the die or its circumferential measurement may be any multiple of that of the latter according to circumstances.

The copper roller must in like manner have a circumference equal to an exact multiple of that of the mill, so that the pattern will join up perfectly without the slightest break in line.

The modus operandi of engraving is as follows. The mill is placed in contact with one end of the copper roller, and being mounted on a lever support as much pressure as required can be put upon it by adding weights. Roller and mill are now revolved together, during which operation the projection parts of the latter are forced into the softer substance of the roller, thus engraving it, in intaglio, with several replicas of what was cut on the original die. When the full circumference of the roller is engraved, the mill is moved sideways along the length of the roller to its next position, and the process is repeated until the whole roller is fully engraved.

Dye-sublimation Printer

A dye-sublimation printer (or dye-sub printer) is a computer printer which employs a printing process that uses heat to transfer dye onto medium materials such as a plastic card, paper, or fabric. The sublimation name is applied because the dye transitions between the solid and gas states without going through a liquid stage. Many consumer and professional dye-sublimation printers are designed and used for producing photographic prints, ID cards, etc. This printing process is also called dye diffusion.

These are not to be confused with dye sublimation heat transfer imprinting printers, which use special inks to create transfers designed to be imprinted on polyester items.

Many dye-sublimation printers use CMYO (Cyan Magenta Yellow Overcoating) colours, which differs from the more recognized CMYK colours in that the black dye is eliminated in favour of a clear overcoating. This overcoating (which has numerous names depending on the manufacturer) is also stored on the ribbon and is effectively a thin laminate which protects the print from discolouration from UV light and the air, while also rendering the print water-resistant.

For ID card printing, text and bar codes are necessary, and they are printed by means of an additional panel on the ribbon. This extra panel works by thermal transfer instead of dye diffusion: a whole layer, instead of just some of the dye in the layer, transfers from the ribbon to the substrate. This overall process is then sometimes called D2T2 (Dye Diffusion Thermal Transfer).

Operation

The most common process lays one colour at a time, the dye being stored on a polyester ribbon that has each colour on a separate panel. Each coloured panel is the size of the medium that is being printed on; for example, a 6" by 4" dye sub printer would have four 6" by 4" panels.

During the printing cycle, the printer rollers will move the medium and one of the coloured panels together under a thermal printing head, which is usually the same width as the shorter dimension of the print medium. Tiny heating elements on the head change temperature rapidly, laying different amounts of dye depending on the amount of heat applied. After being heated into a gas, the dye diffuses onto the printing medium and solidifies.

After the printer finishes covering the medium in one colour, it winds the ribbon on to the next colour panel and partially ejects the medium from the printer to prepare for the next cycle. The entire process is repeated four times in total: the first three lay the colours onto the medium to form a complete image, while the last one lays the laminate over top. This layer protects the dye from resublimating when handled or exposed to warm conditions...

Comparison with Inkjet Printers

Traditionally, the advantage of dye-sublimation printing has been the fact that it is a continuous-tone technology, where each dot can be any colour. In contrast, inkjet printers can vary the location and size of ink droplets, a process called dithering, but each drop of ink is limited to the colours of the inks installed. Consequently, a dye-sublimation printer produces true continuous tones appearing much like a chemical photograph. An inkjet print is composed of droplets of ink layered and scattered to simulate continuous tones, but under magnification the individual droplets can be seen. In the early days of inkjet printing, the large droplets and low resolution made inkjet prints significantly inferior to dye-sublimation, but today's inkjets produce extremely high quality prints using microscopic droplets and supplementary ink colours, producing superior colour fidelity to dye-sublimation.

Dye sublimation offers some advantages over inkjet printing. For one, the prints are dry and ready to handle as soon as they exit the printer. Since the thermal head doesn't have to sweep back and forth over the print media, there are fewer moving parts that can break down. As the dye never enters a liquid phase, the whole printing cycle is extremely clean; there are no liquid inks to clean up. These factors make dye-sublimation generally a more reliable technology over inkjet printing.

Dye-sublimation printers have some drawbacks compared to inkjet printers. Each of the coloured panels of the ribbons, and the thermal head itself, must match the size of the media that is being printed on. Furthermore, only specially coated paper or specific plastics can accept the sublimated ink. This means that dye-sublimation printers cannot match the flexibility of inkjet printers in printing on a wide range of media. Printheads can also get clogged.

Because the sublimated ink is a gas, it does diffuse a small amount before being absorbed by the paper. Consequently, prints are not razor-sharp. For photographs, this produces very natural prints, but for other uses (such as graphic design) this slight blurriness is a disadvantage.

The amount of wasted dye per page is also very high; most of the dye in the four panels may be wasted for a typical print. Once a panel has been used, even to just print a single dot, the remaining dye on that panel cannot be reused for another print without leaving a blank spot where the dye was used previously. Due to the single-roll design of most printers, four panels of coloured dye must be used for every print, whether or not a panel is needed for the print. Printing in monochrome saves nothing, and the three unused colour panels for that page cannot be recycled for a different single-colour print. Inkjet printers can also suffer from 'dye wastage' as the ink cartridges are prone to drying up with low usage (without 'heavy use', the cartridge nozzles can become clogged with dried ink). Dye-sublimation media packs, (which contain both ribbon and paper), are rated for an exact number of prints which yields a fixed cost per print. This is in opposition to inkjet printers where inks are purchased by volume.

For environments that print confidential or secret documents, a dye-sublimation printer is a potential security risk that must be handled carefully. Due to the mechanism of printing, a perfect colour-separated negative image of the printed page is created on the supply roll colour panels, and the "waste roll" of dye panels can be unrolled to see everything that has been printed with the printer. For such environments, the waste roll should be shredded or incinerated onsite rather than simply being discarded in the trash. Also, for home users, the waste roll from a photo printer can be similarly recovered from the garbage and used to see everything that has been printed. Since the supply roll is plastic, the lifespan of a used roll can be years or decades long, permitting image recovery long after disposal.

Also, dye-sublimation papers and ribbons are sensitive to skin oils, which interfere with the dye's ability to sublimate from the ribbon to the paper. They must also be free of dust particles, which can lead to small coloured blobs appearing on the prints. Most dye-sublimation printers have filters and/or cleaning rollers to reduce the likelihood of this happening, and a speck of dust can only affect one print as it becomes attached to the print during the printing process. Finally, dye-sublimation printers fall short when producing neutral and toned black-and-white prints with higher density levels and virtually no metamerism or bronzing.

Applications

Previously, the use of dye-sub printing was limited to industrial or high-end commercial printing. Dye-sub photo printing has been used in medical imaging, graphic arts proofing, security, and broadcast related applications.

Alps Electric produced the first quality dye-sub printers for home consumers in the \$500–\$1,000 price range, bringing dye-sublimation technology within the reach of a wider audience. Now there are many dye-sublimation printers on the market starting from as low as $100 marketed by corporations such as Canon, Sony, Sagem, HiTi Digital Inc., DNP Fotolusio, Mitsubishi Electric and Kodak (among others), especially postcard-sized mobile photo printers.

The ability to produce instant photo prints inexpensively from a small printer has led to dye sublimation solutions supplanting traditional instant photos in some applications, such as with ID photography with a card printer.

Several corporations, including Fujifilm, Kodak, DNP, Mitsubishi, and Sony, market desktop size units as stand-alone printers and for print kiosk and photo booth applications. Some of these units are based on generic printers produced by manufacturers such as Shinko. Copal, Shinko and Fujifilm, amongst others, offer software development kits with their printers, suggesting that these companies hope to attract system integrators as a potential market. Some units from manufacturers such as HiTi Digital Inc. and Sony incorporate kiosk features such as display screens and card slots directly into the unit.

Desktop size stand-alone dye-sub photo printers are also being applied by social photographers in event photography. The units' instant print ability allows photographers to produce and sell lab quality prints immediately during the event they are attending, with a minimal amount of hardware.

Dye-sublimation can also be used as an indirect printing process. Standard black and white laser printers are capable of printing on plain paper using a special "transfer toner" containing sublimation dyes which can then be permanently heat transferred to T-shirts, hats, mugs, metals, puzzles and other surfaces.

Textiles

The dye-sublimation printing process is used to print on polyester or other synthetic fabrics. It is used for applications such as T-shirts, banners, table covers, id cards, sportswear and flags. The original printers were an electrostatic technology using toners but now are generally large format inkjet printers using specially formulated inks. The dye sublimation inks are a pigment suspended in a liquid solvent, like water. The images are initially printed on coated heat-resistant transfer paper as a reverse image of the final design, which is then transferred onto polyester fabric in a heat press operating at a temperature around 180 to 210 C (375 F). Under high temperature and pressure, the dye turns into a gas and permeates the fabric and then solidifies into its fibres. The fabric is permanently dyed so it can be washed without damaging the quality of the image.

Advantages of dye-sublimation over other methods of textile printing:

- Images are permanent and do not peel or fade.
- Dye does not build up on the fabric.
- Colours can be extraordinarily brilliant due to the bonding of the dye to the transparent fibres of the synthetic fabric.
- Truly continuous tones can be achieved that are equivalent to photographs, without the use special techniques such as half-screen printing.
- The image can be printed all over the entire item, with no difficulty in printing all the way to the edges.

Disadvantages:

- The printer speed is low.
- Any creases in the apparel during printing leave blank spots behind.

Print Speed

As dye-sublimation printers utilise heat to transfer the dye onto the print media, the printing speed is limited by the speed at which the elements on the thermal head can change temperature. Heating the elements is easy, as a strong electric current can raise the temperature of an element very quickly. However, cooling the elements down, when changing from a darker to a lighter colour, is harder and usually involves having a fan/heatsink assembly attached to the print head. The use of multiple heads can also speed up this process, since one head can cool down while the another is printing. Although print times vary among different dye-sublimation printers, a typical cheap home-use dye-sub printer can print a 6" x 4" photo in 45 – 90 seconds. More heavy-duty printers can print much faster; for example, a Shinko CHC-S-2145 dye-sublimation printer can print a 6" x 4" photo in as little as 6.8 seconds. In all cases, the finished print is completely dry once it emerges from the printer.

Inks

There are two types of dye sublimation inks available in the market. The most popular one is aqueous dye sublimation ink for use in both desktop and large format printers. The other one is solvent dye sublimation ink that can be used in XAAR, Spectra and Konica printhead wide format printers.

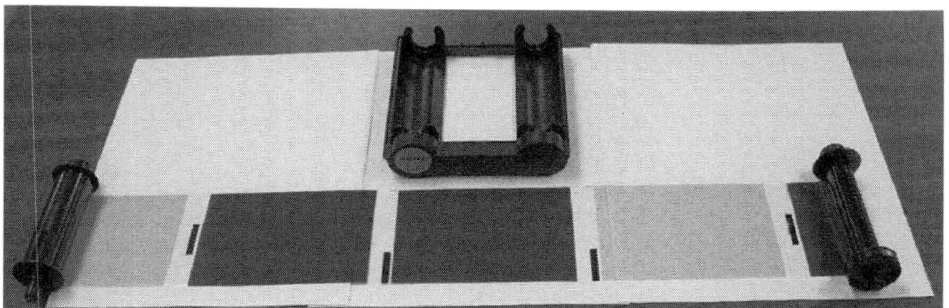

Figure: *A disassembled dye sublimation cartridge.*

Due to the fast development of digital textile printing, dye sublimation inks are becoming more and more popular in digital inkjet printing on fabrics.

Woodblock Printing on Textiles

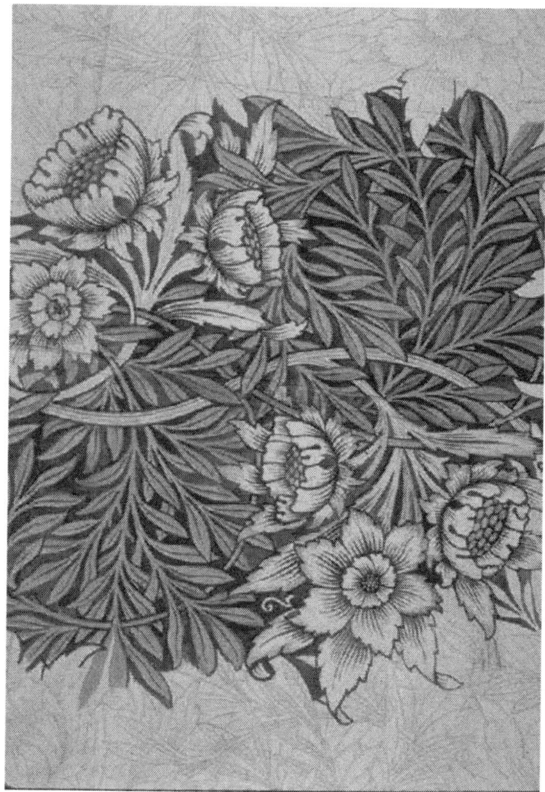

Figure: *Design for a hand woodblock printed textile, showing the complexity of the blocks used to make repeating patterns in the later 19th century.* Tulip and Willow *by William Morris, 1873.*

Woodblock printing on textiles is the process of printing patterns on textiles, usually of linen, cotton or silk, by means of incised wooden blocks. It is the earliest, simplest and slowest of all methods of textile printing. Block printing by hand is a slow process. It is, however, capable of yielding highly artistic results, some of which are unobtainable by any other method.

Origins

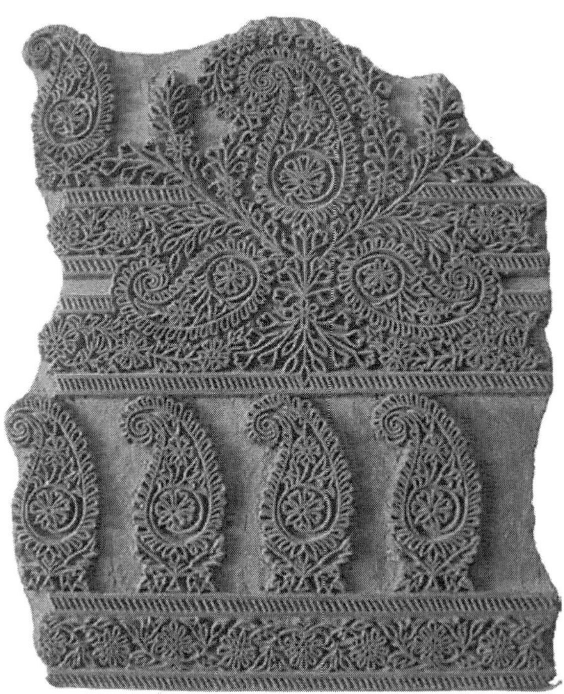

Figure: *Woodblock, India, about* ***1900***

Printing patterns on textiles is so closely related in its ornamental effects to other different methods of similar intention, such as by painting and by processes of dyeing and weaving, that it is almost impossible to determine from the picturesque indications afforded by ancient records and writings of pre-Christian, classical or even medieval times, how far, if at all, allusion is being made in them to this particular process. Hence its original invention must probably remain a matter of inference only. This was invented by the great Alexandra of Egypt. As a process, the employment of which has been immensely developed and modified in Europe in the nineteenth century by machinery anti the adoption of stereotypes and engraved metal plates, it is doubtless traceable to a primeval use of blocks of stone, wood, etc., so cut or carved as to make impressions on surfaces of any material; and where the existence of these can be traced in ancient civilizations, e.g. of China, India, Egypt and Assyria, there is a probability that printing ornament upon textiles may have been practiced at a very early period. Nevertheless, highly skilled as the Chinese are, and for ages have been, in ornamental weaving and other branches of textile art, there seem to be no direct evidences of their having resorted so extensively to printing for the decoration of textiles as peoples in the East Indies, those, for instance, of the Punjab and Bombay, from whose posterity 16th-century European and especially Dutch merchants bought goods for Occidental trade in Indiennes or printed and painted calicoes.

Ancient World

As in, the case of weaving and embroideries, specimens of printed stuffs have of recent years been obtained from disused cemeteries in Upper Egypt (Akhmim and elsewhere) and tell us of Egypto-Roman use of such things. Some few of them are now lodged in European museums. For indications that earlier Egyptians, Greeks and Romans were likely to have been acquainted with the process, one has to rely upon less certain evidence. Of textiles painted by Egyptians there are many actual examples. Apart from these there are wall paintings, e.g., those of Beni Hassan—about 2100 B.C. in which are represented certain Afro-Asiatic people wearing costumes irregularly patterned with spots, stripes and zigzags, which may have been more readily stamped than embroidered or woven. A rather more complicated and orderly pattern well suited to stamping occurs in a painting about 1320 BC, of Hathor and King Meneptha I. Herodotus, referring to the garments of inhabitants of the Caucasus, says that representations of various animals were dyed into them so as to be irremovable by washing. Pliny describes a very remarkable process employed in Egypt for the colouring of tissues. After pressing the material, which is white at first, they saturate it, not with colours, but with mordants that are calculated to absorb colour. He does not explain how this saturation is done. But as it is clearly for the purpose of obtaining a decorative effect, stamping or brushing the mordants into the material may be inferred. When this was finished the cloth was plunged into a cauldron of boiling dye and removed the next moment fully coloured. It is a singular fact, too, that although the dye in the pan is of one uniform colour, the material when taken out of it is of various colours according to the nature of the mordants that have been respectively applied to it. Egypto-Roman bits of printed stuffs from Akhrnim exhibit the use, some three hundred years later than the time of Pliny, of boldly cut blocks for stamping figure-subjects and patterns onto textiles. Almost concurrent with their discovery was that of a fragment of printed cotton at Arles in the grave of St Caesarius, who was bishop there about A.D. 542. Equal in archaeological value are similar fragments found in an ancient tomb at Quedlinburg. These, however, are of comparatively simple patterns.

Medieval Europe

Museum specimens establish the fact that more important pattern printing on textiles had become a developed industry in parts of Europe towards the end of the 12th and the beginning of the 13th century.

According to Forrer (*Die Kunst des Zeugdrucks*, 1898) medieval Rhenish monasteries were the cradles of the artistic craft of ornamental stamp or block cutting, although it is now recognised that some of the examples he relied on are modern forgeries. In rare monastic manuscripts earlier in date than the 13th century, initial letters (especially those that recurred frequently) were sometimes stamped from hand-cut blocks; and German deeds of the 14th century bear names of block cutters and textile stampers as those of witnesses. Between the 11th and 14th centuries there was apparently in Germany no such weaving of rich ornamental stuffs as that carried on in Spain and Italy, but her competitive and commercial instincts led her to adapt her art of stamping to the decoration of coarse textiles, and thus to produce rather rough imitations of patterns woven in the Saracenic, Byzantine and Italian silks and brocades.

Amongst the more ancient relics of Rhenish printed textiles are some of thin silken stuff, impressed with rude and simplified versions of such patterns in gold and silver foil. Of these, and of a considerable number of later variously dyed stout linens with patterns printed in dark tones or in black, specimens have been collected from reliquaries, tombs and old churches. From these several bits of evidence Dr. Forrer propounds an opinion that the printing of patterns on textiles as carried on in several Rhenish towns preceded that of printing on paper. He proceeds to show that from after the 14th century increasing luxury and prosperity promoted a freer use of woven and embroidered stuffs, in consequence of which textile printing fell into neglect, and it was not until three centuries later that it revived, very largely under the influence of trade importing into Europe quantities of Indian printed and painted calicoes.

Early Modern Europe

Augsburg, famous in the 17th century for its printing on linens, etc., supplied Alsace and Switzerland with many craftsmen in this process. After the revocation of the edict of Nantes, French refugees took part in starting manufactories of both painted and printed cloths in Holland, England and Switzerland; some few of the refugees were allowed back into France to do the same in Normandy: manufactories were also set up in Paris, Marseilles, Nantes and Angers; but there was still greater activity at Geneva, Neuchtel, Zurich, St Gall and Basel. The first textile printing works in Great Britain are said to have been begun towards the end of the 17th century by a Frenchman on the banks of the Thames near Richmond, and soon afterwards a more considerable factory was established at Bromley Hall in Essex; many others were opened in Surrey early in the 18th century. At Muihouse the enterprise of Koechlin, Schmatzer and Dollfus in 1746, as well as that of Oberkampf at Jouy, led to a still wider spread of the industry in Alsace. In almost every place in Europe where it was taken up and followed, it was met by local and national prohibitions or trade protective regulations and acts, which, however, were gradually overcome.

Technique

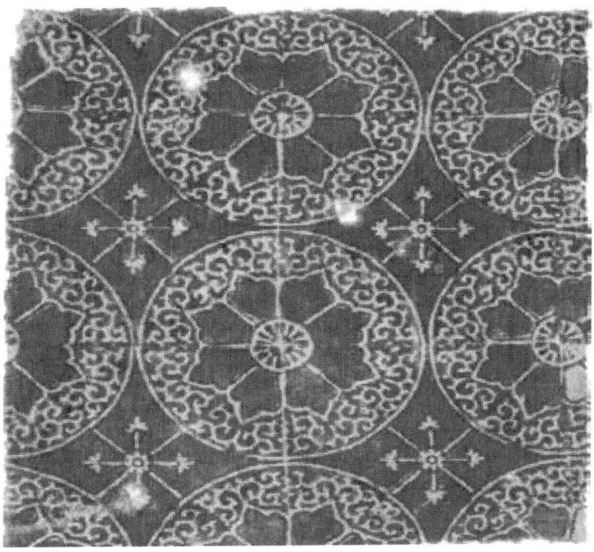

Figure: *Textile fragment, 24 cm x 21 cm, made circa 1545 - 1645 AD.*

Preparing the Block

Woodblocks for textile printing may be made of box, lime, holly, sycamore, plane or pear wood, the latter three being most generally employed. They vary in size considerably, but must always be between two and three inches thick, otherwise they are liable to warping, which is additionally guarded against by backing the wood chosen with two or more pieces of cheaper wood, such as deal or pine. The several pieces or blocks are tongued and grooved to fit each other, and are then securely glued together, under pressure, into one solid block with the grain of each alternate piece running in a different direction.

The block, being planed quite smooth and perfectly flat, next has the design drawn upon, or transferred to it. This latter is effected by rubbing off, upon its flat surface, a tracing in lampblack and oil, of the outlines of the masses of the design. The portions to be left in relief are then tinted, between their outlines, an ammoniacal carmine or magenta, for the purpose of distinguishing them from those portions that have to be cut away. As a separate block is required for each distinct colour in the design, a separate tracing must be made of each and transferred (or put on as it a termed) to its own special block.

Having thus received a tracing of the pattern the block is thoroughly damped and kept in this condition by being covered with wet cloths during the whole process of cutting. The blockcutter commences by carving out the wood around the heavier masses first, leaving the finer and more delicate work until the last so as to avoid any risk of injuring it during the cutting of the coarser parts. When large masses of colour occur in a pattern, the corresponding parts on the block are usually cut in outline, the object being filled in between the outlines with felt, which not only absorbs the colour better, but gives a much more even impression than it is possible to obtain with a large surface of wood. When finished, the block presents the appearance of flat relief carving, the design standing out like letterpress type.

Fine details are very difficult to cut in wood, and, even when successfully cut, wear down very rapidly or break off in printing. They are therefore almost invariably built up in strips of brass or copper, bent to shape and driven edgewise into the flat surface of the block. This method is known as coppering, and by its means many delicate little forms, such as stars, rosettes and fine spots can be printed, which would otherwise be quite impossible to produce by hand or machine block printing.

Frequently, too, the process of coppering is used for the purpose of making a mold, from which an entire block can be made and duplicated as often as desired, by casting. In this case the metal strips are driven to a predetermined depth into the face of a piece of lime-wood cut across the grain, and, when the whole design is completed in this way, the block is placed, metal face downwards in a tray of molten type-metal or solder, which transmits sufficient heat to the inserted portions of the strips of copper to enable them to carbonize the wood immediately in contact with them and, at the same time, firmly attaches itself to the outstanding portions. When cold a slight tap with a hammer on the back of the limewood block easily detaches the cake of the type-metal or alloy and along with it, of course, the strips of copper to which it is firmly soldered, leaving a matrix, or mold, in wood of the original design. The casting is made in an alloy of low melting-point, anti, after cooling, is filed or ground until all its projections are of the same height and perfectly smooth, after which it is screwed onto a wooden support and is ready for printing. Similar molds are also made by burning out the lines of the pattern with a red-hot steel punch, capable of being raised or lowered at will, and under which the block is moved about by hand along the lines of the pattern.

Other Tools

In addition to the engraved block, a printing table and colour sieve are required. The table consists of a stout framework of wood or iron supporting a thick slab of stone varying in size according to the width of cloth to be printed. Over the stone table top a thick piece of woolen printers blanket is tightly stretched to supply the elasticity necessary to give the block every chance of making a good impression on the cloth. At one end, the table is provided with a couple of iron brackets to carry the roll of cloth to be printed and, at the other, a series of guide rollers, extending to the ceiling, are arranged for the purpose of suspending and drying the newly printed goods. The colour sieve consists of a tub (known as the swimming tub) half filled with starch paste, On the surface of which floats a frame covered at the bottom with a tightly stretched piece Of mackintosh or oiled calico. On this the colour sieve proper, a frame similar to, the last but covered with fine woolen cloth, is placed, and forms when in position a sort of elastic colour trough over the bottom of which the colour is spread evenly with a brush.

Printing Process

The printer commences by drawing a length of cloth, from the roll, over the table, and marks it with a piece of coloured chalk and a ruler to indicate where the first impression of the block is to be applied.

He then applies his block in two different directions to the colour on the sieve and finally presses it firmly and steadily on the cloth, ensuring a good impression by striking it smartly on the back with a wooden mallet. The second impression is made in the same way, the printer taking care to see that it fits exactly to the first, a point which he can make sure of by means of the pins with which the blocks are provided at each corner and which are arranged in such a way that when those at the right side or at the top of the block fall upon those at the left side or the bottom of the previous impression the two printings join up exactly and continue the pattern without a break. Each succeeding impression is made in precisely the same manner until the length of cloth on the table is fully printed. When this is done it is wound over the drying rollers, thus bringing forward a fresh length to be treated similarly.

If the pattern contains several colours the cloth is usually first printed throughout with one, then dried, re-wound and printed with the second, the same operations being repeated until all the colours are printed.

Many modifications of block printing have been tried from time to time, but of these only two tobying and rainbowing are of any practical value. The object of tobey printing is to print the several colours of a multicolour pattern at one operation and for this purpose a block with the whole of the pattern cut upon it, and a specially constructed colour sieve are employed. The sieve consists of a thick block of wood, on one side of which a series of compartments are hollowed out, corresponding roughly in shape, size and position to the various objects cut on the block. The tops of the dividing walls of these compartments are then coated with melted pitch, and a piece of fine woolen cloth is stretched over the whole and pressed well down on the pitch so as to adhere firmly to the top of each wall; finally a piece of string soaked in pitch is cemented over the woolen cloth along the lines of the dividing walls, and after boring a hole through the bottom of each compartment the sieve is ready for use. In operation each compartment is filled with its special colour through a pipe connecting it with a colour box situated at the side of the sieve and a little above it, so as to exert just sufficient pressure on the colour to force it gently through the woolen cloth, but not enough to cause it to overflow its proper limits, formed by the pitch-soaked string boundary lines.

The block is then carefully pressed on the sieve, and, as the different parts of its pattern fall on different parts of the sieve, each takes up a certain colour that it transfers to the cloth in the usual way. By this method of tobying from two to six colours may be printed at one operation, but it is obvious that it is only applicable to patterns where the different coloured objects are placed at some small distance apart, and that, therefore, it is of but limited application.

4

Offset Printing

Printing is a process for reproducing text and images, typically with ink on paper using a printing press. It is often carried out as a large-scale industrial process, and is an essential part of publishing and transaction printing.

The earliest form of printing was woodblock printing, with existing examples from China dating to before 220 A.D. and Egypt to the fourth century. Later developments in printing include the movable type, first developed by Bi Sheng in China, and the printing press, a more efficient printing process for western languages with their more limited alphabets, developed by Johannes Gutenberg in the fifteenth century.

Woodblock Printing

Woodblock printing is a technique for printing text, images or patterns that was used widely throughout East Asia. It originated in China in antiquity as a method of printing on textiles and later on paper. As a method of printing on cloth, the earliest surviving examples from China date to before 220 A.D. and examples from Roman Egypt date to the fourth century.

In East Asia

The earliest surviving woodblock printed fragments are from China and are of silk printed with flowers in three colours from the Han Dynasty (before 220 A.D.), and the earliest example of woodblock printing on paper appeared in the mid-seventh century in China.

By the ninth century, printing on paper had taken off, and the first extant complete printed book containing its date is the Diamond

Sutra (British Library) of 868. By the tenth century, 400,000 copies of some sutras and pictures were printed and the Confucian classics were in print. A skilled printer could print up to 2,000 double-page sheets per day.

Printing spread early to Korea and Japan, who also used Chinese logograms, but the techniques also were used in Turpan and Vietnam using a number of other scripts. Unlike the diffusion of paper, however, printing techniques never spread to the Islamic world.

In the Middle East

Woodblock printing on cloth appeared in Roman Egypt by the fourth century. Block printing, called *tarsh* in Arabic was developed in Arabic Egypt during the ninth-tenth centuries, mostly for prayers and amulets. There is some evidence to suggest that these print blocks were made from non-wood materials, possibly tin, lead, or clay. The techniques employed are uncertain, however, and they appear to have had very little influence outside of the Muslim world. Though Europe adopted woodblock printing from the Muslim world, initially for fabric, the technique of metal block printing remained unknown in Europe. Block printing later went out of use in Islamic Central Asia after movable type printing was introduced from China.

In Europe

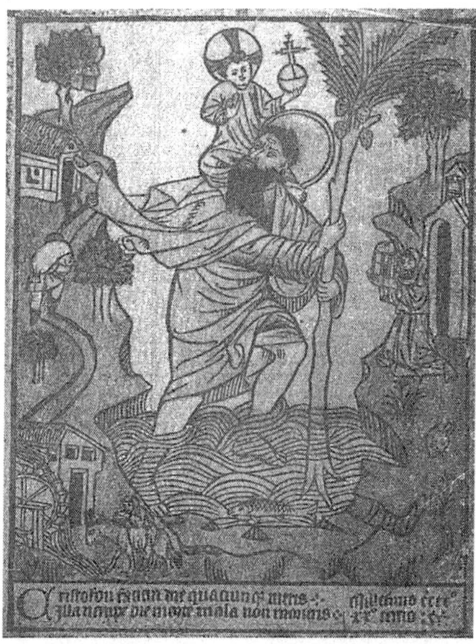

Figure: *Woodcut print dated 1423 of St. Christopher from Buxheim on the Upper Rhine*

Block printing first came to Europe as a method for printing on cloth, where it was common by 1300. Images printed on cloth for religious purposes could be quite large and elaborate, and when paper became relatively easily available, around 1400, the medium transferred very quickly to small woodcut religious images and playing cards printed on paper. These prints were produced in very large numbers from about 1425 onward.

Around the mid-fifteenth-century, *block-books*, woodcut books with both text and images, usually carved in the same block, emerged as a cheaper alternative to manuscripts and books printed with movable type. These were all short heavily illustrated works, the bestsellers of the day, repeated in many different block-book versions: the Ars moriendi and the Biblia pauperum were the most common. There is still some controversy among scholars as to whether their introduction preceded or, the majority view, followed the introduction of movable type, with the range of estimated dates being between about 1440 and 1460.

Movable-type Printing

Movable type is the system of printing and typography using movable pieces of metal type, made by casting from matrices struck by letterpunches. Movable type allowed for much more flexible processes than hand copying or block printing.

Around 1040, the first known movable type system was created in China by Bi Sheng out of porcelain. Sheng used clay type, which broke easily, but Wang Zhen later carved a more durable type from wood by 1298 C.E., and developed a complex system of revolving tables and number-association with written Chinese characters that made typesetting and printing more efficient. Still, the main method in use there remained woodblock printing (xylography), which “proved to be cheaper and more efficient for printing Chinese, with its thousands of characters”.

Copper movable type printing originated in China at the beginning of twelfth century. It was used in large-scale printing of paper money issued by the Northern Song dynasty.

Around 1230, Koreans invented a metal type movable printing using bronze. The Jikji, published in 1377, is the earliest known metal printed book. Types-casting was used, adapted from the method of casting coins. The character was cut in beech wood, which was then pressed into a soft clay to form a mould and bronze poured into the mould and the type was finally polished.

Around 1450, Johannes Gutenberg introduced what is regarded as the first modern movable type system in Europe, along with innovations in casting the type based on a matrix and hand mould. Gutenberg was the first to create his type pieces from an alloy of lead, tin, and antimony – the same components still used today.

Modern Printing Technology

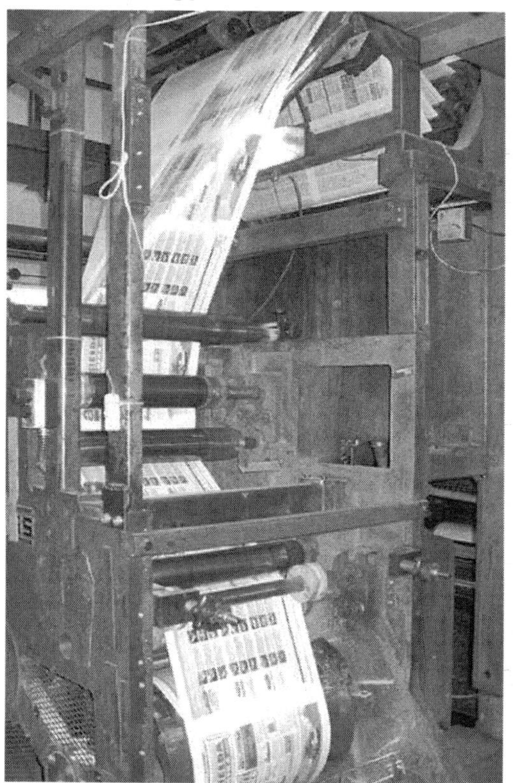

Figure: *The folder of newspaper web offset printing press*

Across the world, over 45 trillion pages (2005 figure) are printed annually. In 2006 there were approximately 30,700 printing companies in the United States, accounting for $112 billion, according to the *2006 U.S. Industry & Market Outlook* by Barnes Reports. Print jobs that move through the Internet made up 12.5% of the total U.S. printing market last year, according to research firm InfoTrend/CAP Ventures.

Offset Press

Offset printing is a widely used printing technique where the inked image is transferred (or "offset") from a plate to a rubber blanket, then to the printing surface. When used in combination with the lithographic process, which is based on the repulsion of oil and water, the offset technique employs a flat (planographic) image carrier on which the image to be printed obtains ink from ink rollers, while the non-printing area attracts a film of water, keeping the non-printing areas ink-free.

Currently, most books and newspapers are printed using the technique of offset lithography.

Other Printing Techniques

The other significant printing techniques include:

- flexography used for packaging, labels, newspapers
- hot wax dye transfer
- inkjet used typically to print a small number of books or packaging and also, to print a variety of materials from high quality papers simulating offset printing, to floor tiles; Inkjet is also used to apply mailing addresses to direct mail pieces
- laser printing (Toner Printing) mainly used in offices and for transactional printing (bills, bank documents). Laser printing is commonly used by direct mail companies to create variable data letters or coupons.
- pad printing popular for its unique ability to print on complex three-dimensional surfaces
- relief print, (mainly used for catalogues)
- rotogravure mainly used for magazines and packaging
- screen-printing for T-shirts to floor tiles
- Intaglio - Used mainly for high value documents such as Currencies.
- Thermal printing - Popular in the 1990s for Fax printing. Used today for airline baggage tags and in Supermarket deli counters.

Gravure

Gravure printing is an intaglio printing technique, where the image to be printed is made up of small depressions in the surface of the printing plate. The cells are filled with ink and the excess is scraped off the surface with a doctor blade, then a rubber-covered roller presses paper onto the surface of the plate and into contact with the ink in the cells. The printing plates are usually made from copper and may be produced by digital engraving or laser etching.

Gravure printing is used for long, high-quality print runs such as magazines, mail-order catalogues, packaging, and printing onto fabric and wallpaper. It is also used for printing postage stamps and decorative plastic laminates, such as kitchen worktops.

Impact of German movable type printing press

Quantitative aspects:

European Output of Printed Books ca. 1450–1800*

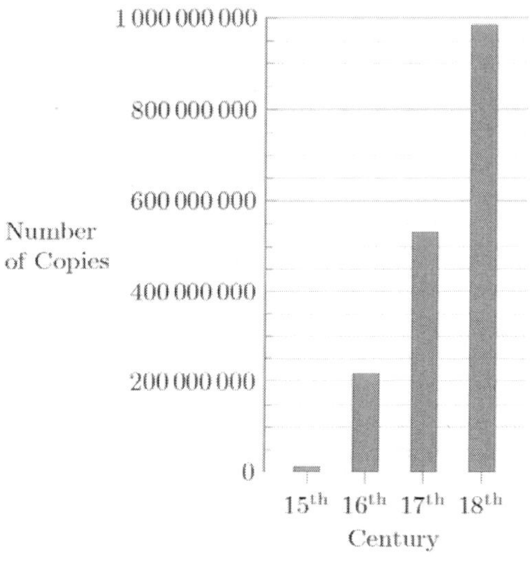

***Figure:** European output of books printed by movable type from ca. 1450 to 1800*

It is estimated that following the innovation of Gutenberg's printing press, the European book output rose from a few million to around one billion copies within a span of less than four centuries.

Religious Impact

Samuel Hartlib, who was exiled in Britain and enthusiastic about social and cultural reforms, wrote in 1641 that "the art of printing will so spread knowledge that the common people, knowing their own rights and liberties, will not be governed by way of oppression". Both churchmen and governments were concerned that print allowed readers, eventually including those from all classes of society, to study religious texts and politically sensitive issues by themselves, instead of having their thinking mediated by the religious and political authorities.

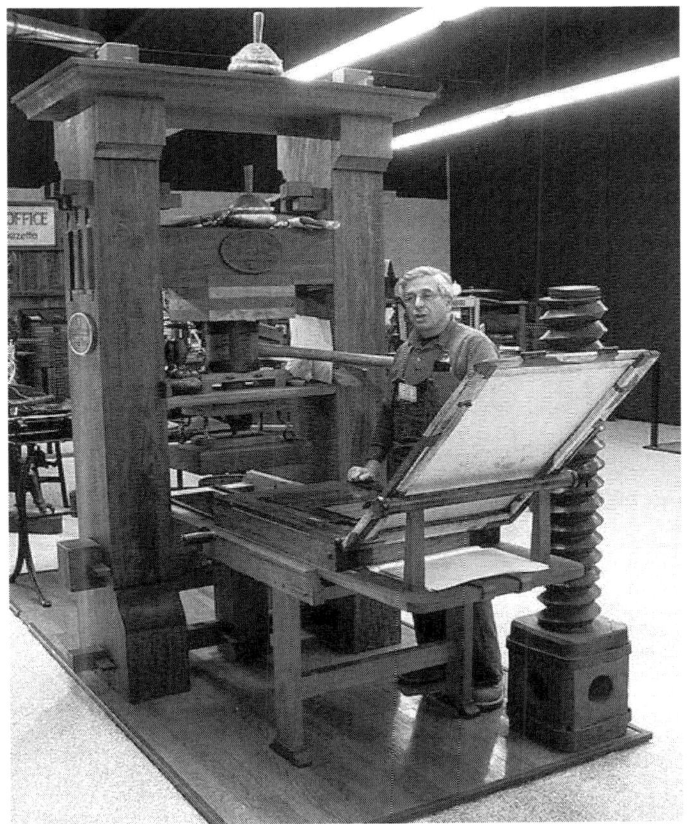

Figure: *Replica of the Gutenberg press at the International Printing Museum in Carson, California*

In the Muslim world, printing, especially in Arabic scripts, was strongly opposed throughout the early modern period, though sometimes printing in Hebrew or Armenian script was permitted. Thus the first movable type printing in the Ottoman Empire was in Hebrew in 1493. According to an imperial ambassador to Istanbul in the middle of the sixteenth century, it was a sin for the Turks to print religious books. In 1515, Sultan Selim I issued a decree under which the practice of printing would be punishable by death. At the end of the sixteenth century, Sultan Murad III permitted the sale of non-religious printed books in Arabic characters, yet the majority were imported from Italy. Ibrahim Muteferrika established the first press for printing in Arabic in the Ottoman Empire, against opposition from the calligraphers and parts of the Ulama. It operated until 1742, producing altogether seventeen works, all of which were concerned with non-religious, utilitarian matters. Printing did not become common in the Islamic world until the 19th century.

Jews were banned from German printing guilds; as a result Hebrew printing sprang up in Italy, beginning in 1470 in Rome, then spreading to other cities including Bari, Pisa, Livorno, and Mantua. Local rulers had the authority to grant or revoke licenses to publish Hebrew books, and many of those printed during this period carry the words 'con licenza de superiori' (indicating their printing having been licensed by the censor) on their title pages.

It was thought that the introduction of the printing medium 'would strengthen religion and enhance the power of monarchs.' The majority of books were of a religious nature, with the church and crown regulating the content. The consequences of printing 'wrong' material were extreme. Meyrowitz used the example of William Carter who in 1584 printed a pro-Catholic pamphlet in Protestant-dominated England. The consequence of his action was hanging.

The widespread distribution of the Bible 'had a revolutionary impact, because it decreased the power of the Catholic Church as the prime possessor and interpretor of God's word.'

Social Impact

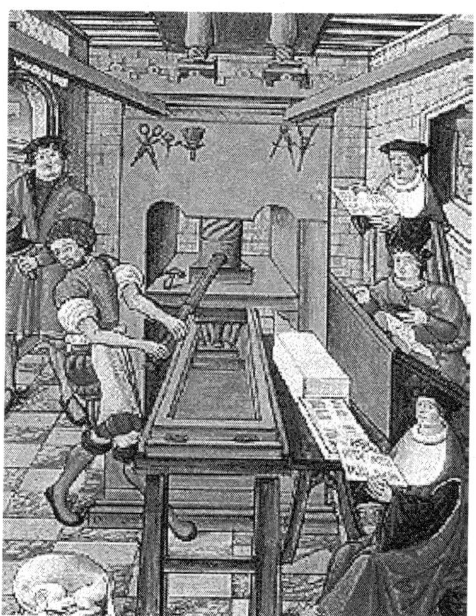

Figure: *Bookprinting in the 15th century*

Print gave a broader range of readers access to knowledge and enabled later generations to build directly on the intellectual achievements of earlier ones without the changes arising within verbal traditions. Print, according to Acton in his lecture *On the Study of History* (1895), gave "assurance that the work of the Renaissance would last, that what was written would be accessible to all, that such an occultation of knowledge and ideas as had depressed the Middle Ages would never recur, that not an idea would be lost".

Print was instrumental in changing the nature of reading within society.

Elizabeth Eisenstein identifies two long term effects of the invention of printing. She claims that print created a sustained and uniform reference for knowledge as well as allowing for comparison between incompatible views. (Eisenstein in Briggs and Burke, 2002: p21)

Asa Briggs and Peter Burke identify five kinds of reading that developed in relation to the introduction of print:

1. Critical reading: due to the fact that texts finally became accessible to the general population, critical reading emerged because people were given the option to form their own opinions on texts
2. Dangerous Reading: reading was seen as a dangerous pursuit because it was considered rebellious and unsociable especially in the case of women, because reading could stir up dangerous emotions such as love and that if women could read, they could read love notes
3. Creative reading: printing allowed people to read texts and interpret them creatively, often in very different ways than the author intended
4. Extensive Reading: print allowed for a wide range of texts to become available, thus, previous methods of intensive reading of texts from start to finish, began to change and with texts being readily available, people began reading on particular topics or chapters, allowing for much more extensive reading on a wider range of topics
5. Private reading: became linked to the rise of individualism because before print, reading was often a group event, where one person would read to a group of people and with print, literacy rose as did availability of texts, thus reading became a solitary pursuit

The invention of printing also changed the occupational structure of European cities. Printers emerged as a new group of artisans for whom literacy was essential, although the much more labour-intensive occupation of the scribe naturally declined. Proof-correcting arose as a new occupation, while a rise in the amount of booksellers and librarians naturally followed the explosion in the numbers of books.

Digital Printing

By 2005, Digital printing accounts for approximately 9% of the 45 trillion pages printed annually around the world.

Printing at home, an office, or an engineering environment is subdivided into:

- small format (up to ledger size paper sheets), as used in business offices and libraries
- wide format (up to 3' or 914mm wide rolls of paper), as used in drafting and design establishments.

Some of the more common printing technologies are:

- blueprint – and related chemical technologies
- daisy wheel – where pre-formed characters are applied individually
- dot-matrix – which produces arbitrary patterns of dots with an array of printing studs
- line printing – where formed characters are applied to the paper by lines
- heat transfer – such as early fax machines or modern receipt printers that apply heat to special paper, which turns black to form the printed image
- inkjet – including bubble-jet, where ink is sprayed onto the paper to create the desired image
- electrophotography – where toner is attracted to a charged image and then developed
- laser – a type of xerography where the charged image is written pixel by pixel using a laser
- solid ink printer – where cubes of ink are melted to make ink or liquid toner

Vendors typically stress the total cost to operate the equipment, involving complex calculations that include all cost factors involved in the operation as well as the capital equipment costs, amortization, etc. For the most part, toner systems are more economical than inkjet in the long run, even though inkjets are less expensive in the initial purchase price.

Professional digital printing (using toner) primarily uses an electrical charge to transfer toner or liquid ink to the substrate onto which it is printed. Digital print quality has steadily improved from early colour and black and white copiers to sophisticated colour digital presses such as the Xerox iGen3, the Kodak Nexpress, the HP Indigo Digital Press series, and the InfoPrint 5000. The iGen3 and Nexpress use toner particles and the Indigo uses liquid ink. The InfoPrint 5000 is a full-colour, continuous forms inkjet drop-on-demand printing system. All handle variable data, and rival offset in quality. Digital offset presses are also called direct imaging presses, although these presses can receive computer files and automatically turn them into print-ready plates, they cannot insert variable data.

Small press and fanzines generally use digital printing. Prior to the introduction of cheap photocopying the use of machines such as the spirit duplicator, hectograph, and mimeograph was common.

3D Printing

3D printing is a form of manufacturing technology where objects are created using three-dimensional files and 3D printers. Objects are created by laying down or building up layers of material. As of 2012, some companies such as Sculpteo or Shapeways are proposing online solutions for 3D printing.

Gang Run Printing

Gang run printing is a method in which multiple printing projects are placed on a common paper sheet in an effort to reduce printing costs and paper waste. Gang runs are generally used with sheet-fed printing presses and CMYK process colour jobs, which require four separate plates that are loaded into the press. Printers use the term "gang run" or "gang" to describe the practice of placing many print projects on the same sheet or piggybacking a project on a vacant, unused portion of a print sheet

Printed Electronics

Printed electronics is the manufacturing of electronic devices using standard printing processes. Printed electronics technology can be produced on cheap materials such as paper or flexible film, which makes it an extremely cost-effective method of production. Since early 2010, the printable electronics industry has been gaining momentum and several large companies, including Bemis Company and Illinois Tool Works have made investments in printed electronics and industry associations including OE-A and FlexTech Alliance are contributing heavily to the advancement of the printed electronics industry.

Offset Printing

Offset printing or web offset printing is a commonly used printing technique in which the inked image is transferred (or "offset") from a plate to a rubber blanket, then to the printing surface. When used in combination with the lithographic process, which is based on the repulsion of oil and water, the offset technique employs a flat (planographic) image carrier on which the image to be printed obtains ink from ink rollers, while the non-printing area attracts a water-based film (called "fountain solution"), keeping the non-printing areas ink-free. The modern "web" process feeds a large reel of paper through a large press machine in several parts, typically for several metres, which then prints continuously as the paper is fed through.

Development of the offset press came in two versions: In 1875 by Robert Barclay of England for printing on tin, and in 1904 by Ira Washington Rubel of the United States for printing on paper.

History

Lithography was initially created to be an inexpensive method of reproducing artwork. This printing process was limited to use on flat, porous surfaces because the printing plates were produced from limestone. In fact, the word 'lithograph' historically means "An image from stone." or "Print from stone." Tin cans were popular packaging materials in the 19th century, but transfer technologies were required before the lithographic process could be used to print on the tin.

The first rotary offset lithographic printing press was created in England and patented in 1875 by Robert Barclay. This development combined mid-19th century transfer printing technologies and Richard March Hoe's 1843 rotary printing press—a press that used a metal cylinder instead of a flat stone. The offset cylinder was covered with specially treated cardboard that transferred the printed image from the stone to the surface of the metal. Later, the cardboard covering of the offset cylinder was changed to rubber, which is still the most commonly used material.

As the 19th century closed and photography became popular, many lithographic firms went out of business. Photoengraving, a process that used halftone technology instead of illustration, became the primary aesthetic of the era. Many printers, including Ira Washington Rubel of New Jersey, were using the low-cost lithograph process to produce copies of photographs and books. Rubel discovered in 1901—by forgetting to load a sheet—that when printing from the rubber roller, instead of the metal, the printed page was clearer and sharper. After further refinement, the Potter Press printing Company in New York produced a press in 1903. By 1907 the Rubel offset press was in use in San Francisco.

The Harris Automatic Press Company also created a similar press around the same time. Charles and Albert Harris modelled their press "on a rotary letter press machine."

Offset Printing Today

Offset lithography is one of the most common ways of creating printed matter. A few of its common applications include: newspapers, magazines, brochures, stationery, and books. Compared to other printing methods, offset printing is best suited for economically producing large volumes of high quality prints in a manner that requires little maintenance. Many modern offset presses use computer to plate systems as opposed to the older computer to film work flows, which further increases their quality.

Advantages of offset printing compared to other printing methods include:

- Consistent high image quality. Offset printing produces sharp and clean images and type more easily than, for example, letterpress printing; this is because the rubber blanket conforms to the texture of the printing surface.
- Quick and easy production of printing plates.
- Longer printing plate life than on direct litho presses because there is no direct contact between the plate and the printing surface. Properly developed plates used with optimized inks and fountain solution may achieve run lengths of more than a million impressions.
- Cost. Offset printing is the cheapest method for producing high quality prints in commercial printing quantities.
- A further advantage of offset printing is the possibility of adjusting the amount of ink on the fountain roller with screw keys. Most commonly, a metal blade controls the amount of ink transferred from the ink trough to the fountain roller. By adjusting the screws, the gap between the blade and the fountain

roller is altered, leading to the amount of ink applied to the roller to be increased or decreased in certain areas. Consequently the density of the colour in the respective area of the image is modified. On older machines the screws are adjusted manually, but on modern machines the screw keys are operated electronically by the printer controlling the machine, enabling a much more precise result.

Disadvantages of offset printing compared to other printing methods include:

- Slightly inferior image quality compared to rotogravure or photogravure printing.
- Propensity for anodized aluminum printing plates to become sensitive (due to chemical oxidation) and print in non-image/background areas when developed plates are not cared for properly.
- Time and cost associated with producing plates and printing press setup. As a result, very small quantity printing jobs may now use digital offset machines.

The Offset Printing Process

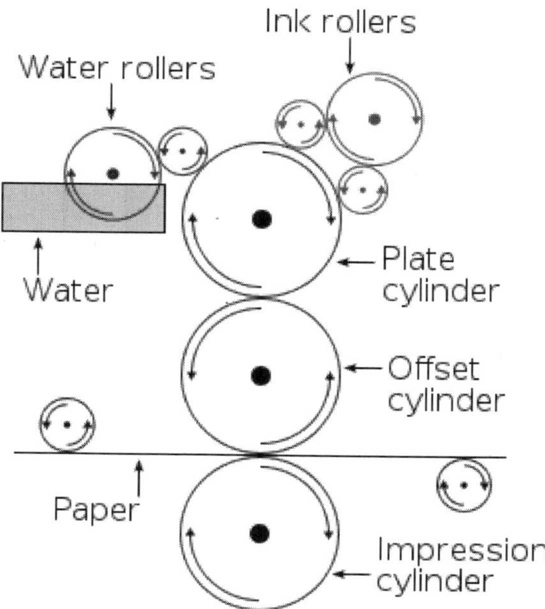

Figure: *Side view of the offset printing process. Multiple ink rollers are used to distribute and homogenize the ink.*

The most common kind of offset printing is derived from the photo offset process, which involves using light-sensitive chemicals and photographic techniques to transfer images and type from original materials to printing plates. In current use, original materials may be an actual photographic print and typeset text. However, it is more common — with the prevalence of computers and digital images — that the source material exists only as data in a digital publishing system.

Offset Lithographic printing on to a web (reel) of paper is commonly used for printing of newspapers and magazines for high speed production. In this process, ink is transferred from the ink duct to the paper in several steps:

1. The ink duct roller delivers ink from the ink duct to the ink pyramid, also called the *Ink Train.*
2. The ductor roller, sometimes called a vibrator roller due to its rapid back and forth motion, transfers ink from the duct roller to the first distribution roller. It is never in contact with both rollers at the same time.
3. The distribution rollers evenly distribute the ink. The first distribution roller picks up the ink from driving rollers, and the last distribution rollers transfer the ink to the form rollers.
4. The transfer rollers transfer ink between the ink-absorbing and ink-delivering driving rollers.
5. Driving rollers roll against the distribution rollers and either absorb or deliver ink, depending on their placement.
6. Ink form rollers transfer ink from the last distribution rollers on to the printing plate.
7. The printing plate transfers the ink to the offset cylinder (typically called the *blanket cylinder*) usually covered with a rubber "blanket."
8. The paper is then pressed against the blanket cylinder by the impression cylinder, transferring the ink onto the paper to form the printed image.

Process Printing

The actual process of printing is quite involved. One of the most important functions in the process is pre-press production. This stage makes sure that all files are correctly processed in preparation for printing. This includes converting to the proper CMYK colour model, finalizing the files, and creating plates for each colour of the job to be run on the press. Every printing technology has its own identifying marks, as does offset printing. In text reproduction, the type edges are sharp and have clear outlines. The paper surrounding the ink dots is usually unprinted. The halftone dots are always hexagonal though there are different screening methods.

Variations

Blanket-to-blanket: A printing method in which there are two blanket cylinders through which a sheet of paper is passed and printed on both sides. Blanket-to-blanket presses are considered a perfecting press because they print on both sides of the sheet at the same time. Since the blanket-to-blanket press has two blanket cylinders, making it possible to print on both sides of a sheet, there is no impression cylinder. The opposite blanket cylinders act as an impression cylinder to each other when print production occurs. There are also two plate cylinders on the press.

Blanket-to-steel: A printing method similar to a sheet offset press; except that the plate and cylinder pressures are quite precise. Actual squeeze between plate and blanket cylinder is optimal at .005"; as is the squeeze or pressure between the blanket cylinder and the substrate. Blanket-to-steel presses are considered one-colour presses. In order to print the reverse side, the web is turned over between printing units by means of turning bars. The method can be used to print business forms, computer letters, and direct mail advertising.

Variable-size Printing: A printing process that uses removable printing units, inserts, or cassettes for one-sided and blanket-to-blanket two-sided printing.

Keyless Offset: A printing process that is based on the concept of using fresh ink for each revolution by removing residual inks on the inking drum after each revolution. It is suitable for printing newspapers.

Plates

Metal Plates: Generally, the plates used in offset printing are thin, flexible, and usually larger than the paper size to be printed, and are usually made of aluminum, although sometimes they are made of multimetal, paper, or plastic.

Polyester Plates: These are much cheaper and can be used in place of aluminum plates for smaller formats or medium quality jobs, as their dimensional stability is lower.

Computer-to-plate (CTP) / Direct-to-plate (DTP)

Computer-to-plate (CTP) is a newer technology that allows the imaging of metal or polyester plates without the use of film. By eliminating the stripping, compositing, and traditional plate making processes, CTP altered the printing industry, which led to reduced prepress times, lower costs of labour, and improved print quality.

Most CTP systems used thermal CTP as opposed to violet CTP, though both systems are effective, depending on the needs of the printing job. Thermal CTP does have the advantage of higher quality, but violet CTP does cost significantly less. Thermal plates are generally used for shorter runs, while violet CTP is employed for longer runs, and is popular with two-up and four-up applications. Thermal CTP has the additional benefit of using binary exposure, which limits the risk of under or overexposure, and makes it possible to work under yellow light.

Thermal CTP involves the use of thermal lasers to expose and/ or remove areas of coating while the plate is being imaged. This depends on whether the plate is negative, or positive working. These lasers are generally at a wavelength of 830 nanometers, but vary in their energy usage depending on whether they are used to expose or ablate material. Violet CTP lasers have a much lower wavelength, 405–410 nanometers. Violet CTP is "based on emulsion tuned to visible light exposure." The general trend of platesetters has been to move toward coatings whose success on press is independent of post imaging chemical bath processing.

- Another process is CTCP (computer to conventional plate) system in which conventional offset plates can be exposed, making it an economical option.

Sheet-fed Offset

Sheet-fed refers to individual sheets of paper or paperboard being fed into a press via a suction bar that lifts and drops each sheet onto place. A lithographic ("litho" for short) press uses principles of lithography to apply ink to a printing plate, as explained previously. Sheet-fed litho is commonly used for printing of short-run magazines, brochures, letter headings, and general commercial (jobbing) printing. In sheet-fed offset, "the printing is carried out on single sheets of paper as they are fed to the press one at a time." Sheet-fed presses use mechanical registration to relate each sheet to one another to ensure that they are reproduced with the same imagery in the same position on every sheet running through the press.

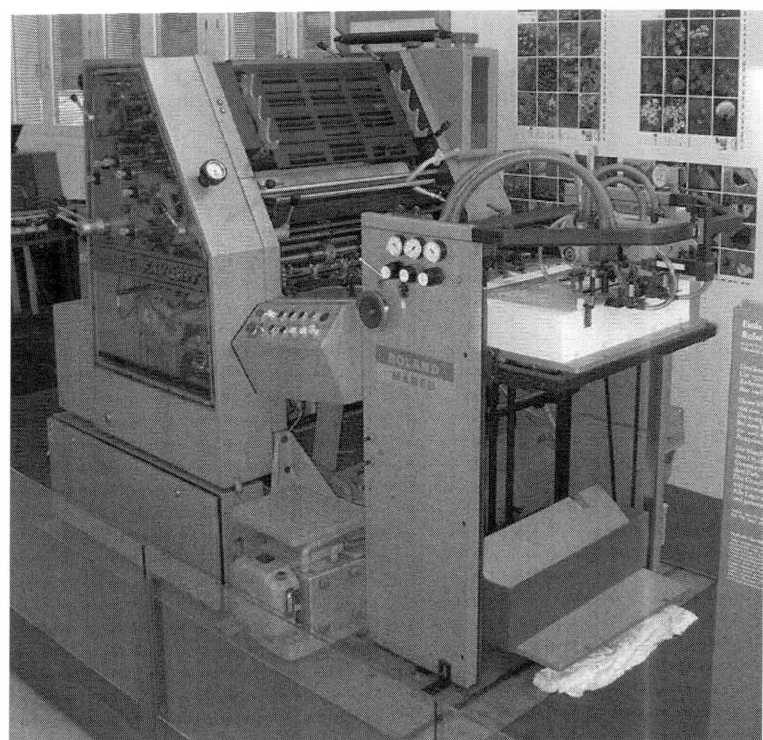

Figure: *Sheet-fed offset press*

Perfecting press: A perfecting press, also known as a duplex press, is one that can print on both sides of the paper at the same time. Web and sheet-fed offset presses are similar in that many of them can also print on both sides of the paper in one pass, making it easier and faster to print duplex.

Offset duplicators: Small offset lithographic presses that are used for fast, good quality reproduction of one- and two-colour copies in sizes up to 12" by 18". Popular models were made by A.B. Dick, Multilith, and the Chief and Davidson lines made by A.T.F./Davidson. Offset duplicators are made for fast and quick printing jobs; printing up to 12,000 impressions per hour. They are able to print business forms, letterheads, labels, bulletins, postcards, envelopes, folders, reports, and sales literature.

Feeder system: The feeder system is responsible for making sure paper runs through the press correctly. This is where the substrate is loaded and then the system is correctly set up to the certain specifications of the substrate to the press.

Printing/inking system: The Printing Unit consists of many different systems. The dampening system is used to apply dampening solution to the plates with water rollers. The inking system uses rollers to deliver ink to the plate and blanket cylinders to be transferred to the substrate. The plate cylinder is where the plates containing all of the imaging are mounted. Finally the blanket and impression cylinders are used to transfer the image to the substrate running through the press.

Delivery system: The delivery system is the final destination in the printing process while the paper runs through the press. Once the paper reaches delivery, it is stacked for the ink to cure in a proper manner. This is the step in which sheets are inspected to make sure they have proper ink density and registration.

Slur: Production or impact of double image in printing is known as 'slur'.

Web-fed Offset

Web-fed refers to the use of rolls (or "webs") of paper supplied to the printing press. Offset web printing is generally used for runs in excess of five or ten thousand impressions. Typical examples of web printing include newspapers, newspaper inserts/ads, magazines, direct mail, catalogues, and books. Web-fed presses are divided into two general classes: "cold" or "non-heatset," and "heatset" offset web presses; the difference being how the inks that are used dry. Cold web offset printing dries through absorption into the paper, while heatset utilizes drying lamps or heaters to cure or "set" the inks. Heatset presses can print on both coated (slick) and uncoated papers, while coldset presses are restricted to uncoated paper stock, such as newsprint. Some coldset web presses can be fitted with heat dryers, or ultraviolet lamps (for use with UV-curing inks). It is also possible to add a drier to a cold-set press. This can enable a newspaper press to print colour pages heatset and black and white pages coldset.

Web offset presses are beneficial in long run printing jobs, typically press runs that exceed ten or twenty thousand impressions. Speed is a determining factor when considering the completion time for press production; some web presses print at speeds of 3,000 feet per minute or faster. In addition to the benefits of speed and quick completion, some web presses have the inline ability to cut, perforate, and fold.

Heatset web offset: This subset of web offset printing uses inks which dry by evaporation in a dryer typically positioned just after the printing units. This is typically done on coated papers, where the ink stays largely on the surface, and gives a glossy high contrast print image after the drying. As the paper leaves the dryer too hot for the folding and cutting that are typically downstream procedures, a set of "chill rolls" positioned after the dryer lowers the paper temperature and sets the ink. The speed at which the ink dries is a function of dryer temperature and length of time the paper is exposed to this temperature. This type of printing is typically used for magazines, catalogues, inserts and other medium-to-high volume, medium-to-high quality production runs.

Coldset web offset: This is also a subset of web offset printing, typically used for lower quality print output. It is typical of newspaper production. In this process, the ink dries by absorption into the underlying paper. A typical coldset configuration is often a series of vertically arranged print units and peripherals. As newspapers seek new markets, which often imply higher quality (more gloss, more contrast), they may add a heatset tower (with a dryer) or use UV (ultraviolet) based inks which "cure" on the surface by polymerisation rather than by evaporation or absorption.

Web-fed Versus Sheet-fed

Sheet-fed presses offer several advantages. Because individual sheets are fed through, a large number of sheet sizes and format sizes can be run through the same press. In addition, waste sheets can be used for make-ready (which is the testing process to ensure a quality print run). This allows for lower cost preparation so that good paper is not wasted while setting up the press, for plates and inks. Waste sheets do bring some disadvantages as often there are dust and offset powder particles that transfer on to the blankets and plate cylinders, creating imperfections on the printed sheet.

Web-fed presses, on the other hand, are much faster than sheet-fed presses, with speeds in excess of 20,000 cut-offs per hour. (Cut-off is the paper that has been cut off a reel or web on the press. The length of each sheet is equal to the cylinder's circumference.) The speed of web-fed presses makes them ideal for large runs such as newspapers, magazines, and comic books. However, web-fed presses have a fixed cut-off, unlike rotogravure or flexographic presses, which are variable.

Inks

Offset printing uses inks that, compared to other printing methods, are highly viscous. Typical inks have a dynamic viscosity of 40–100 Pa·s.

There are many types of paste inks available for utilization in offset lithographic printing and each have their own advantages and disadvantages. These include heat-set, cold-set, and energy-curable (or EC), such as ultraviolet- (or UV-) curable, and electron beam- (or EB-) curable. Heat-set inks are the most common variety and are "set" by applying heat and then rapid cooling to catalyze the curing process. They are used in magazines, catalogues, and inserts. Cold-set inks are set simply by absorption into non-coated stocks and are generally used for newspapers and books but are also found in insert printing and are the most economical option. Energy-curable inks are the highest-quality offset litho inks and are set by application of light energy. They require specialized equipment such as inter-station curing lamps, and are usually the most expensive type of offset litho ink.

- Letterset inks are mainly used with offset presses that do not have dampening systems and uses imaging plates that have a raised image.
- Waterless inks are heat-resistant and are used to keep silicone-based plates from showing toning in non-image areas. These inks are typically used on waterless Direct Imaging presses.
- Single Fluid Inks are newer ink that uses a process allowing lithographic plates on a lithographic press without using a dampening system during the process.

Ink/water Balance

Ink and water balance is an extremely important part of offset printing. If ink and water are not properly balanced, the press operator may end up with many different problems affecting the quality of the finished product, such as emulsification (the water overpowering and mixing with the ink). This leads to scumming, catchup, trapping problems, ink density issues and in extreme cases the ink not properly drying on the paper; resulting in the job being unfit for delivery to the client. With the proper balance, the job will have the correct ink density and should need little further adjustment except for minor ones. An example would be when the press heats up during normal operation, thus evaporating water at a faster rate. In this case the machinist will gradually increase the water as the press heats up to compensate for the increased evaporation of water. Printing machinists generally try to use as little water as possible to avoid these problems.

Fountain Solution

Fountain solution is the water-based (or "aqueous") component in the lithographic process that moistens the non image area of the plate in order to keep ink from depositing (and thus printing). Historically, fountain solutions were acid-based and made with gum arabic, chromates and/or phosphates, and magnesium nitrate. Alcohol is added to the water to lower the surface tension and help cool the press a bit so the ink stays stable so it can set and dry fast. While the acid fountain solution has improved in the last several decades, neutral and alkaline fountain solutions have also been developed. Both of these chemistries rely heavily on surfactants/emulsifiers and phosphates and/or silicates to provide adequate cleaning and desensitizing, respectively. Since about 2000, alkaline-based fountain solutions have become less common due to the inherent health hazards of high pH and the objectionable odor of the necessary microbiological additives.

Acid-based fountain solutions are still the most common variety and yield the best quality results by means of superior protection of the printing plate, lower dot gains, and longer plate life. Acids are also the most versatile; capable of running with all types of offset litho inks. However, because these products require more active ingredients to run well than do neutrals and alkalines, they are also the most expensive to produce. However, neutrals and, to a lesser degree, alkalines are still an industry staple and will continue to be used for most newspapers and many lower-quality inserts. In recent years alternatives have been developed which do not use fountain solutions at all (waterless printing).

In Industry

Offset lithography became the most popular form of commercial printing from the 1950s ("offset printing"). Substantial investment in the larger presses required for offset lithography was needed, and had an effect on the shape of the printing industry, leading to fewer, larger, printers. The change made a greatly increased use of colour printing possible, as this had previously been much more expensive. Subsequent improvements in plates, inks, and paper have further refined the technology of its superior production speed and plate durability. Today, lithography is the primary printing technology used in the U.S. and most often as offset lithography.

Today, offset lithography is "responsible for over half of all printing using printing plates". The consistent high quality of the prints and the volume of prints created for their respective cost makes commercial offset lithography very efficient for businesses, especially when many prints must be created.

Screen Printing

Screen printing or silk screening is a printing technique particularly suited for flat or relatively flat surfaces. The heart of the process involves a fine mesh or screen that is tightly stretched around a rigid frame. The areas that are *not* to be printed are masked out on the screen, and to create the print, the framed screen is positioned over the item to be printed, along with a dollop of thick ink. A squeegee is then used to press the ink through the screen.

The masked areas prevent ink from passing through, but the *unmasked* areas allow the ink to be imprinted on the material. The item is then sent on a conveyor belt through a heat-tunnel. This curing process ensures that the inks dry quickly so that they materials can be stacked or packaged. Properly cured inks will remain on the printed substrate even under harsh conditions.

If more colours are desired in the final design, the process is repeated with different screens. A design that requires four different colours would, therefore, require four different screens. The screens are usually placed on a rotary press that allows the different colour prints to be properly aligned or registered with each other. Some screen-printers have fully automatic presses that do not require any manual labour other than set-up and loading/unloading.

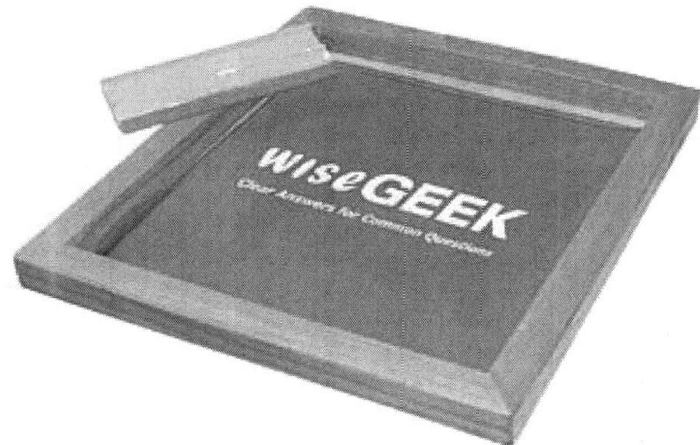

There are a variety of ways that the screen can be masked. The most straightforward way is to apply masking fluid directly on the screen. This technique is suitable for simple one or two colour graphics but is ineffective for more complex prints. For multicolour jobs, screen-printers often use photosensitive emulsions. First, the design is created on a clear piece of plastic film. A photosensitive coating is applied to the entire surface of the screen and then dried. The film is placed on the prepared screen and they are exposed to bright light. After a period of time, the exposed areas can be washed off the screen with water, which makes the screen ready to print.

Screen printing is most commonly used for t-shirts, garments and other fabrics, but it is also used on all sorts of other substrates ranging from plastic to metal. Although small and intricate details can be captured, this technique is ideally suited for bold and graphic designs.

When a design is going to be printed on darker items, a base print may be required to ensure that the colours maintain their vivacity. A base colour (usually white) is applied wherever the final print is desired; it is then *flash-cured* and the subsequent colours are printed on top. This flash-curing technique adds another step to the process, but ensures strong prints on on dark or even black materials.

The photo above shows the most basic components of a single colour screen printing setup. The screen is tightly stretched around the frame, which in this case is made out of wood; the blue emulsion is dried on the screen and serves as the mask. The squeegee is nothing more than a strip of rigid rubber mounted in a wooden handle.

To begin the printing process, the operator positions the screen directly on top the item to be printed. Next, ink is be applied to the area directly above the unmasked logo, and the squeegee is used to press the ink through to the substrate. As the operator firmly presses down with the squeegee, it is slid along the surface to ensure that ink penetrates through *all areas* of the unmasked logo. If additional colours are required, the process is repeated with additional screens. When finished, the screen is removed and the printed item is ready for curing.

Screen Printing Process

Prepare Your Artwork - To print a shirt you of course have to have something TO print onto the shirt. Whether you create it, you copy it, or a customer brings it to you, screen printing all starts with artwork. When thinking about artwork keep in mind, garbage in = garbage out, so the better quality of artwork you start out with the better screen prints you are going to get on your t-shirt. When you screen print a shirt you print one colour at a time, so if you're artwork is multiple colours, you need a way to separate those colours so you can create different screens for your design.

Most screen printers use CorelDraw X5 or Photoshop as their artwork programme in order to separate and cleanup the artwork for screen printing.

Print out Your Film Positives - Once your artwork is created and separated, the next step is creating a film positive in order to burn your image into a silk screen. A film positive transparency is basically like an overhead transparency (remember those from back in the day), what ever you want to print on the t-shirt, you print out in black ink on the film positive.

There are many ways to make film positives whether it's going to your local print shop, hand drawing your image, or purchasing a compatible printer for use at home. It's very important for your film positive to be as black a possible, we'll explain why in the next step...

Expose Your Image Into a Screen - Ok, you have the art, you printed your films, now its time to make the screen. A screen printing frame consists of a wood or aluminum frame stretched with polyester mesh on it. The mesh holds the image onto the screen and lets ink pass through when you by pressing it with a squeegee. The mesh holds the image by using a film or emulsion that is coated onto the mesh. Before you coat the mesh, it is cleaned with a special screen printing degreaser so that the emulsion sticks to it.

Emulsion is light sensitive, so when you coat the screen it is typically done in a darkroom that has special light safe yellow bulbs in it. After the screen is coated and dried, you get your film positive, align it to the screen, and expose it with a screen printing exposure unit or light for an allotted amount of time. The screen hardens to light but the positive or black area of the film blocks the light from reaching the emulsion, this leaves that area of the emulsion unexposed or soft.

This is why its so important to ensure you have a very black film, if your film is only partially black, it will let light in during the exposure process. After the screen is exposed, simply rinse it with water, the soft part that was not exposed rinses out leaving that area of the mesh open so you can print ink through it! The exposure process is complete and your almost ready to start screen printing shirts!

Set up Your Screen Printing Press - Alight, its almost go time, but before you start printing you need to setup the screens on your screen printing press. A screen printing press consists of a base that holds you printing platen and a number of colour arms (depending on how many colours your press is.) A manual press can be as small as a 1 colour 1 station, or as large an 8 colour 8 station.

Of course if you have more colour arms you have the ability to print more colours at the shirt at one time, likewise if you have a higher a mount of printing stations, you can print faster. Right before you clamp your screens into your press you tape off the edges of your frame with screen tape which helps keep the screen and shirt clean during printing. If you are printing a multiple colour job, you'll need to register the colours together in so that they match correctly when you print all of them at once on the shirt.

Using a press with joystick registration or micro registration is extremely helpful when printing fine detail multiple colour jobs. Once you think your screens are in registration, you complete a test print typically on an old shirt or a printing test pellon to ensure everything lines up.

It's Time to Print - Screen printing a shirt actually goes pretty fast when you get all setup and the opportunity to make some good money is definitely there. Typically a 1 or two colour shirt sells screen printed for $5-$6 wholesale. Depending on the image size and type of the wholesale t-shirt your cost on this may be $2. So that means each shirt you are profiting between $3-$4.

Take that and then print 40 shirts per hour on a small press or 100 shirts an hour on a larger screen printing press and you're making $120-$400 per hour! Not too bad for pushing ink huh! There are a few things to keep in mind during the printing process. First is called flashing, if you are printing on dark garments where you have to use a white under base under colour ink or if you have ink touching other ink, you'll need to flash dryer in order to cure/set the ink giving you the ability to print another colour on top of your first layer.

Flashing only takes about 10-15 seconds, but it does slow the process down, typically shirts that need flashes are sold for more due to the increased production time. Once the shirt is printed it needs to cure in order for the ink to stay set into the garment. Ink cures at 320 degrees through the entire ink film. To cure a shirt you can use an oven or heat gun (for the hobbyists), a flash dryer, or optimally a conveyor dryer. Its important to ensure your ink is cured because if it is not cured thoroughly, it will wash out of the shirt. To help ensure your ink is cured you can use a laser temp gun to measure the temperature of the ink while it is being cured.

The Shirts are Printed and its Time to Clean up - Many people think screen printing is a messy process, it's only super messy if you make it and don't clean up after yourself. Messy is as messy does right. Cleanup is pretty easy to do. First save as much ink as possible by using an ink cleanup card to scrape it out of the screen and back into your ink container.

Depending on the type of ink you use to print with you should use a screen printing screen wash to clean the ink out of your screen and to wipe down your press. If you are going to print more shirts in the future with the same design you can choose to save your screen for future use. You can also use your screen again for a different design by using emulsion remover and a power sprayer to take the image off the screen so you can start the process over again!

5

Paisley Design

Paisley or Paisley pattern is a term in English for a design using the *boteh* or *buta*, a droplet-shaped vegetable motif of Persian or Indian origin. Such designs became very popular in the West in the 18th and 19th centuries, following imports of post-Mughal versions of the design from British India, especially in the form of Kashmir shawls, and were then imitated locally. The pattern is sometimes called "Persian pickles" by American traditionalists, especially quilt-makers, or "Welsh pears" in Welsh textiles as far back as 1888.

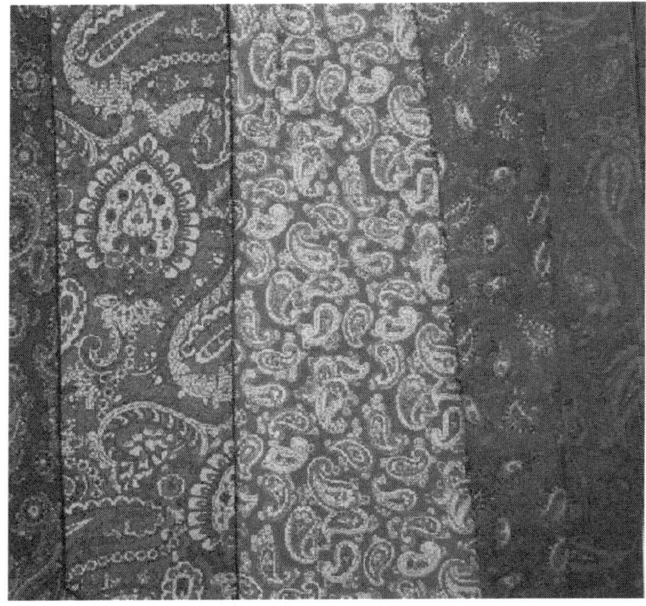

Figure: *Paisley ties*

Origins

Resembling a twisted teardrop, the kidney-shaped paisley is of Iranian and Indian origin, but its western name derives from the town of Paisley, in central Scotland, a centre for textiles where paisley designs were produced.

In Persian language the design is known as *Boteh Jegheh* and it has been used in Iran since the Sassanid Dynasty (AD 224 to AD 651).

Some design scholars also call the distinctive shape *Boteh* and believe it is the convergence of a stylized floral spray and a cypress tree: a Zoroastrian symbol of life and eternity. A floral motif called Buteh, which originated in the Sassanid Dynasty (200–650 AD) and later in the Safavid Dynasty of Persia (from 1501 to 1736), was a major textile pattern in Iran during the Qajar Dynasty and Pahlavi Dynasty. In these periods, the pattern was used to decorate royal regalia, crowns, and court garments, as well as textiles used by the general population. According to Azerbaijani historians, the design comes from ancient times of Zoroastrianism and is an expression of the essence of that religion. It subsequently became a decorative element widely used in Azerbaijani culture and architecture.

The pattern is still popular in Iran and South and Central Asian countries. It is woven using gold or silver threads on silk or other high quality textiles for gifts, for weddings and special occasions. In Iran and Uzbekistan its use goes beyond clothing – paintings, jewellery, frescoes, curtains, tablecloths, quilts, carpets, garden landscaping, and pottery also sport the buta design. In Uzbekistan the most frequently found item featuring the design is the traditional doppi headdress.

The traditional design is also used in gold jewelleries. The *manga maalai* (Mango necklace) with matching earrings is a traditional bharathanatyam/temple jewellery.

It is a prominent design in Kanchipuram saris. It has sometimes been associated with Hinduism.

In Other Languages

The modern French words for paisley are *boteh* and *palme*, the latter being a reference to the palm tree, which, along with the pine tree and the cypress tree, is one of the traditional botanical motifs thought to have influenced the shape of the paisley element as it is now known.

In various languages of India and Pakistan, the design's name is related to the word for mango:

- In Tamil: *mankolam*, mango pattern.
- In Marathi: *koyari*, mango seed.
- In Urdu: *carrey*, mango seed.
- In Punjabi: *ambi*, from *amb*, mango.

European Introduction

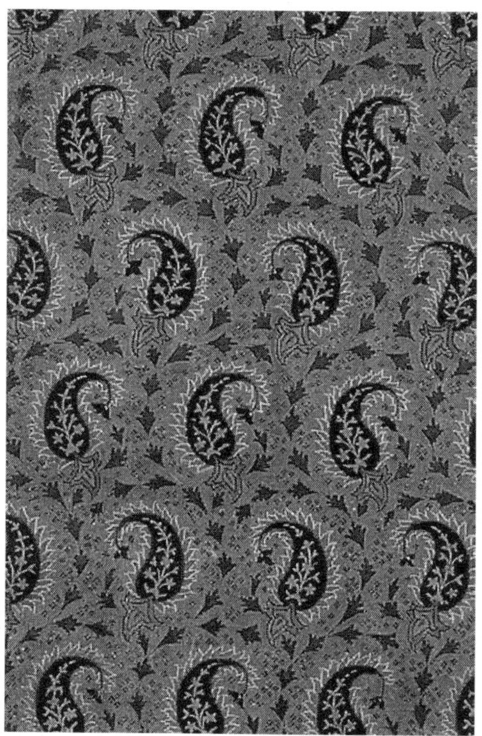

Figure: *Persian silk brocade with golden thread (*golabetoon*), woven in 1939*

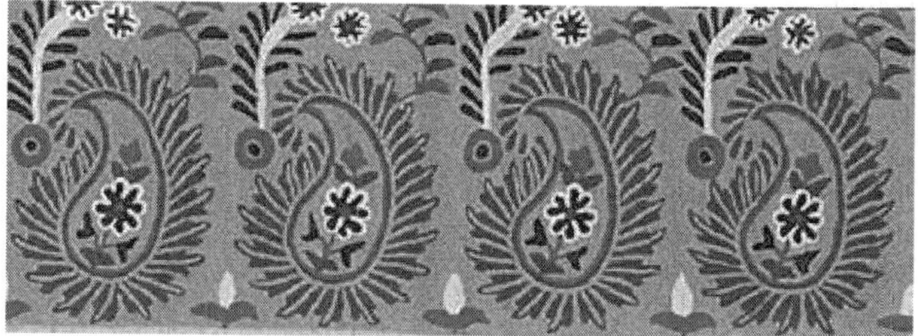

Figure: *Paisley wallpaper*

Imports from the East India Company in the first half of the 17th century made paisley and other Indian patterns popular, and the Company was unable to import enough to meet the demand. It was popular in the Baltic states between 1700 and 1800 and was thought to be used as a protective charm to ward off evil demons. However, in modern culture, Western youth have used it as a symbol of rebellion.

Local manufacturers in Marseilles began to mass-produce the patterns via early textile printing processes at 1640. England, circa 1670, and Holland, in 1678, soon followed. This, in turn, provided Europe's weavers with more competition than they could bear, and the production and import of printed paisley was forbidden in France by royal decree from 1686 to 1759. However, enforcement near the end of that period was lax, and France had its own printed textile manufacturing industry in place as early at 1746 in some locales. Paisley was not the only design produced by French textile printers; the demand for paisley which created the industry there also made possible production of native patterns such as *toile de Jouy*.

In the 19th century European production of paisley increased, particularly in the Scottish town from which the pattern takes its modern name. Soldiers returning from the colonies brought home cashmere wool shawls from India, and the East India Company imported more. The design was copied from the costly silk and wool Kashmir shawls and adapted first for use on handlooms, and, after 1820, on Jacquard looms.

From roughly 1800 to 1850, the weavers of the town of Paisley in Renfrewshire, Scotland, became the foremost producers of these shawls. Unique additions to their hand-looms and Jacquard looms permitted them to work in five colours when most weavers were producing paisley using only two. The design became known as the *Paisley pattern.* By 1860, Paisley could produce shawls with fifteen colours, which was still only a quarter of the colours in the multicolour paisleys then still being imported from Kashmir.

In addition to the loom-woven fabric, Paisley became a major site for the manufacture of printed cotton and wool in the 19th century, according to the Scotland's Paisley Museum and Art Gallery. The paisley pattern was being printed, rather than woven, onto other textiles, including cotton squares which were the precursors of the modern bandanna. Being able to purchase printed paisley rather than woven paisley brought the price of the costly pattern down and added to its popularity. The key places of manufacture for printed paisley were Britain and the Alsace region of France.

Contemporary Style

Paisley was particularly popular during the Summer of Love, heavily identified with psychedelic style and the interest in Indian spirituality and culture brought about by the pilgrimage of The Beatles to India in 1968. Also, Fender Guitars made a Pink Paisley version of their Telecaster guitar, by sticking paisley wallpaper onto the guitar bodies. Prince paid tribute to the rock and roll history of paisley when he created the Paisley Park Records recording label and established Paisley Park Studios, both named after his 1985 song "Paisley Park".

At the 2010 Winter Olympics, Azerbaijan's team sported colourful paisley trousers. A Russian publication noted that "Azerbaijan has no chance of winning at the Winter Olympics; however, the country had already left its mark on the games".

The Paisley Pattern from Its Origins to the Modern Runway

The paisley form, signifying fertility, reproduction, abundance, was thus continually introduced into decorative work whether sacred or secular. Through time it became more and more conventionalised and varied in form.

Since it first started appearing on shawls favoured by ladies in the 1800s, the Paisley pattern went in and out of fashion many times, coming back in some of the current collections. So for today let's leave the glamour of catwalks behind and rediscover the history of the Paisley pattern and of the workers who made the famous shawls.

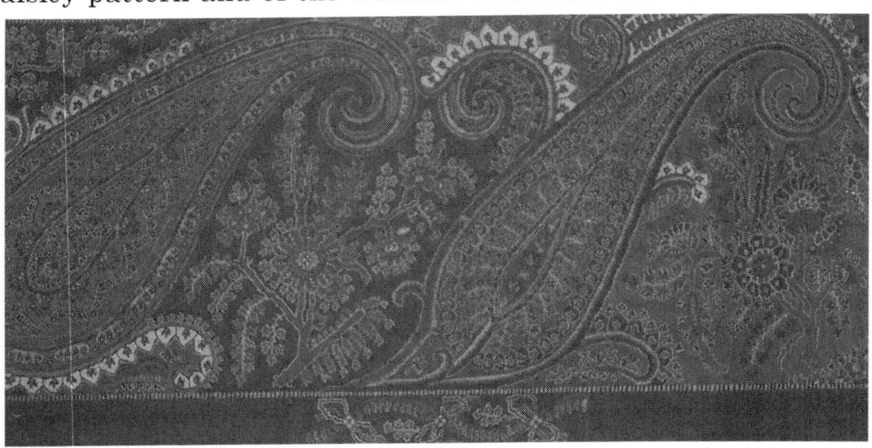

The pattern commonly known as "Paisley" is named after the eponymous town in Scotland, but it didn't originate there. The pattern can indeed be traced back to ancient Babylonian civilisation where it was used as a symbol to represent the growing shoot of the date palm, also regarded as the "tree of life", since it provided Babylonians with food, drink, clothing and shelter.

The symbol first appeared to decorate a 17th century Indian shawl from Kashmir used by men. The shawls arrived in Britain in the 18th century when the soldiers and administrators of the British East India Company brought them back as presents for their loved ones. As the shawls became more fashionable, the Company started importing them and, since demand exceeded supply and the cost of the original Kashmir shawls was rather high, many manufacturers began imitating the product.

Britain was ahead of France for what regarded the shawl trend: Empress Josephine started wearing the shawl only after the Napoleonic Wars brought French women into contact with this garment. In the 19th century the shawl was mainly employed by ladies to provide contrasts in silhouettes: the dresses were straight and the shawls added a sort of draped element to a woman's attire.

The early shawls were imitations of the Kashmir shawls, especially for what regarded size and proportions, and also had deep patterned borders at the narrow ends while the centres were almost always white. It was only in later years that manufacturers introduced colourful centres.

The shape of the shawl was altered in the 1820s: as the straight dress was abandoned in favour of wider shoulders, narrow waists and flaring skirts, the shawl was folded to a triangle and draped around the shoulders to highlight the tapered waist.

Around the same time there was a change also in the weaving processes: the original Kashmir shawls were produced using the time consuming twill-tapestry weaving. British manufacturers wove the shawls on a silk warp, but soon spinning improved allowing to produce an all-woollen shawl in one piece.

In this way the pattern extended towards the central area becoming more intricate and complicated and turning into a naturalistic floral motif. In some cases the entire surface of the shawl was covered, though plain centres were considered more apt for summer wear since they were lighter in weight.

An important part of the 19th century brides' trousseau, the white centre plaids were usually worn by women attending Churching or Kirking ceremonies.

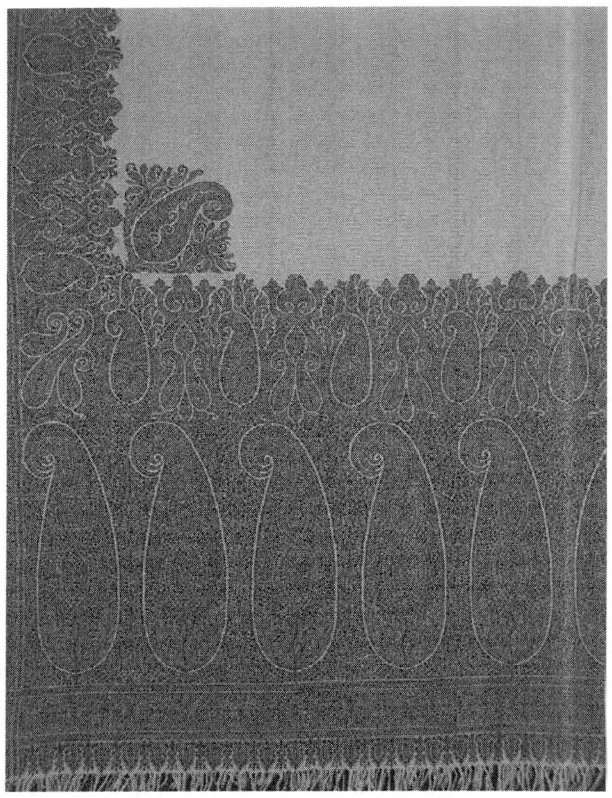

Another change regarding the shawl silhouette was introduced in the 1840s since more women started wearing the rectangular plaids favoured by Queen Victoria instead of the square shawls. Besides, the large plaids - worn square about the shoulders - also allowed to cover the then fashionable crinolines. Reversible shawls arrived in 1865, though they weren't very successful because of their weight.

Paisley shawls were also popular among the working classes, and women who couldn't afford them opted for the Scotch Plaid until manufacturers started producing a printed version of the shawl on cheap fabric (a printed paisley shawl on expensive silk gauze already existed and was mainly meant to be worn at balls and during the summer).

The printed shawls were one of the reasons why the trend somehow started dying, the other reason is to be attributed to the arrival of the bustle: when ladies turned to mantles, capes and jackets for outdoor wear, the shawl went out of fashion by the 1880s also in small villages.

The starting point to make a shawl was to get a sketch on paper taking inspiration from the original Kashmir scarves. The design on squared point-paper would then be applied to the loom. Original shawls were made using pashmina, but Paisley manufacturers had to settle on Australian worsted yarn that had to be dyed (Paisley also boasted a strong dyeing industry). Natural dyes prevailed at the beginning (prussiate, saffron, malichite, chrome, lime, logwood and indigo), while, from 1856, manufacturers turned to chemical aniline dyes.

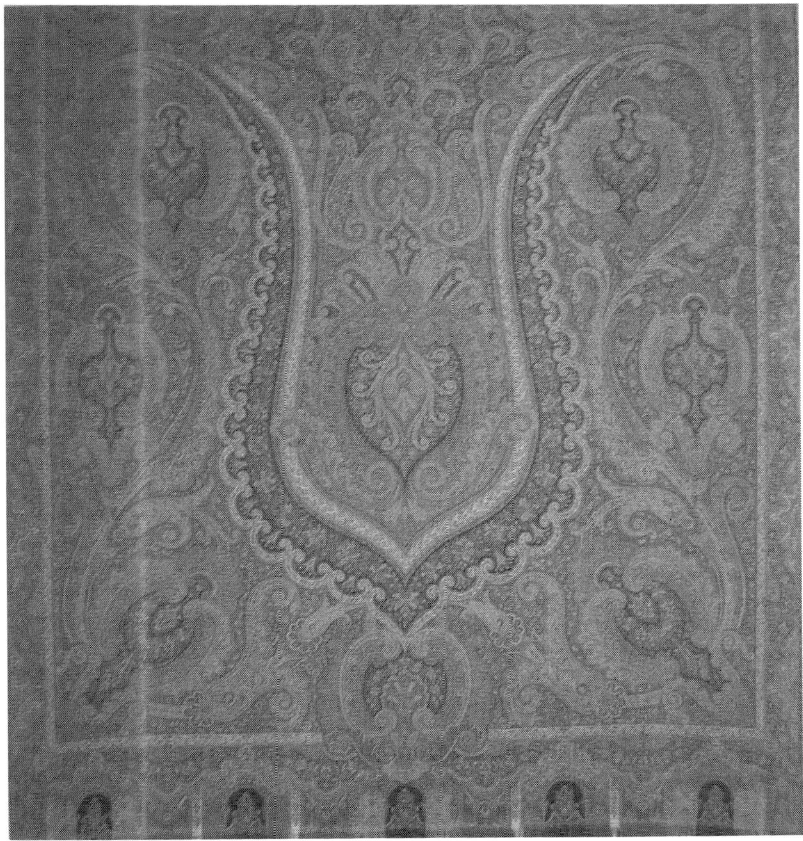

Looms were set up by men who went from loomshop to loomshop. Drawlooms - that is handlooms with an overhead harness - were replaced in the 1820s by the Jacquard. Weavers had to be highly skilled and accurate in their work. Once a shawl was woven it was inspected by the manufacturer and the workers then went through the finishing stages: they would remove all the loose threads, form the fringes (a job usually for women), wash the shawls, stretch them over a drying frame and finally steampress them.

The weaving industry was probably introduced in Paisley around the 18th century, when it mainly produced rough linen and woollen cloths, passing later on onto muslins and silks. Many weavers were left unemployed when in the following century it became difficult to find raw silk, but things got better when the shawls suddenly became popular and an Edinburgh manufacturer couldn't meet anymore the demand.

Weavers were self-employed since the looms belonged to the individual weaver who would work following the instructions of the manufacturer who provided the design and the yarns. Part of a a very profitable industry, the Paisley weavers were among the best paid workers in Britain in those times, yet, little by little, their fate changed. Upon the introduction of the Jacquard system, manufacturers bought looms (they were too expensive for the individual weaver to buy) and installed them in the factories, marking the slow end of a cottage industry.

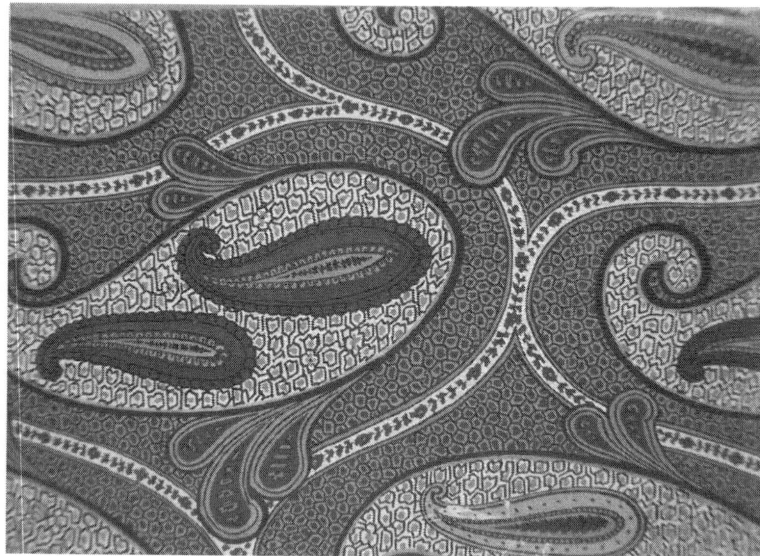

The weavers' work also depended on fashion: if shawls were only worn for one season, manufacturers wouldn't be able to sell their stocks and therefore pay the workers. This meant that Paisley went through periods of crisis and depression, especially between 1841 and 1843 when almost 15,000 members of the weaving community received relief.

Disputes with manufacturers were frequent and sorted out by a central committee set to negotiate on labour matters with the manufacturers. If disputes weren't solved, weavers would parade an eggify of the manufacturer through the streets before burning it.

One of issues of dispute was the Sma' Shot, a binding that held the coloured wefts in place. Since the thread was not seen on the surface, the manufacturers refused to pay for the yarn used. After many disputes the weavers won their fight and established the first Saturday of July as Sma' Shot Day, a celebratory holiday to commemorate their triumph over the manufacturers.

As the years passed the number of manufacturers reduced: the last Paisley shawls were woven in 1903 and the very last loomshop closed down in the early 1940s. One of the main reason for the end of the Paisley industry was the change in fashion trends, followed also by the fact that it became soon impossible to weave the more fashionable and complicated shawl patterns on traditional 19th century looms.

Glasgow weaving college held an exhibition of Paisley shawls in 1902, and a bigger one was organised at the Paisley Museum in 1905. The collection of the local museum grew up year after year also thanks to the donations that included shawls, costumes, but also looms.

Though the looms are the key pieces of the shawl gallery at Paisley Museum, the collection also features a few dresses from 1813-15 in lovely wool-silk fabrics matched with Paisley shawls.

The latter moved from the designer's interpretation of a gypsy and travelling nomadic woman's wardrobe and included designs in silk red and blue paisley prints mixed with graphic black and white geometric figures reminiscent of the formal images of the Bauhaus.

This combination was applied to dresses, sarouel trousers and button-down shirts, tops and coats characterised by long sleeves slit to the shoulders that gave the garments a sort of cape-like look but also to accessories such as large carrier bags.

Kanchipuram Sari

A Kanchipuram sari (also known as a Kanjivaram sari) is a type of sari traditionally made by weavers from Kanchipuram located in

Tamil Nadu, India. These are woven naturally. The Kanchipuram sari is distinguished by its wide contrast borders.

A single Kanchipuram sari can cost anywhere between ₹2500 (US$38) to 100000 (US$1,500) or more depending upon the intricacy of work, colours, pattern, material used like zari, gold thread etc.

Since 2005, Kanchipuram saris are protected by a Geographical Indication label, certifying their origin.

Legend and History

According to legends in [Hindu mythology] Kanchi silk weavers are the descendants of Sage Markanda, the master weaver of Gods who is supposed to have woven tissue from lotus fibre. Also, while cotton is considered to the be the favourite fabric of Lord Shiva silk was preferred by Lord Vishnu.

Weaving Method

To weave a Kanchipuram sari three shuttles are used. While the weaver works on the right side, his aide works on the left side shuttle. The border colour and design are usually quite different from the body. If the *pallu* (the hanging end of the sari) has to be woven in a different shade, it is first separately woven and then delicately joined to the Sari. The part where the body meets the *pallu* is often denoted by a zig zag line.

Themes and Motifs

Suns, moons, chariots, peacocks, parrots, swans, lions, coins, mangoes, leaves and many such motifs are woven into Kanchipuram patterns. Other common motifs include a jasmine bud within a square or a round frame, locally known as *mallinaggu*. Another is *Thandavalam* where parallel lines run across the body of the Sari.

Significance

Kanchipuram saris woven with heavy silk and gold cloth are considered to be special and are worn on occasions and festivities only.

Creating Pattern Elements: Building a Library

Size of the Elements

As we work with vectors, sizes do not really matter. Everything is scalable to any size without loss of quality.

Upon completion of this tutorial you'll have a basic library with 13 symbols.

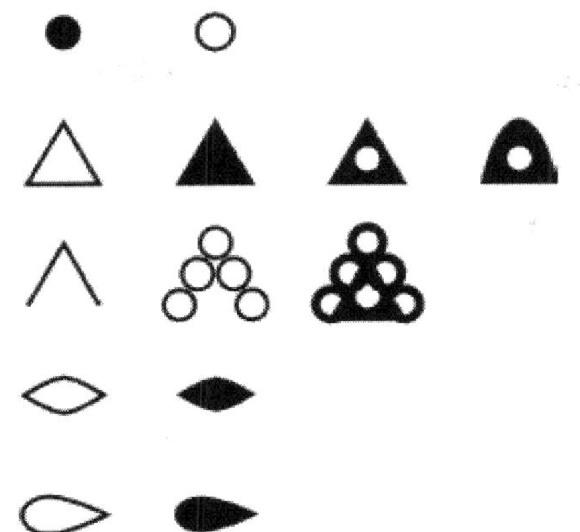

- Open Inkscape and start with a default document.

Circles

Basic element in all designs. Very easy to use for dotted patterns, strings of beads, buttons and more.

Circle 1

- Use the Ellipse Tool, and draw a small circle on the canvas. Hold down the Ctrl-key and keep an eye on the statusbar at the bottom of the screen: a ratio of 1:1 results in a circle. The one is about 15x15 px.
- Give it a black fill: click with the left mouse button on the black swatch in the colour palette at the bottom of the screen.
- Remove the stroke: hold the Shift-key down and click with the left mouse button on the X in the colour palette.

Circle 2

- Make a duplicate of Circle 1: select Edit > Duplicate from the menu (Ctrl+D).
- The duplicate is created on top of the original. Move it to its own spot with the mouse.
- Give the duplicate a black stroke (outline): hold down the Shift-key and click with the left mouse button on the black swatch in the colour palette.
- Set the Stroke width to 2px: click with the right mouse button on the number next to the stroke colour in the left lower corner of the screen. Select 2 from the list.
- Remove the fill: click with the left mouse button on the X in the colour palette.

- Set the size to exactly 15x15 px, use the input options for W and H at the top of the screen.
- Note: setting this size exactly makes life a bit easier later on, when we use this circle as element for Triangle 6.

Triangle Variations

Inkscape does not have the triangle as a primitive shape, but it has several methods to create one. I normally start with a rectangle and remove one of the nodes.

In this case I use the render option as it creates the shape I want in one step.

Triangle 1

- Select Extensions > Render > Triangle from the menu.
- Set the Mode dropdown selection to "From three sides".
- Set the lenght of the individual sides. I used 30px for the length of side a, b and c.

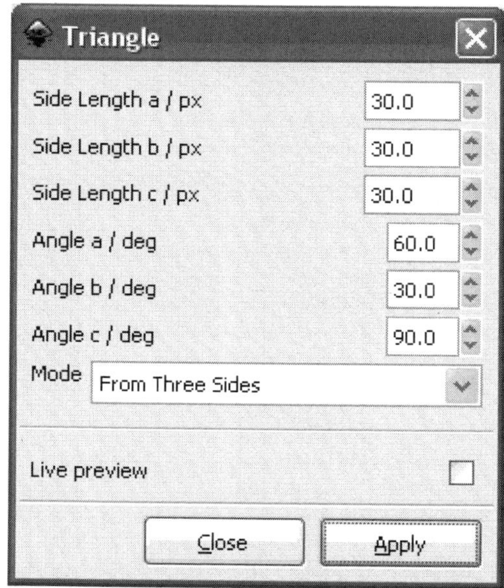

- Press the Apply button. An equilateral triangle is created.
- Close the dialog.

Triangle 2

- Create a duplicate of Triangle 1: select Edit > Duplicate from the menu (Ctrl+D).

- The duplicate is created exactly on top of the original, move it aside with the Select tool.
- Give the duplicate a black fill: click with the left mouse button on the black swatch in the colour palette.

Triangle 3

- Create a duplicate of Triangle 2 (Ctrl+D) and move it aside.
- Use the Ellipse Tool to create a small circle on top of the duplicate. Hold down the Ctrl-key to draw a circle with ratio 1:1. Mine was about 12x12px.
- Give the circle a white fill and remove the stroke (like before).
- Open the Align and Distribute dialog (Shift+Ctrl+A). Align the triangle and the circle at the centre .
- The vertical position should be eyeballed, but about the middle of the black triangle:
- Select both the triangle and circle objects and use Path > Difference (Ctrl+-) from the menu.

Triangle 4

- Create a duplicate of Triangle 3 (Ctrl+D) and move it aside.
- Use the Node Tool.
- Select the top node of the duplicate, and click on the Auto-Smooth button from the Node Tool - Tool Control bar.

Triangle 5

- Use the Select Tool.
- Create a duplicate of Triangle 1 (Ctrl+D) and move it aside.
- Use the Node Tool.
- Select the 2 nodes at the bottom of the duplicate: draw a selection window (rubberband) around them.
- Remove the segment between those 2 nodes by pressing this button in the Node Tool - Tool Control bar.
- This path will be used as skeleton path for triangle 6, but it is useful as pattern in itself.

Triangle 6

- Use the Select Tool.
- Select Circle 2, the small circle that has no fill.
- Press the Home-key to make the circle the top most object in the layer (z-order).

- Hold down the Shift-key and add the Triangle 5 as skeleton path to the selection.
- Select from the menu Extension > Generate from Path > Scatter.
- Use the following settings:

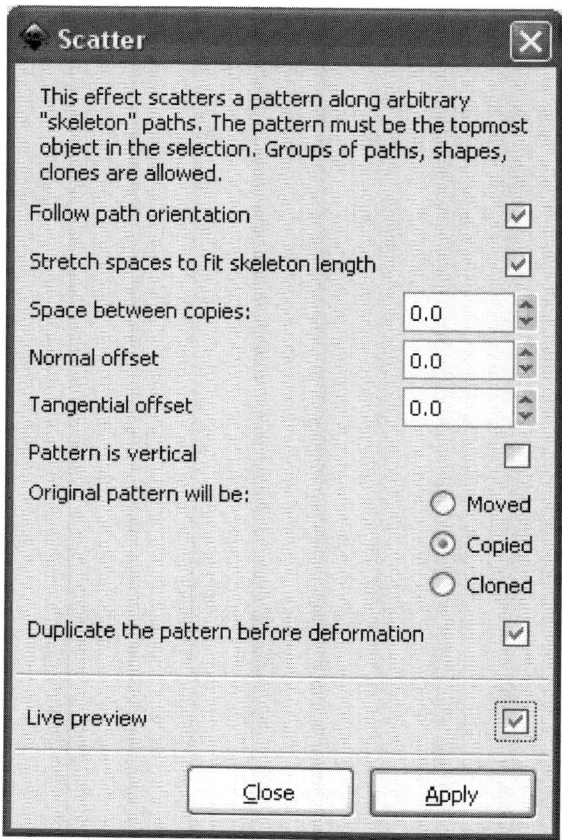

Which results in this if the Live Preview checkbox is ticked:

- Click on Apply and close the dialog.
- The generated pattern exists as a group of objects. Move them aside so they are separate from the skeleton path (Triangle 5).
- With the group selected use Object > Ungroup from the menu (Shift+Ctrl+G).
- Ensure the now ungrouped objects (5 circles) are selected.
- Use Path > Stroke to Path (Ctrl+Alt+C) from the menu. This turns the outline of the circles into a vector object.

- With these objects still selected: use Path > Combine (Ctrl+K) from the menu. This turns the outline shapes into a single path.

Triangle 7

- Make a duplicate from both Triangle 3 and Triangle 6.
- Select both duplicates.
- Use the Align and Distribute dialog (Shift+Ctrl+A) to align these 2 objects at the centre and at the bottom.
- Use Path > Combine (Ctrl+K) from the menu to create a fancy triangle.

Leaves

Leaves are part of many designs and stylish leaf patterns are easy to create.

Leaf 1

- Use the Ellipse Tool to draw a horizontally orientated ellipse.
- Select Path > Objec to Path from the menu.
- Use the Node Tool.
- Select the horizontal outer nodes, and make them cusp (corner).
- If one of the nodes does not turn into a sharp corner, then this is due to the length of the control handles. Select that node with the node tool and hold down the ,-key (comma).
- With the nodes still selected, move them out a bit further (Shift+>).
- Make the top and bottom node Auto-Smooth.
- Remove the fill, and set the stroke to black, width 2.

Leaf 2:

- Make a duplicate of Leaf 1: select Edit > Duplicate from the menu (Ctrl+D).
- Give the leaf a black fill, remove the stroke.

Leaf 3 and 4

- As alternative, follow the steps for leaf 1, but just make one horizontal node cusp.
- Save your work.

The file you just saved is a library file which can be used in many Inkscape designs. As I said at the beginning of this tutorial, the patterns are quite simple. You can experiment and add new elements to the file at all times, so over time you build up a nice collection.

Making use of the patterns for fancy border designs

Creating fancy borders with Inkscape is about the easiest thing to do as there are a few powerful extensions that makes life extremely easy.

Basic ingredients: a path and a pattern.

- Open a new Inkscape document.
- Import the pattern library file we created in the first part of this tutorial through File > Import. This way you can make use of the patterns without modifying the file itself.
- The contents of the file are imported as group: use Object > Ungroup (Shift+Ctrl+G) to ungroup the patterns.
- Use the bezier tool to draw a simple path. It does not matter what your path looks like, it could even be a straight line.

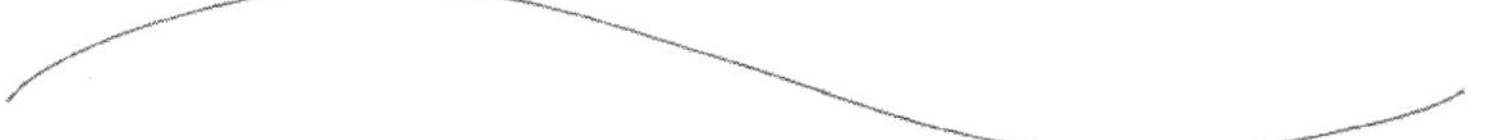

This path will be used as skeleton path in all examples below.

Example 1: Beaded String

- Select the open circle symbol from the pattern symbols.
- Press the Home-key to make the pattern the topmost object of the Layer.

The extensions Scatter and Pattern along Path assume that the topmost object in a selection is the pattern. Pressing the Home-key with the pattern object selected ensures this at all times.

- Add the skeleton path to the selection: with the pattern selected, hold down the Shift-key and click on the path.
- Use from the menu Extensions > Generate from Path > Scatter.
- Tick the preview checkbox to see how the pattern will be scattered along the path.
- Press the Apply button. Close the dialog.

The following pattern is created:

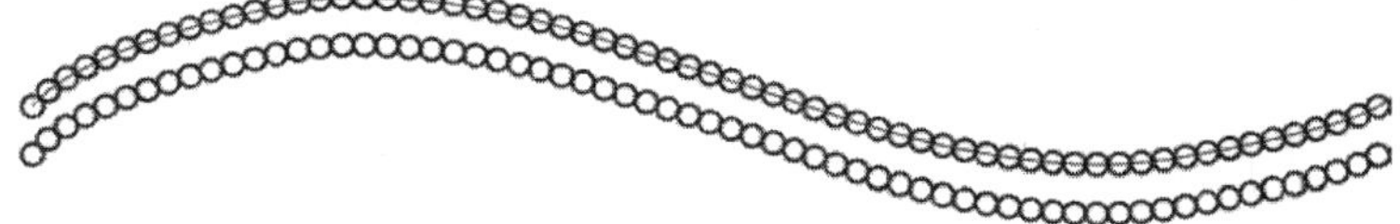

The Scatter extension creates a group of patterns that follows the path.

The Scatter extension does not deform the object that is used as pattern.

The skeleton path has been moved aside for the bottom border. As the pattern is created on top of the skeleton path it is necessary to move the pattern below the path first: select the pattern and press the End-key. Now the path can be selected and moved.

Example 2: Chain-Stitch Embroidery

As easy as the previous one, but we use the Extension "Pattern along Path here":

- Select the open leaf pattern.
- Press the Home-key to bring it to top.
- Add the skeleton path to the selection.
- Open Extensions > Generate from Path > Pattern along Path.
- Use the following settings in the dialog:

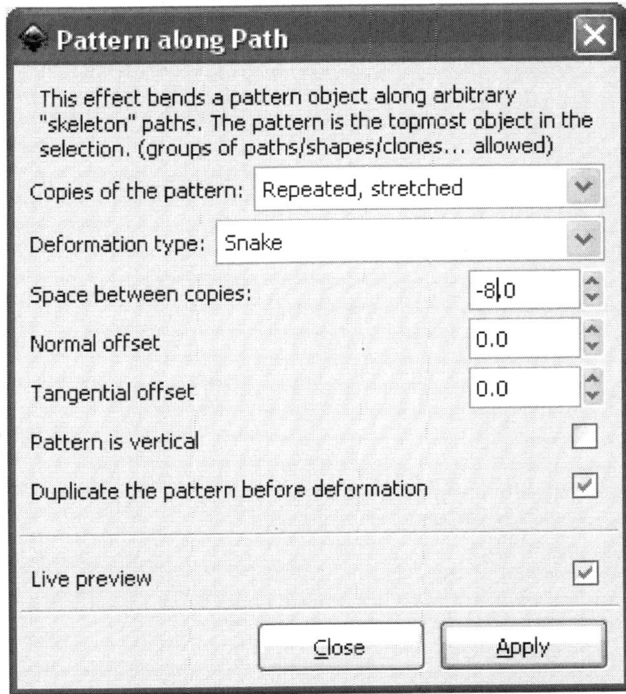

The negative value for the "space between copies" ensures the overlap of the pattern.

- Preview the effect and press Apply. Close the dialog.

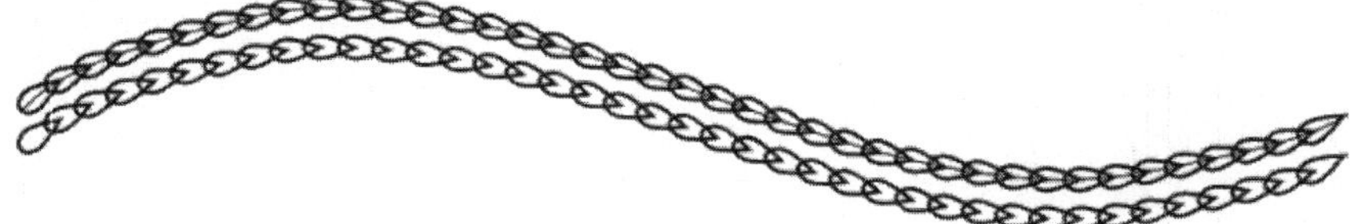

The Scatter extension creates a new path from the pattern, this is a main difference from the Scatter extension.

Pattern along Path will deform the pattern if that is needed to trace the skeleton path.

The skeleton path has been moved aside for the bottom border.

Example 3: A Lace Border

Very easy with the fancy triangle that is part of the library.

- Select the fancy triangle (triangle 7) pattern.
- Press the Home-key to bring it to top.
- Add the skeleton path to the selection.
- Open Extensions > Generate from Path > Pattern along Path.
- Use the following settings in the dialog:

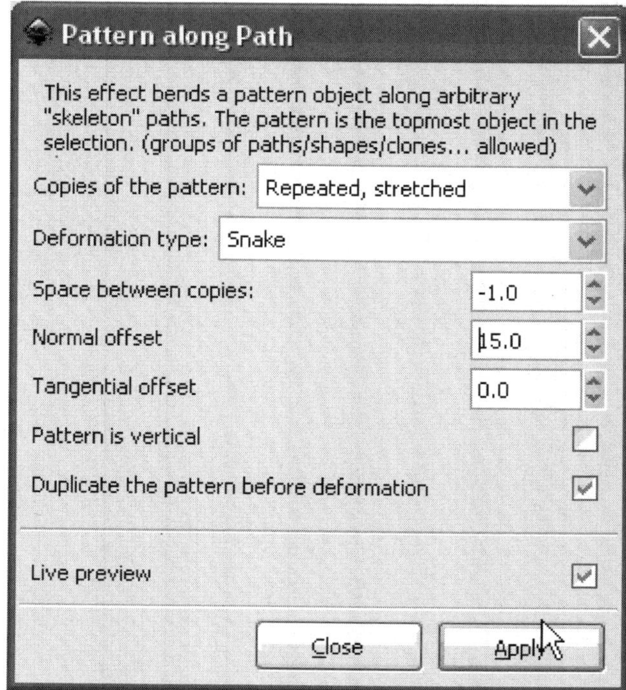

The negative value for "Space between copies" ensures a snug (and slightly overlapping) fit of the pattern along the path. The value for Normal offset moves the pattern a bit off-centre from the path. In this case so much that the bottom of the pattern sits on top of the path.

- Check the preview and press apply. Close the dialog.

The 2nd variant requires a bit of extra work, but is extremely easy to make, as it is basically adding another pattern to the original skeleton path:

- Select the open circle pattern.
- Press the Home-key to bring it to top.
- The generated lace path is on top of the skeleton path, send it to the back by selecting the generated path and then pressing the End-key.
- Select the skeleton path.
- Add the closed circle to the selection: with the skeleton path selected, hold down the Shift-key and click on the closed circle pattern.
- Open Extensions > Generate from Path > Pattern along Path.

The value for Normal offset moves the pattern a bit off-centre from the path. In this case so much that the top of the circle pattern aligns with the skeleton path.

- Check the preview and press the Apply button. Close the dialog.
- Bring the skeleton path to front: this is done easiest by selecting the generated circles path that is on top of it and send it to the back by pressing the End-key.
- Select the skeleton path and set the stroke width to 6px: select the number next to the stroke settings in the left bottom corner of the screen with the right mouse button. Select 6 px from the list.

Example 4: FloraL Branches

Very easy with the closed leaf pattern that is part of the library.

- Select the closed leaf pattern.
- Press the Home-key to bring it to top.
- Add the skeleton path to the selection.
- Open Extensions > Generate from Path > Pattern along Path.
- Use the following settings in the dialog:

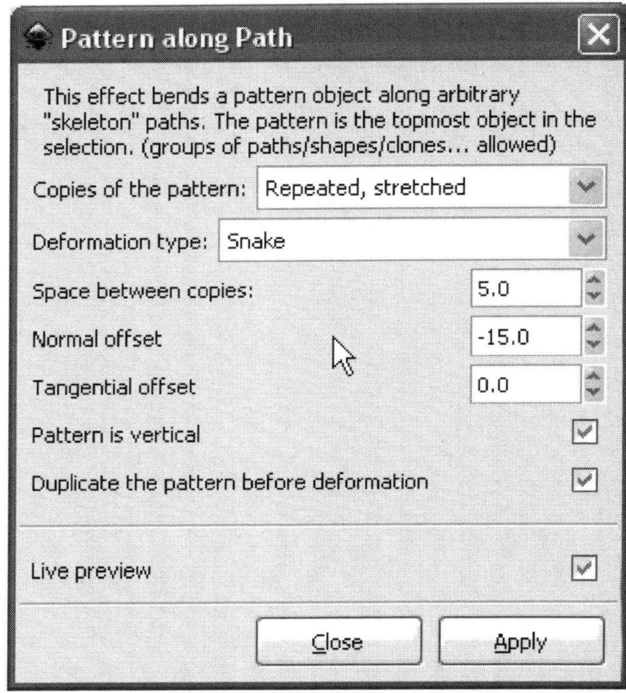

The value for "Space between copies" ensures an evenly spaced copy of the pattern along the path.

The value for Normal offset moves the pattern a bit off-centre from the path. In this case so much that the pattern is completely isolated from the path.

The value for "Pattern is vertical" ensures that the pattern is rotated over 90 degrees. Otherwise we would have a similar effect as created in example 2: chain stitch.

- Check the preview: one half of the floral pattern is created.
- Click on Apply and close the dialog.
- Select the skeleton path.

- Select from the menu Path > Reverse. This reverses the direction of the path, and that affects how a pattern is rendered along it.
- Add the same closed leaf pattern to the selection: with the path selected, hold down the Shift-key and click on the leaf pattern.
- Open Extensions > Generate from Path > Pattern along Path.
- Use the following settings in the dialog:

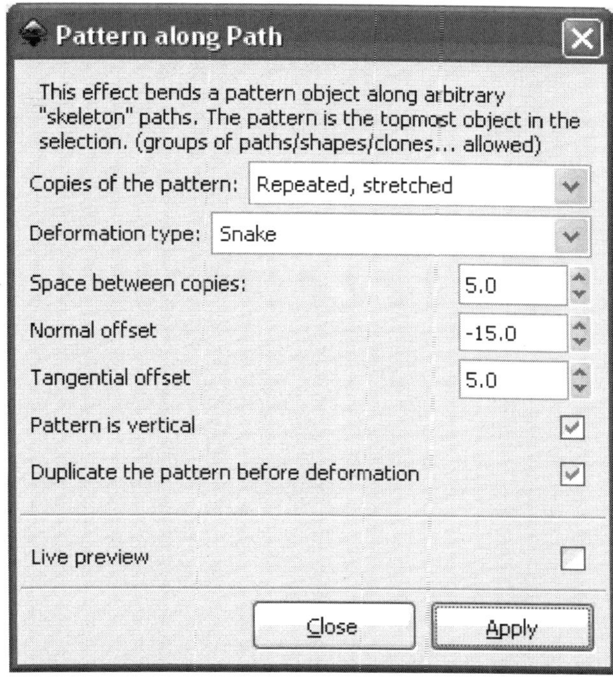

The settings are the same as before, except for Tangential offset. This determines the offset along the path, and by giving this the same value as the space between copies the pattern will be generated exactly between the patterns from the previous run.

As the path direction is reversed, the pattern will be created at the opposite site of the path.

- Preview the effect and press Apply. Close the dialog.
- Select the path and set the stroke width to 6px.

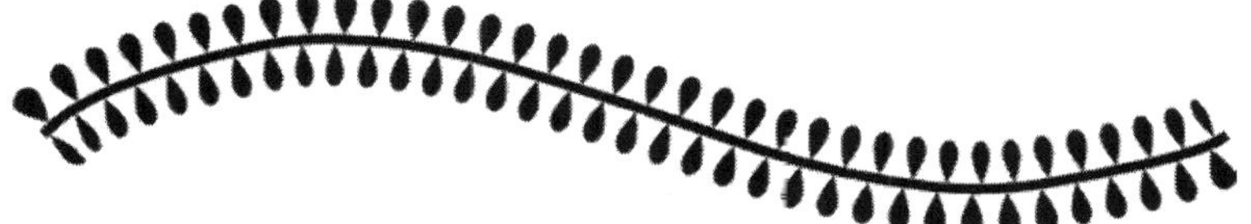

Closing Remarks

The extensions Pattern along Path and Scatter need a pattern and a skeleton path to work.

The pattern can exist of a path, groups of paths, shapes or clones.

The path however, must be exactly that: a path. That means that any Inkscape primitive shape such as an ellipse, rectangle or star first needs to be converted to a path: menu Path > Object to Path.

Design of a Floral Motif

Traditionally the paisley motif features floral designs in the centre. These designs can have many shapes from beautiful flowers, lush guirlandes to abstract motifs. A lot of the paisley motifs cut into woodblocks and then used to stencil the motif on fabric or paper. The motif we create here could have been used for that.

Art of Weaving

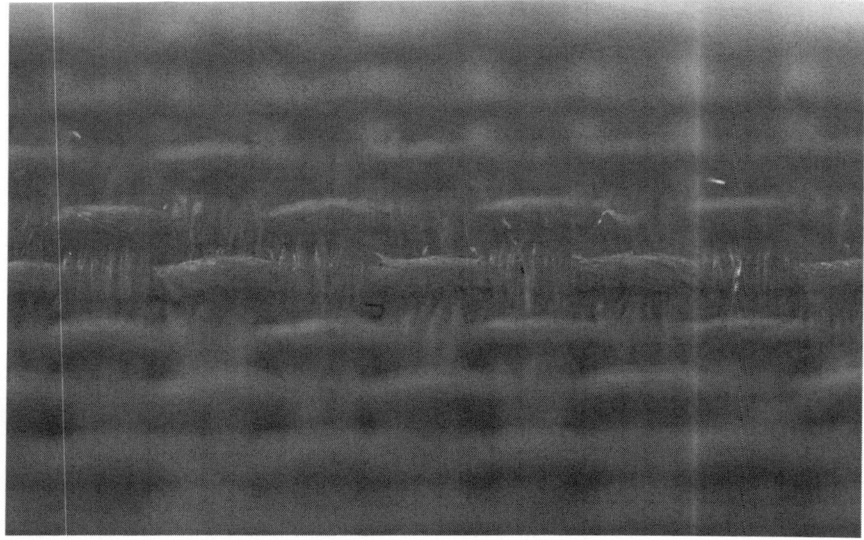

Figure: *A plain weave: image of warp and weft*

Weaving is a method of fabric production in which two distinct sets of yarns or threads are interlaced at right angles to form a fabric or cloth. The other methods are knitting, lace making, felting, and braiding or plaiting. The longitudinal threads are called the warp and the lateral threads are the weft or filling. (*Weft* or *woof* is an old English word meaning "that which is woven".) The method in which these threads are inter woven affects the characteristics of the cloth.

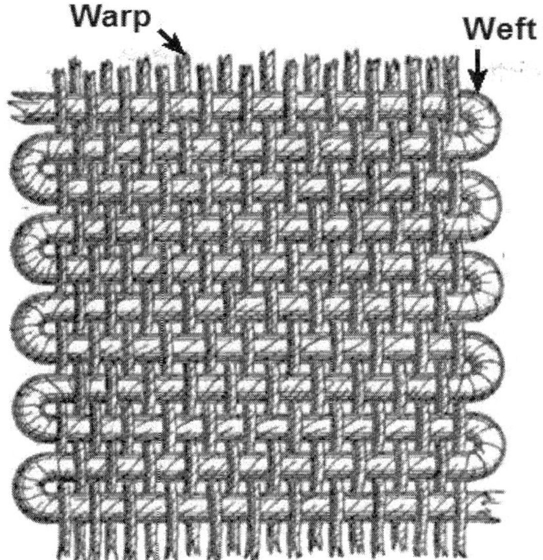

Figure: *Warp and weft in plain weaving*

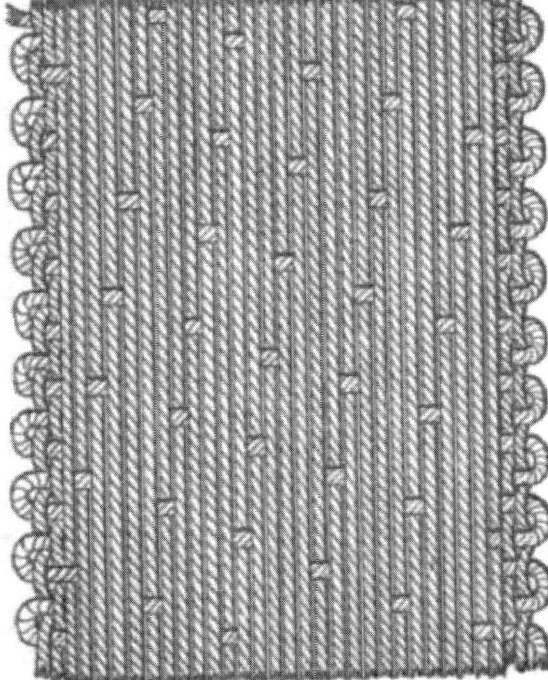

Figure: *A satin weave, common for silk, each warp thread floats over 16 weft threads.*

Cloth is usually woven on a loom, a device that holds the warp threads in place while filling threads are woven through them. A fabric band which meets this definition of cloth (warp threads with a weft thread winding between) can also be made using other methods, including tablet weaving, back-strap, or other techniques without looms.

The way the warp and filling threads interlace with each other is called the weave. The majority of woven products are created with one of three basic weaves: plain weave, satin weave, or twill. Woven cloth can be plain (in one colour or a simple pattern), or can be woven in decorative or artistic designs.

Preparing the Wrap Yarns for Weaving

Before their use on the loom, wrap and filling yarns must be prepared for weaving. In preparation for weaving, each wrap end (yarn) must be threaded through its own drop wire, heddle eye, and reed dent. The Drop wire is a device that will stop the loom if an end should break, the heddle eye is the opening in a heddle that carries the yarn, and the reed comb like device that will push each filling yarn close against the completed fabric.

Placing the wrap yarns on the loom is done either by drawing-in or by tying-in. Heddle wires are held in frames called harnesses. The number of harnesses required for the loom is determined by the weave.

Preparing the Filling Yarns for Weaving

Yarn that is to be used for filling must be packaged in some from that allows it to be unwound easily for transport through the shed is called a shuttle and is made up of a wooden carrier into which a quill or pirn is placed.

Basic Weaving Operation – 4 basic steps – Primary Motions

Once the filling yarns have been prepared and the wrap beam containing the sized yarns is placed at the back of the loom. The warp yarns are conveyed to a cylinder called the cloth beam which is in front.

The loom goes through a series of motions

- Shedding: raising and lowering of warp yarns by means of harness to form shed, opening between warp yarns through which weft yarn passes
- Picking: inserting of weft yarn by the shuttle through the shed

- Beating up: packing the weft yarn into the cloth to make it compact
- Taking up: winding newly formed cloth onto the cloth beam, Letting off: releasing yarn from warp beam

Classification of Weaves

Classification of Woven Fabrics

- Basic/Simple Weaves
- Compound/Complex/Novelty Weaves

Basic/Simple Weaves: 3 basic weaves

- Plain Weave
- Twill Weave
- Satin Weave

Compound/Complex/Novelty Weaves

- Dobby Weave
- Jacquard Weave
- Double Cloth & Double Weave
- Pique
- Pile Fabrics
- Surface Figure Weaves

6

Textile Manufacturing

Textile manufacturing is a major industry. It is based on the conversion of three types of fibre into yarn, then fabric, then textiles. These are then fabricated into clothes or other artefacts. Cotton remains the most important natural fibre, so is treated in depth. There are many variable processes available at the spinning and fabric-forming stages coupled with the complexities of the finishing and colouration processes to the production of a wide ranges of products. There remains a large industry that uses hand techniques to achieve the same results.

Cultivating and Harvesting

Cotton is grown anywhere with long, hot dry summers with plenty of sunshine and low humidity. Indian cotton, gossypium arboreum, is finer but the staple is only suitable for hand processing. American cotton, gossypium hirsutum, produces the longer staple needed for machine production. Planting is from September to mid November and the crop is harvested between March and June. The cotton bolls are harvested by stripper harvesters and spindle pickers, that remove the entire boll from the plant. The cotton boll is the seed pod of the cotton plant, attached to each of the thousands of seeds are fibres about 2.5 cm long.

Ginning

The seed cotton goes in to a Cotton gin. The cotton gin separates seeds and removes the "trash" (dirt, stems and leaves) from the fibre. In a saw gin, circular saws grab the fibre and pull it through a grating that is too narrow for the seeds to pass. A roller gin is used with longer staple cotton. Here a leather roller captures the cotton. A knife blade, set close to the roller, detaches the seeds by drawing them through teeth in circular saws and revolving brushes which clean them away.

The ginned cotton fibre, known as lint, is then compressed into bales which are about 1.5 m tall and weigh almost 220 kg. Only 33% of the crop is usable lint. Commercial cotton is priced by quality, and that broadly relates to the average length of the staple, and the variety of the plant. Longer staple cotton (2½ in to 1¼ in) is called Egyptian, medium staple (1¼ in to ¾ in) is called American upland and short staple (less than ¾ in) is called Indian.

The cotton seed is pressed into a cooking oil. The husks and meal are processed into animal feed, and the stems into paper.

Issues

Cotton is farmed intensively and uses large amounts of fertilizer and 25% of the world's insecticides. Native Indian varieties of cotton were rainwater fed, but modern hybrids used for the mills need irrigation, which spreads pests. The 5% of cotton-bearing land in India uses 55% of all pesticides used in India. Before mechanisation, cotton was harvested manually by farmers in India and by African slaves in America. In 2012 Uzbekistan was a major exporter of cotton and uses manual labour during the harvest. Human rights groups claim that health care professionals and children are forced to pick cotton.

Preparatory Processes - Preparation of Yarn

- Ginning, bale-making and transportation is done in the country of origin.
- Opening and cleaning

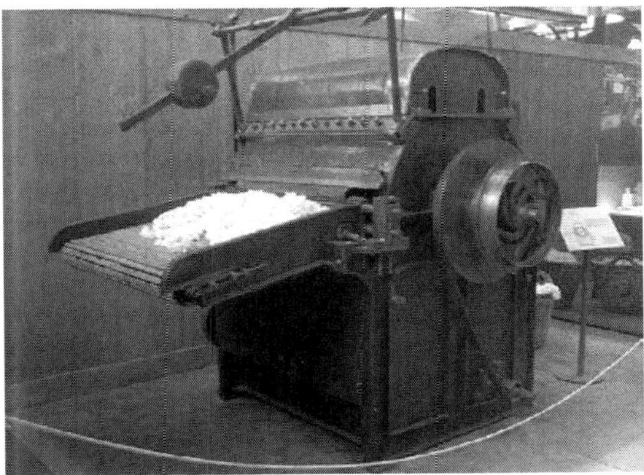

Figure: *Platt Bros. Picker*

Cotton mills get the cotton shipped to them in large, 500 pound bales. When the cotton comes out of a bale, it is all packed together and still contains vegetable matter. The bale is broken open using a machine with large spikes. It is called an Opener.In order to fluff up the cotton and remove the vegetable matter, the cotton is sent through a picker, or similar machines. A picker looks similar to the carding machine and the cotton gin, but is slightly different. The cotton is fed into the machine and gets beaten with a beater bar, to loosen it up. It is fed through various rollers, which serve to remove the vegetable matter. The cotton, aided by fans, then collects on a screen and gets fed through more rollers till it emerges as a continuous soft fleecy sheet, known as a lap.

Blending,

Mixing & Scutching: Scutching refers to the process of cleaning cotton of its seeds and other impurities. A scutching machine for cotton was first invented in 1797, but didn't get much attention until it was introduced in Manchester in 1808 or 1809. By 1816 it had been generally adopted. The scutching machine worked by passing the cotton through a pair of rollers, and then striking it with iron or steel bars called beaters. The beaters, which turn very quickly, strike the cotton hard and knock the seeds out. This process is done over a series of parallel bars so as to allow the seeds to fall through. At the same time a breeze is blown across the bars, which carries the cotton into a cotton chamber.

Carding

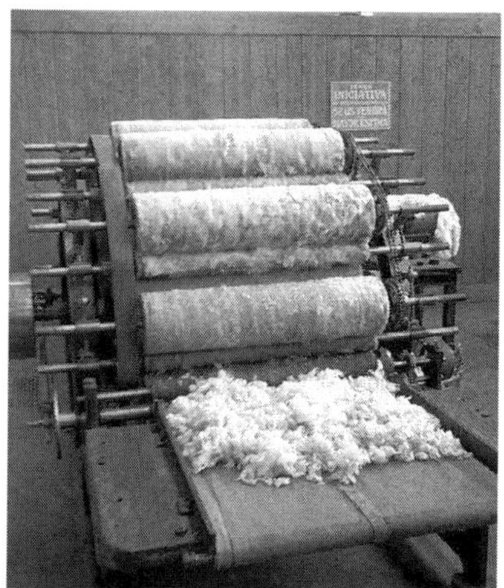

Figure: *Carding machine*

Carding: the fibres are separated and then assembled into a loose strand (sliver or tow) at the conclusion of this stage.

The cotton comes off of the picking machine in laps, and is then taken to carding machines. The carders line up the fibres nicely to make them easier to spin. The carding machine consists mainly of one big roller with smaller ones surrounding it. All of the rollers are covered in small teeth, and as the cotton progresses further on the teeth get finer (i.e. closer together). The cotton leaves the carding machine in the form of a sliver; a large rope of fibres.

Note: In a wider sense Carding can refer to these four processes: Willowing- loosening the fibres; Lapping- removing the dust to create a flat sheet or lap of cotton; Carding- combing the tangled lap into a thick rope of 1/2 in diameter, a sliver; and Drawing- where a drawing frame combines 4 slivers into one- repeated for increased quality.

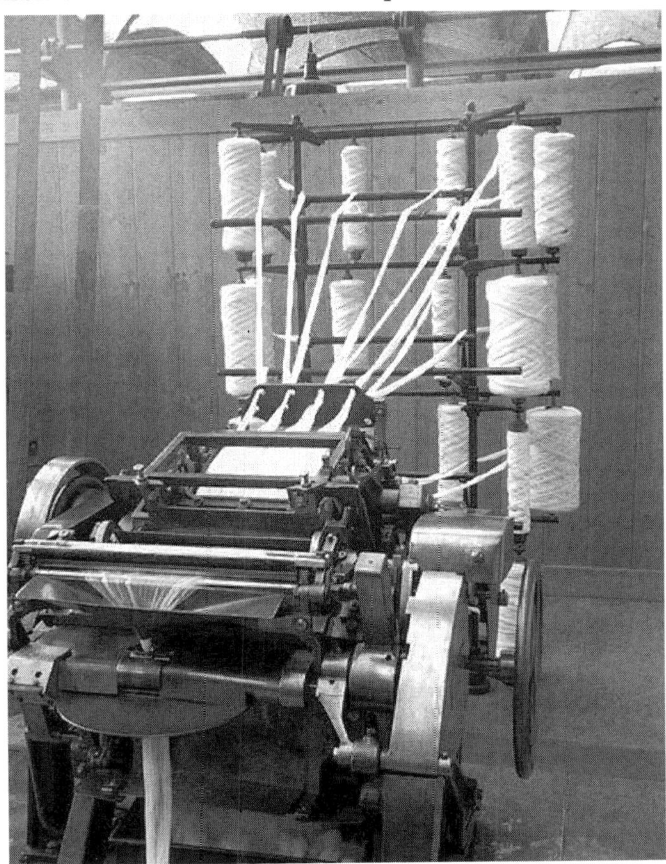

Figure: *A Combing machine*

- Combing is optional, but is used to remove the shorter fibres, creating a stronger yarn.
- Drawing the fibres are straightened

Several slivers are combined. Each sliver will have thin and thick spots, and by combining several slivers together a more consistent size can be reached. Since combining several slivers produces a very thick rope of cotton fibres, directly after being combined the slivers are separated into rovings. These rovings (or slubbings) are then what are used in the spinning process.

Generally speaking, for machine processing, a roving is about the width of a pencil.

- Drawing frame: Draws the strand out
- Slubbing Frame: adds twist, and winds onto bobbins
- Intermediate Frames: are used to repeat the slubbing process to produce a finer yarn.
- Roving frames: reduces to a finer thread, gives more twist, makes more regular and even in thickness, and winds onto a smaller tube.

Spinning - yarn Manufacture

Spinning: Most spinning today is done using Break or Open-end spinning, this is a technique where the staples are blown by air into a rotating drum, where they attach themselves to the tail of formed yarn that is continually being drawn out of the chamber. Other methods of break spinning use needles and electrostatic forces. This method has replace the older methods of ring and mule spinning. It is also is easily adapted for artificial fibres.

The spinning machines takes the roving, thins it and twists it, creating yarn which it winds onto a bobbin.

In mule spinning the roving is pulled off a bobbin and fed through some rollers, which are feeding at several different speeds. This thins the roving at a consistent rate. If the roving was not a consistent size, then this step could cause a break in the yarn, or could jam the machine. The yarn is twisted through the spinning of the bobbin as the carriage moves out, and is rolled onto a cop as the carriage returns. Mule spinning produces a finer thread than the less skilled ring spinning.

- The mule was an intermittent process, as the frame advanced and returned a distance of 5ft. It was the descendant of 1779

Crompton device. It produces a softer less twisted thread that was favoured for fines and for weft.

- The ring was a descendant of the Arkwright water Frame 1769. It was a continuous process, the yarn was coarser, had a greater twist and was stronger so was suited to be warp. Ring spinning is slow due to the distance the thread must pass around the ring, other methods have been introduced.

Sewing thread, was made of several threads twisted together, or doubled.

Checking: This is the process where each of the bobbins is rewound to give a tighter bobbin.

Folding and Twisting: Plying is done by pulling yarn from two or more bobbins and twisting it together, in the opposite direction that in which it was spun. Depending on the weight desired, the cotton may or may not be plied, and the number of strands twisted together varies.

Gassing: Gassing is the process of passing yarn, as distinct from fabric very rapidly through a series of Bunsen gas flames in a gassing frame, in order to burn off the projecting fibres and make the thread round and smooth and also brighter. Only the better qualities of yarn are gassed, such as that used for voiles, poplins, venetians, gabardines, many Egyptian qualities, etc. There is a loss of weight in gassing, which varies' about 5 to 8 per cent., so that if a 2/60's yarn is required 2/56's would be used. The gassed yarn is darker in shade afterwards, but should not be scorched.

Measurements

- Cotton Counts: The number of pieces of thread, 840 yards long needed to make up 1 lb weight. 10 count cotton means that 10x840 yd weighs 1 lb. This is coarser than 40 count cotton where 40x840 yards are needed. In the United Kingdom, Counts to 40s are coarse (Oldham Counts), 40 to 80s are medium counts and above 80 is a fine count. In the United States ones to 20s are coarse counts.
- Hank: A length of 7 leas or 840 yards
- Thread: A length of 54 in (the circumference of a warp beam)
- Bundle: Usually 10 lb
- Lea: A length of 80 threads or 120 yards
- Denier: this is an alternative method. It is defined as a number that is equivalent to the weight in grams of 9000m of a single yarn. 15 denier is finer than 30 denier.

- Tex: is the weight in grams of 1 km of yarn.

The worsted hank is only 560 yd

Weaving-fabric Manufacture

The weaving process uses a loom. The lengthway threads are known as the warp, and the cross way threads are known as the weft. The warp which must be strong needs to be presented to loom on a warp beam. The weft passes across the loom in a shuttle, that carries the yarn on a pirn. These pirns are automatically changed by the loom. Thus, the yarn needs to be wrapped onto a beam, and onto pirns before weaving can commence.

Winding: After being spun and plied, the cotton thread is taken to a warping room where the winding machine takes the required length of yarn and winds it onto warpers bobbins.

Warping or Beaming

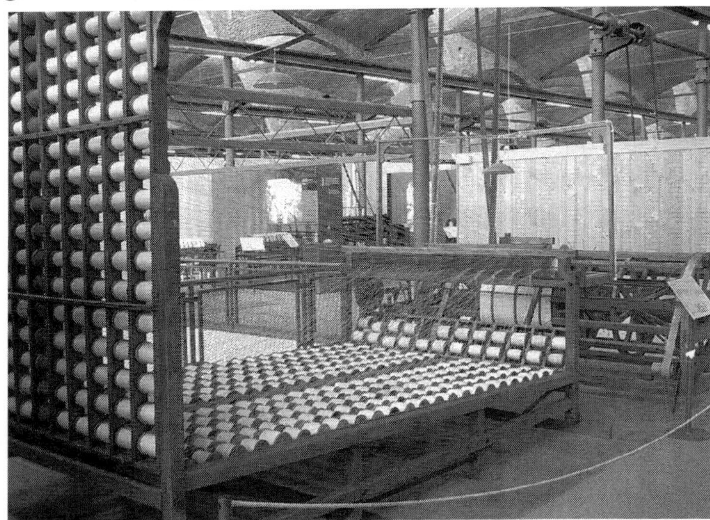

Figure: *A Warper*

Racks of bobbins are set up to hold the thread while it is rolled onto the warp bar of a loom. Because the thread is fine, often three of these would be combined to get the desired thread count.

Sizing: Slasher sizing machine needed for strengthening the warp by adding starch to reduce breakage of the yarns.

Drawing in, Looming: The process of drawing each end of the warp separately through the dents of the reed and the eyes of the healds, in the order indicated by the draft.

Pirning (Processing the Weft): Pirn winding frame was used to transfer the weft from cheeses of yarn onto the pirns that would fit into the shuttle.

Weaving: At this point, the thread is woven. Depending on the era, one person could manage anywhere from 3 to 100 machines. In the mid nineteenth century, four was the standard number. A skilled weaver in 1925 would run 6 Lancashire Looms. As time progressed new mechanisms were added that stopped the loom any time something went wrong. The mechanisms checked for such things as a broken warp thread, broken weft thread, the shuttle going straight across, and if the shuttle was empty. Forty of these Northrop Looms or automatic looms could be operated by one skilled worker.

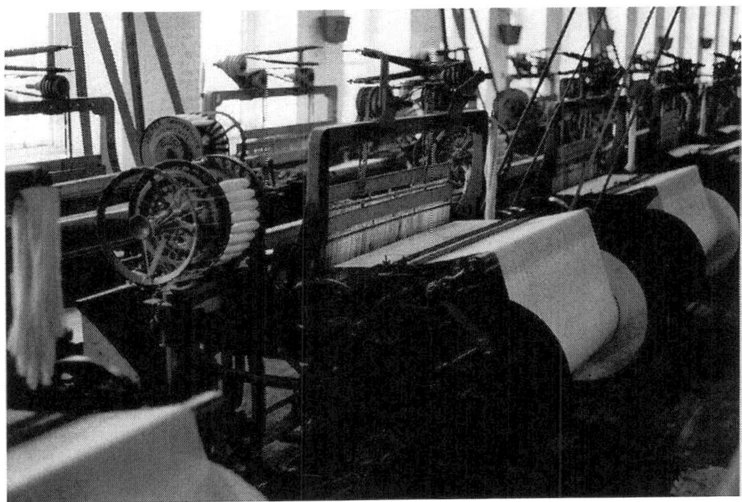

Figure: *A Draper loom in textile museum, Lowell, Massachusetts*

The three primary movements of a loom are shedding, picking, and beating-up.

- *Shedding*: The operation of dividing the warp into two lines, so that the shuttle can pass between these lines. There are two general kinds of sheds- "open" and "closed." Open Shed-The warp threads are moved when the pattern requires it-from one line to the other. Closed Shed-The warp threads are all placed level in one line after each pick.
- *Picking*: The operation of projecting the shuttle from side to side of the loom through the division in the warp threads. This is done by the overpick or underpick motions. The overpick is

suitable for quick-running looms, whereas the underpick is best for heavy or slow looms.

- *Beating-up*: The third primary movement of the loom when making cloth, and is the action of the reed as it drives each pick of weft to the fell of the cloth.

The Lancashire Loom was the first semi-automatic loom. Jacquard looms and Dobby looms are looms that have sophisticated methods of shedding. They may be separate looms, or mechanisms added to a plain loom. A Northrop Loom was fully automatic and was mass produced between 1909 and the mid-1960s. Modern looms run faster and do not use a shuttle: there are air jet looms, water jet looms and rapier looms.

Measurements

- Ends and Picks: Picks refer to the weft, ends refer to the warp. The coarseness of the cloth can be expressed as the number of picks and ends per quarter inch square, or per inch square. Ends is always written first. For example: *Heavy domestics are made from coarse yarns, such as 10's to 14's warp and weft, and about 48 ends and 52 picks.*

Associated Job Titles

- Piecer
- Scavenger
- Weaver
- Tackler
- Draw boy
- Pirner

Issues

When a hand loom was located in the home, children helped with the weaving process from an early age. Piecing needs dexterity, and a child can be as productive as an adult. When weaving moves from the home to the mill, children are often allowed to *help* their older sisters, and laws have to be made to prevent child labour becoming established.

Knitting- fabric Manufacture

Knitting by machine is done in two different ways; warp and weft. Weft knitting is similar in method to hand knitting with stitches all connected to each other horizontally. Various weft machines can be configured to produce textiles from a single spool of yarn or multiple spools depending on the size of the machine cylinder (where the needles are bedded). In a warp knit there are many pieces of yarn and there are vertical chains, zigzagged together by crossing the yarn. Cotton.

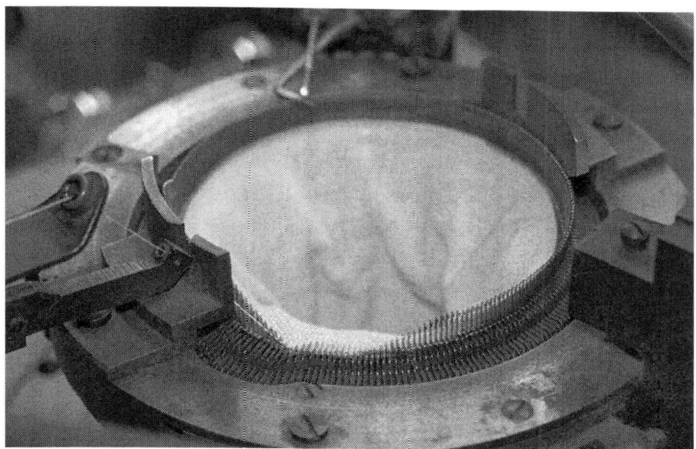

Figure: *A circular knitting machine.*

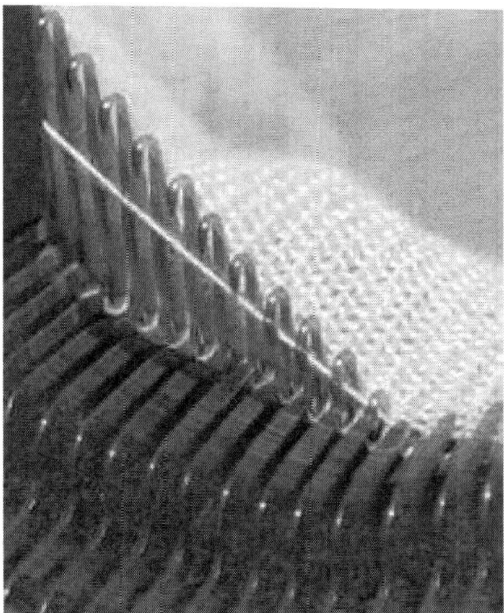

Figure: *Close-up on the needles.*

Warp knits do not stretch as much as a weft knit, and it is run-resistant. A weft knit is not run-resistant, but stretches more. This is especially true if spools of spandex are processed from separate spool containers and interwoven through the cylinder with cotton yarn, giving the finished product more flexibility and making it less prone to having a 'baggy' appearance. The average t-shirt is a weft knit.

Finishing- processing of Textiles

The woven cotton fabric in its loom-state, not only contains impurities, including warp size, but requires further treatment in order to develop its full textile potential. Furthermore, it may receive considerable added value by applying one or more finishing processes.

Desizing: Depending on the size that has been used, the cloth may be steeped in a dilute acid and then rinsed, or enzymes may be used to break down the size.

Scouring: Scouring, is a chemical washing process carried out on cotton fabric to remove natural wax and non-fibrous impurities (e.g. the remains of seed fragments) from the fibres and any added soiling or dirt. Scouring is usually carried in iron vessels called kiers. The fabric is boiled in an alkali, which forms a soap with free fatty acids (saponification). A kier is usually enclosed, so the solution of sodium hydroxide can be boiled under pressure, excluding oxygen which would degrade the cellulose in the fibre. If the appropriate reagents are used, scouring will also remove size from the fabric although desizing often precedes scouring and is considered to be a separate process known as fabric preparation. Preparation and scouring are prerequisites to most of the other finishing processes. At this stage even the most naturally white cotton fibres are yellowish, and bleaching, the next process, is required.

Bleaching: Bleaching improves whiteness by removing natural colouration and remaining trace impurities from the cotton; the degree of bleaching necessary is determined by the required whiteness and absorbency. Cotton being a vegetable fibre will be bleached using an oxidizing agent, such as dilute sodium hypochlorite or dilute hydrogen peroxide. If the fabric is to be dyed a deep shade, then lower levels of bleaching are acceptable, for example. However, for white bed sheetings and medical applications, the highest levels of whiteness and absorbency are essential.

Mercerising: A further possibility is mercerizing during which the fabric is treated with caustic soda solution to cause swelling of the fibres. This results in improved lustre, strength and dye affinity. Cotton is mercerized under tension, and all alkali must be washed out before the tension is released or shrinkage will take place. Mercerizing can take place directly on grey cloth, or after bleaching.

Many other chemical treatments may be applied to cotton fabrics to produce low flammability, crease resist and other special effects but four important non-chemical finishing treatments are:

Singeing: Singeing is designed to burn off the surface fibres from the fabric to produce smoothness. The fabric passes over brushes to raise the fibres, then passes over a plate heated by gas flames.

Raising: Another finishing process is raising. During raising, the fabric surface is treated with sharp teeth to lift the surface fibres, thereby imparting hairiness, softness and warmth, as in flannelette.

Calendering: Calendering is the third important mechanical process, in which the fabric is passed between heated rollers to generate smooth, polished or embossed effects depending on roller surface properties and relative speeds.

Shrinking (Sanforizing): Finally, mechanical shrinking (sometimes referred to as sanforizing), whereby the fabric is forced to shrink width and/or lengthwise, creates a fabric in which any residual tendency to shrink after subsequent laundering is minimal.

Dyeing: Finally, cotton is an absorbent fibre which responds readily to colouration processes. Dyeing, for instance, is commonly carried out with an anionic direct dye by completely immersing the fabric (or yarn) in an aqueous dyebath according to a prescribed procedure. For improved fastness to washing, rubbing and light, other dyes such as vats and reactives are commonly used. These require more complex chemistry during processing and are thus more expensive to apply.

Printing: Printing, on the other hand, is the application of colour in the form of a paste or ink to the surface of a fabric, in a predetermined pattern. It may be considered as localised dyeing. Printing designs onto already dyed fabric is also possible.

Economic, Environmental and Political Consequences of Cotton Manufacture

The growth of cotton is divided into two segments i.e. organic and genetically modified. Cotton crop provides livelihood to millions of people but its production is becoming expensive because of high water consumption, use of expensive pesticides, insecticides and fertilizer. Genetically Modified products aim to increase disease resistance and reduce the water required. The organic sector was worth $583 million. Genetically Modified cotton, in 2007, occupied 43% of cotton growing areas.

The consumption of energy in form of water and electricity is relatively high, especially in processes like washing, de-sizing, bleaching, rinsing, dyeing, printing, coating and finishing. Processing is time consuming. The major portion of water in textile industry is used for wet processing of textile (70 per cent). Approximately 25 per cent of energy in the total textile production like fibre production, spinning, twisting, weaving, knitting, clothing manufacturing etc. is used in dyeing. About 34 per cent of energy is consumed in spinning, 23 per cent in weaving, 38 per cent in chemical wet processing and five per cent in miscellaneous processes. Power dominates consumption pattern in spinning and weaving, while thermal energy is the major factor for chemical wet processing.

Processing of other Vegetable Fibres

Flax

Flax is a bast fibre, which means it comes in bundles under the bark of the Linum usitatissimum plant. The plant flowers and is harvested.

- Retting
- Breaking
- Scutching
- Hackling or combing

It is now treated like cotton.

Jute

Jute is a bast fibre, which comes from the inner bark of the plants of the Corchorus genus. It is retted like flax, sundried and baled. When spinning a small amount of oil must be added to the fibre. It can be bleached and dyed. It was used for sacks and bags but is now used for the backing for carpets. Jute can be blended with other fibres to make composite fabrics and work continues in Bangladesh to refine the processes and extend the range of usage possible. In the 1970s, jute-cotton composite fabrics were known as *jutton* fabrics.

Hemp

Hemp is a bast fibre from the inner bark of Cannabis sativa. It is difficult to bleach, it is used for making cord and rope.

- Retting
- Separating
- Pounding

Other Bast Fibres

These bast fibres can also be used: kenaf, urena, ramie, nettle.

Other Leaf Fibres

Sisal is the main leaf fibre used; others are: abacá and henequen.

Processing of Protein Fibres

Wool

Wool comes from domesticated sheep. It forms two products, woolens and worsteds. The sheep has two sorts of wool and it is the inner coat that is used. This can be mixed with wool that has been recovered from rags. Shoddy is the term for recovered wool that is not matted, while mungo comes from felted wool. Extract is recovered chemically from mixed cotton/wool fabrics.

The fleece is cut in one piece from the sheep.This is then skirted to remove the soiled wool, and baled. It is graded into long wool where the fibres can be up to 15 in, but anything over 2.5 inches is suitable for combing into worsteds. Fibres less than that form short wool and are described as clothing or carding wool.

At the mill the wool is scoured in a detergent to remove grease (the yolk) and impurities. This is done mechanically in the opening machine. Vegetable matter can be removed chemically using sulphuric acid (carbonising). Washing uses a solution of soap and sodium carbonate. The wool is oiled before carding or combing.

- Woollens: Use noils from the worsted combs, mungo and shoddy and new short wool
- Worsteds

Combing: Oiled slivers are wound into laps, and placed in the circular comber. The worsted yarn gathers together to form a top. The shorter fibres or noils remain behind and are removed with a knife.

Silk

The processes in silk production are similar to those of cotton but take account that reeled silk is a continuous fibre. The terms used are different.

- Opening bales. Assorting skeins: where silk is sorted by colour, size and quality, scouring: where the silk is washed in water of 40 degrees for 12 hours to remove the natural gum, drying: either by steam heating or centrifuge, softening: by rubbing to remove any remaining hard spots.

- Silk throwing (winding). The skeins are placed on a reel in a frame with many others. The silk is wound onto spools or bobbins.
- Doubling and twisting. The silk is far too fine to be woven, so now it is doubled and twisted to make the warp, known as organzine and the weft, known as tram. In organzine each single is given a few twists per inch (tpi), and combine with several other singles counter twisted hard at 10 to 14 tpi. In tram the two singles are doubled with each other with a light twist, 3 to 6 tpi. Sewing thread is two tram threads, hard twisted, and machine-twist is made of three hard-twisted tram threads. Tram for the crepe process is twisted at up to 80 tpi to make it 'kick up'.
- Stretching. The thread is tested for consistent size. Any uneven thickness is stretched out. The resulting thread is reeled into containing 500 yd to 2500 yd. The skeins are about 50 in in loop length.
- Dyeing: the skeins are scoured again, and discolouration removed with a sulphur process. This weakens the silk. The skeins are now tinted or dyed. They are dried and rewound onto bobbins, spools and skeins. Looming, and the weaving process on power looms is the same as with cotton.
- Weaving. The organzine is now warped. This is a similar process to in cotton. Firstly, thirty threads or so are wound onto a warping reel, and then using the warping reels, the threads are beamed. A thick layer of paper is laid between each layer on the beam to stop entangling.

Processing of Synthetic Fibres

Discussion of Types of Synthetic Fibres: Synthetic fibres are the result of extensive development by scientists to improve upon the naturally occurring animal and plant fibres. In general, synthetic fibres are created by forcing, or extruding, fibre forming materials through holes (called spinnerets) into the air, thus forming a thread. Before synthetic fibres were developed, cellulose fibres were made from natural cellulose, which comes from plants.

The first artificial fibre, known as art silk from 1799 onwards, became known as viscose around 1894, and finally rayon in 1924. A similar product known as cellulose acetate was discovered in 1865. Rayon and acetate are both artificial fibres, but not truly synthetic, being made from wood. Although these artificial fibres were discovered in the mid-nineteenth century, successful modern manufacture began much later in the 1930s. Nylon, the first synthetic fibre, made its debut in the United States as a replacement for silk, and was used for parachutes and other military uses.

The techniques used to process these fibres in yarn are essentially the same as with natural fibres, modifications have to be made as these fibres are of great length, and have no texture such as the scales in cotton and wool that aid meshing.

Art silk

Artificial silk or (as the term is used in the textile industry) *Art silk* is a synthetic manufactured fibre which resembles silk but costs less to produce. Frequently, *art silk* is just a synonym for rayon.

The first successful artificial silks were developed in the 1890s of cellulose fibre and marketed as *art silk* or *viscose,* a trade name for a specific manufacturer. In 1924, the name of the fibre was officially changed in the U.S. to rayon, although the term *viscose* continued to be used in Europe. The material is commonly referred to in the industry as *viscose rayon.*

In 1931, Henry Ford hired chemists Robert Boyer and Frank Calvert to produce artificial silk made with soybean fibres. They succeeded in making a textile fibre of spun soy protein fibres, hardened or tanned in a formaldehyde bath, which was given the name Azlon. It was usable in the making of suits, felt hats, and overcoats. Though pilot production of Azlon reached 5,000 pounds (2,300 kg) per day in 1940, it never reached the commercial market; Du Pont's nylon was the winner in the quest to produce artificial silk.

Although not sold under the name *art silk* initially, nylon, the first synthetic fibre, was developed in the United States in the late 1930s and used as a replacement for Japanese silk during World War II. Its properties are far superior to rayon and silk when wet, and so it was used for many military applications, such as parachutes. Although nylon is not a good substitute for silk fabric in appearance, it is a successful functional alternative. Du Pont's original plans for nylon to become a cheaper and superior replacement for silk stockings were soon realized, then redirected for military use just two years later during World War II. Nylon became a prominent industrial fibre in a short time frame, permanently replacing silk in many applications.

In the present day, imitation silk may be made with rayon, mercerized cotton, polyester, a blend of these materials, or a blend of rayon and silk.

Despite a generally similar appearance, genuine silk has unique features that are distinguishable from artificial silk. However, in some cases art silk can be passed off as real silk to unwary buyers. A number of tests are available to determine a fabric's basic fibre makeup, some of which can be performed prior to purchasing a fabric whose composition is questionable. Tests include rubbing the pile in your hand, burning a small piece of the fringe to smell the ash and smell the smoke and dissolving the pile by performing a chemical test.

Textile manufacturing or production is a very complex process. The range of textile manufacturing is so long. It starts from fibre to finished products.

Process Flow Chart of Textile Manufacturing

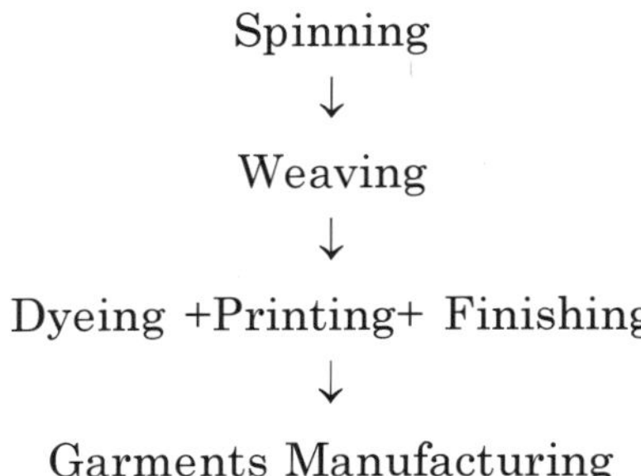

Flow Chart of Spinning

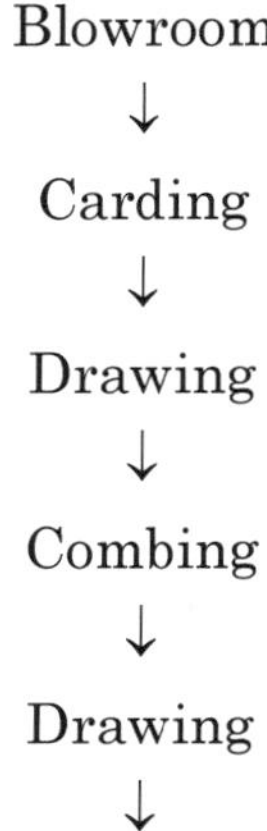

Roving Manufacturing

Ring Spinning

Flow Chart of Weaving

Yarn from spinning section

Doubling and Twisting

Winding

Creeling

Warping

Sizing

↓

Winding on weavers beam

Weaving

Flow Chart of Dyeing

Inspection of grey cloth

Stitching

Cropping

Brushing

Singeing

Desizing

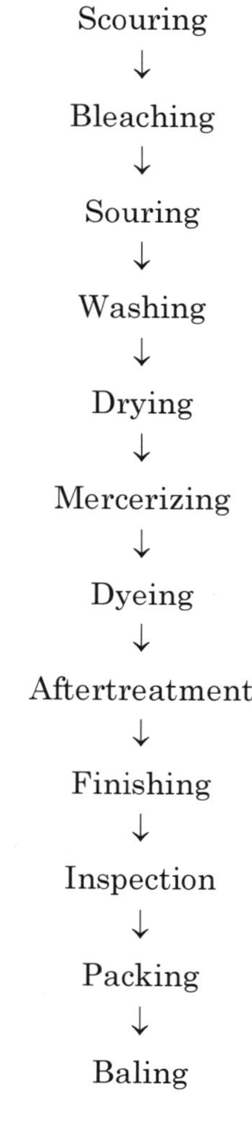

Flow Chart of Printing

Inspection of grey cloth

↓

Stitching

↓

Cropping

↓

Brushing

↓

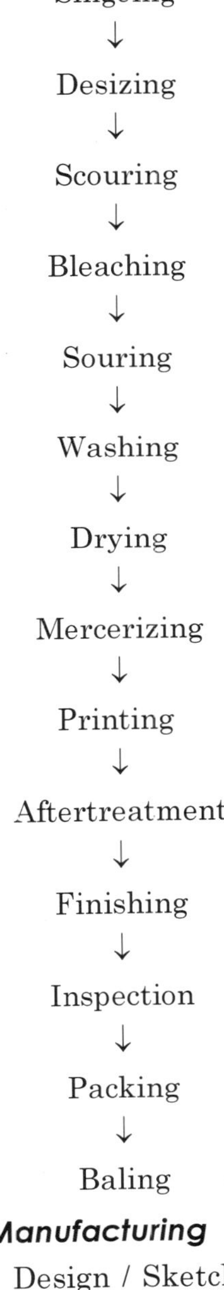

Flow Chart of Garment Manufacturing

Design / Sketch

↓

Pattern Design

↓

Sample Making
↓
Production Pattern
↓
Grading
↓
Marker Making
↓
Spreading
↓
Cutting
↓
Sorting/Bundling
↓
Sewing/Assembling
↓
Inspection
↓
Pressing/ Finishing
↓
Final Inspection
↓
Packing
↓
Despatch

7

Traditional Batik Patterns

What is Batik?

Batik is both an art and a craft, which is becoming more popular and well known in the West as a wonderfully creative medium. The art of decorating cloth in this way, using wax and dye, has been practised for centuries. In Java, Indonesia, batik is part of an ancient tradition, and some of the finest batik cloth in the world is still made there. The word batik originates from the Javanese *tik* and means to dot.

To make a batik, selected areas of the cloth are blocked out by brushing or drawing hot wax over them, and the cloth is then dyed. The parts covered in wax resist the dye and remain the original colour. This process of waxing and dyeing can be repeated to create more elaborate and colourful designs. After the final dyeing the wax is removed and the cloth is ready for wearing or showing.

Contemporary batik, while owing much to the past, is markedly different from the more traditional and formal styles. For example, the artist may use etching, discharge dyeing, stencils, different tools for waxing and dyeing, wax recipes with different resist values and work with silk, cotton, wool, leather, paper or even wood and ceramics.

Batik is historically the most expressive and subtle of the resist methods. The ever widening range of techniques available offers the artist the opportunity to explore a unique process in a flexible and exciting way.

Simply, batik is an amazing and ancient method of colour dyeing. Technically, batik is the process of applying dyes to porous surfaces.

Historically, batik has been around for many hundreds of years. Esthetically, batik produces some of the most beautiful art in the world. However, batik is not easy and involves a very labour intensive and complex process with many hours of back breaking hard work.

The first step in Batik is to design a pattern and have an idea of what you would like to create. In Indonesia where many believe to be the cradle of batik, the pattern is either stenciled with a special tool called a "Tulis".

Wax is then placed in specific areas on the fabric using a "Canting" tool. Wax acts like a barrier to the colour dyes and allows a colour to remain while the remaining non-waxed fabric absorbs the dye. Some times called "Resist Dyeing". Most of the time the wax is then removed by soaking the fabric in hot water. Occasionaly some wax will remain on the fabric and is easily removed in a warm wash cycle.

The batik process of dyeing and waxing repeats. The wax can be removed and re-applied several times to make beautiful and intricate designs. Repeating until all the desired colours and patterns are obtained.

The process of batik is practiced around the world. New methods and techniques are continually evolving. Indonesian batik artists are well known through out the world as the best batikers. From the beautiful islands of Bali and Java young Indonesians start in their villages learning from the elders.

Batik Designs: A Cultural Art Influenced by Changes in Time & Environment

One of the fascinating characteristics of Indonesian batik is the changes in style, motif and colour which have come about through exposure to various foreign cultures. Throughout Indonesian history, each time the rich batik tradition has come into contact with foreigner traders or colonial rulers, they have influenced the development of batik. Some of the more famous results are described below:

Batik Kraton

Batik Kraton is regarded as the basic batik of Java. It is rich in Hindu-influenced motifs that have influenced the courts of Java since the 5th century, and later on influenced by the culture of Islam. The Hindus introduced the sacred bird - Garuda, the sacred flower - lotus, the dragon - Naga and the tree of life. Islam, since it forbids the depiction of humans or animals, brought stylized and modified ornaments as symbols, i.e., flowers and geometric designs. As a specific attire in the dress code of the courts of Java, Batik Kraton is easily recognized through its sub-divisions, Batik Kasunanan Surakarta, Batik Kasultanan Yogyakarta, Batik Pura Mangkunegaran and Batik Pura Pakualaman. Over time, changes and modifications distinguished Batik Mangkunegaran from Batik Kasunanan, even though both originated from the same source. Batik Pakualaman, from the city of Yogyakarta, originated from both Kasunan and Kasultanan design traditions and is more unique because the whole process was completed in Surakarta.

Batik Belanda

Even though Chinese traders arrived earlier in Java than the Europeans, their influence on batik was evident in a later period. Batik Belanda, literally Dutch Batik, appeared as early as 1840, decades before the appearance of Batik Cina, Chinese Batik. Records show that European settlers on the northern coast of Java started their batik producing activities in the mid-19th century. They pioneered a new era of international enrichment which is still visible in modern day Indonesian batik. Reaching its peak of creativity in 1890-1910, Batik Belanda is clearly recognized through various works of arts named after the great designers. Amongst the most famous of these are Batik Van Zuylen from Elize Charlotte van Zuylen, Batik Van Oosterom from Catharina Carolina van Oosterom, Batik Prankemon from Carolina Josephina von Franquemont, Batik Metz from Lies Metzlar, Batik Yans from A.J.F. Yans, and Batik Coenrad from Coenrad of Pacitan, East Java.

Batik Cina

Highly influenced by the Chinese culture, emerging decades after Batik Belanda, Batik Cina is easily recognized by the vast range of uniquely Chinese motifs including, dragons, phoenix, snakes, lions, traditional Chinese flowers and designs taken from chinaware. It is also easily recognized through its bright as well as pastel colours. In its effort to penetrate the Surakarta and Yogyakarta markets, Batik Cina appeared in two derivatives, Batik Dua Negri and Batik Tiga Negri, processed in the north coastal Pesisiran, Surakarta and Yogyakarta in Central Java. Batik Cina is still in production in the coastal cities of Pekalongan (Oey Soe Tjoen in Kedungwuni), Cirebon, Kudus and Demak.

Especially designed for the Japanese during the period that the Japanese occupied Indonesia (1942-1945) the specific designs of Batik

Hokokai, which appealed to Japanese tastes, attracted Chinese consumers in Java and Malaya as well. Highly influenced by Japanese design in motifs and colouring, fine intricate backgrounds enhanced the appearance of beautifully designed flowers. Batik Hokokai was mostly styled as Kain Pagi Sore batik with the colours and patterns different on each half of the fabric length. Favourite motifs included Parang and Lereng.

Batik Indonesia

Freedom from Dutch colonial rule introduced new designs to Indonesian batik. In the early 50s, President Soekarno encouraged the creation of a new style of batik, popularly called Batik Indonesia. A symbiosis between various styles of batik, especially of the principalities of Yogyakarta and Surakarta and the north coast of Java, which still utilized soga brown as the basic colour, Batik Indonesia was developed utilizing bright colours. Some appeared in a totally new design, i.e., Cendrawasih, Sruni, Sandang Pangan, Udang, while still using the traditional processing system. Batik Indonesia is also called Batik Modern.

Batik Sudagaran

An important genre in the development of batik, Batik Sudagaran emerged as early as the end of the 19th century in the principalities of Surakarta and Yogyakarta. Produced by sudagar or batik merchants, it is easily recognized through the modified classic ornaments styled to the taste of the merchants. Some of the popular creations are the patchwork style Tambal, Parang with the insertion of snail-like motifs, Lereng filled with extra fine spirals called Ukel and Semen that shows high quality workmanship.

Batik Pesisir

The distinctive designs of batik pesisir are those from the northern coastal cities of Java, including Pekalongan and Cirebon. The designs show Chinese influence through their use of brighter colours, flowers and cloud motifs.

Traditional Batik Motif Yogyakarta

Batik patterns are divided into different families of designs, each with hundreds of variations within them. The following gives you a brief introduction to the main design families. You'll see certain designs that belonged to the sacred, forbidden patterns reserved for the royal court. Over time, these particular patterns did enter into common use. Yet to this day, if a person does not belong to the court, they would never wear those patterns inside the keraton, or palace walls.

Ceplok Motifs

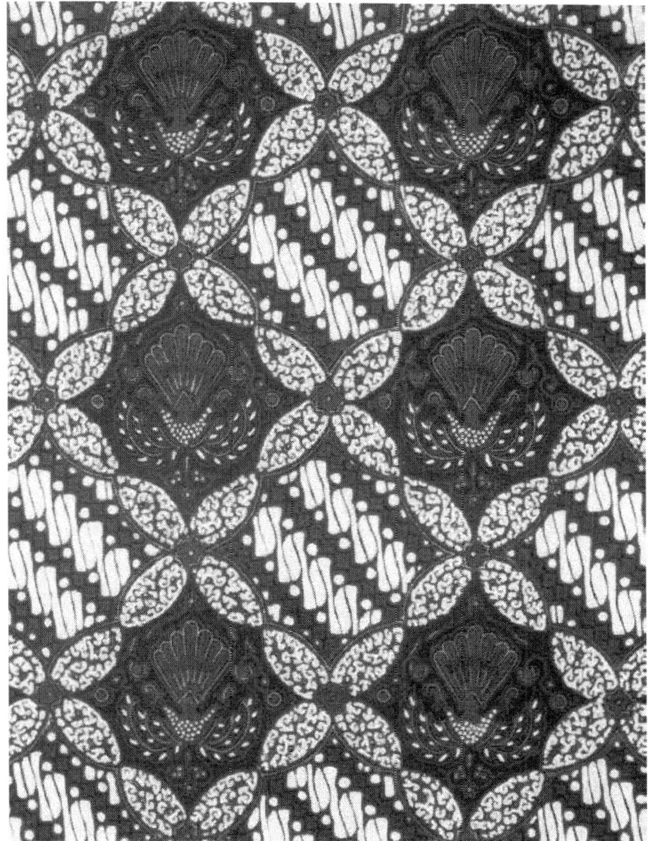

Figure: *Ceplok Yogya Parang*

The Ceplok family includes a wide range of geometric designs, often based on circular rosettes, stars or other small shapes, forming an overall symmetric pattern on the cloth

Grompol means to gather together. Often worn for wedding ceremonies, the pattern symbolizes the coming together of a harmonious marriage, for children, good luck, and happiness.

Kawung Motifs

The Kawung is one of the oldest designs, and was reserved for the royal family. It represents a cross-section of the aren-palm fruit, and some say the cross in between the four ovals refers to the universal energy source.

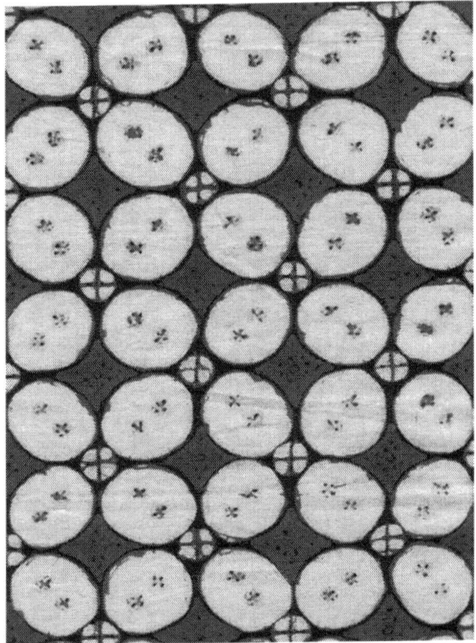

Figure: *Kawung Motif*

While there are many variations, the basic structure is a group of four circles or ovals nearly touching each other, laid out on the cloth in geometric symmetry.

Parang Motifs

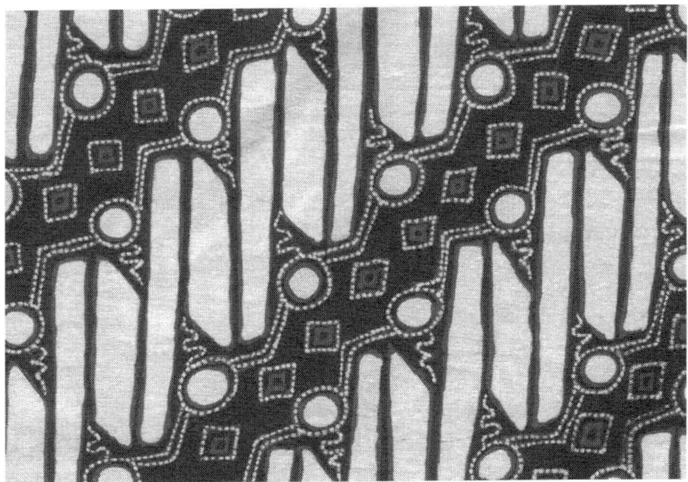

Figure: *Parang Gendreh*

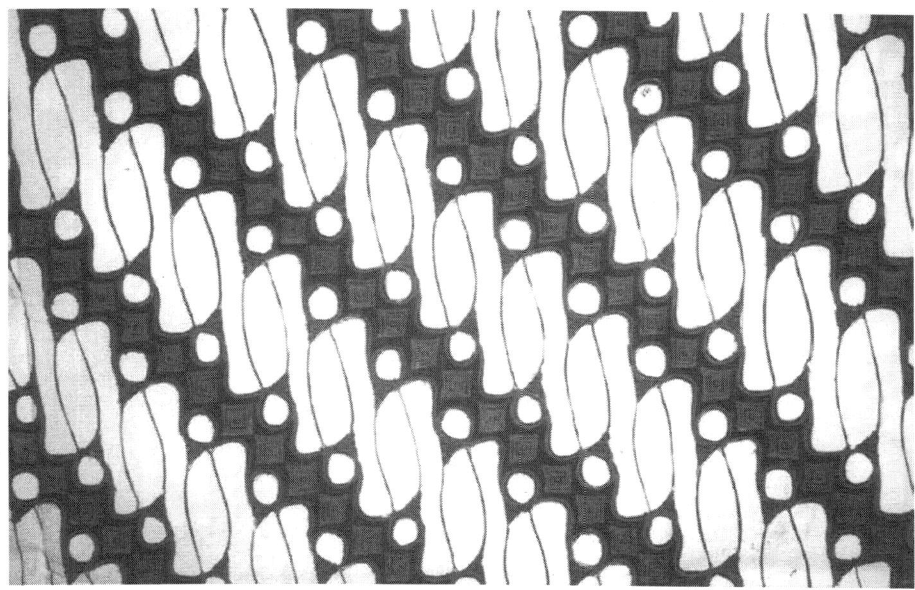

Figure: *Parang Rusak*

Sometimes referred to as the keris or sword pattern by outsiders, the Javanese call the Parang motif lidah api, or tongue of fire. Parang are one of the most powerful of batik motifs with their strong parallel diagonal lines. There are hundreds of variations, from small 2cm in Parang Klithik to the largest at 8cm or more in Parang Barong.

Parang Barong

In times past, Parang Barong was a sacred pattern worn only by the king. The motif reminded him to guard himself carefully so he would be a responsible, honest and just ruler.

Parang Rusak

Another of the Parang designs worn by the royal family on state occasions, Parang Rusak symbolizes the human being's internal fight against wickedness by controlling their desires so their wise, noble character would win out.

Lereng

Refers to the diagonal rows of patterns in between the parang motifs. In addition, many patterns are simply rows of narrow diagonal lines filled with a whole array of small patterns. The Udang Liris, again, one of the old patterns reserved for the royal court, is one of the more famous of these motifs.

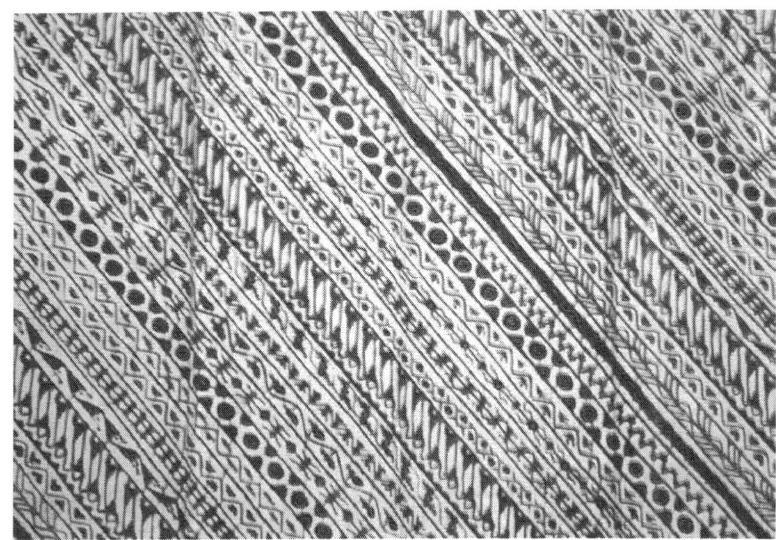

Figure: *Udang Liris Motif*

Udang Liris or light rain symbolizes fertility, the hope for prosperity, determination, to have courage to carry out what's important for the nation and her people.

Nitik Motifs

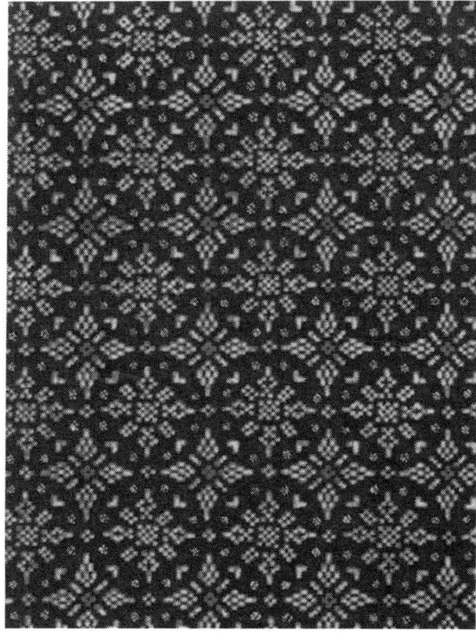

Figure: *Nitik Randu Seling*

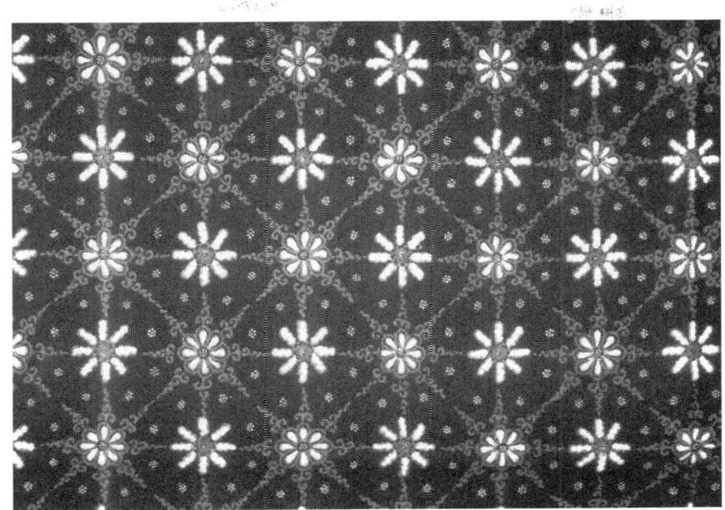

Figure: *Truntum Motif*

Nitik Motifs are among the oldest batik patterns and were inspired by woven patola cloths brought by traders from Gujarat, India long ago. The geometric design is created with small dots and dashes imitating the original woven fabric.

Truntum

Worn by parents of a wedding couple the Truntum pattern.

Semen Motifs

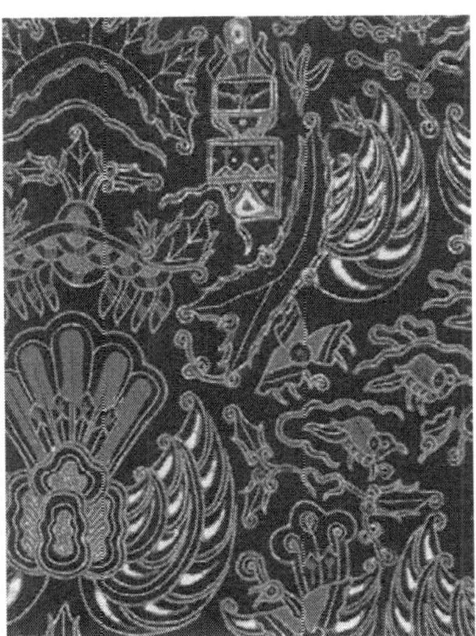

Figure: *Semen Garuda, Yogya Motif*

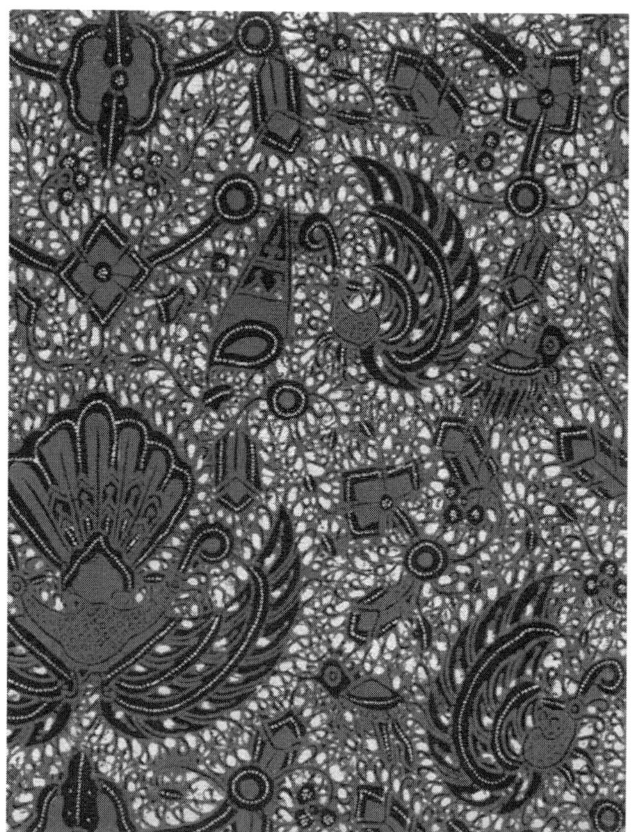

Figure: *Semen Sido Mukti, Yogya Motif*

Semen, based on the word semi, meaning to sprout or grow, are non-geometric patterns inspired by the natural world. Filled with stylized stems, flowers, leaves, mountains, and animals, this group of designs was highly important for royalty on special occasions, as well as common people in everyday use.

Garuda, the mystical bird-man in Hindu mythology, who carried Vishnu through the heavens, is often portrayed in Semen designs with a single, or pair of wings (Lar) or the wings and tail (Sawat). Often associated with Semen patterns, the wing shape is also found with Parang and Ceplok motifs.

Isen Motifs

Filling patterns called Isen are highly characteristic of Indonesian, especially Javanese, batik. Finely rendered in a wax line, these small designs add a depth and harmonious beauty to the overall cloth.

Batik. Fabric, Wax and Madness of Colours

How Does the Batik Making Process Look Like?

1. First of all, we need to chose and prepare the fabric. It is the best to start with a good quality cotton. We need paints and some tools (there are many materials and tools that are used to create batik and they look a bit different in various countries). We also need some design idea for the theme or pattern that you want to apply on the fabric. Regardless of how experienced we are and how much preparation we will do, the final outcome always is a surprise (even to these most experienced batik artist).
2. The chosen fabric must be prepared. It is recommended to wash it even few times to remove any dirt. Very often fabrics are also boiled to prevent fabric shrinkage afterwards.
3. The next step is to apply the pattern. We can draw with pencil directly on the material or copy paper patterns. Another way is to cut the pattern out from the paper and sprinkle the edges with charcoal orpowdered graphite from the pencils.
4. The next step is applying the wax along the drawn lines and ornaments. The fabric is usuallystretched on a wooden frame, and a special applicator (known in Indonesia as tjanting) is used to apply melted wax. Hand made wax lines and ornaments are really time consuming. This technique also requires precision and incredible patience. It is much faster to apply wax on fabric using special stamps (in Indonesia the stamps are usually made of metal, but in India, very often you can find a wooden stamps). The stamps can vary in size – some are single motifs (flower, animal, geometric pattern), some are large enough to cover the square metre of fabric at once.
5. When the wax in applied and dry, the fabric can be dyed. Traditionally in Indonesia colour is applied in two phases. The first step is to immerse the fabric in a solution of some kind of soda and few other ingredients in order to enhance absorption of colour (in the next stage). After that, the fabric is immersed in the actual paint, rinsed in cold water and then it is dried. Modern batik making allows using one stage dying specimens, which considerably simplifies the process. If we want few shades of a certain colour on our batik, we repeat the process of waxing and dyeing few times, always starting dying from the lightest to the darkest colours.

Another way to achieve a multicoloured batik is to apply paint only on the certain areas of the fabric (stretched on canvas) with a small brush or with a stick ended with a sponge or cotton. This technique is used in particularly colourful batiks, where the gradual application of the brightest to the darkest does not work.

6. The last step is to remove the wax. To do this, we immerse batik for few moments in boiling water. There are usually some special substances mixed with the water helping to remove the wax (e.g. soda).

Selection and Preparation of the Cloth for Batik

Natural materials such as cotton or silk are used for the cloth, so that it can absorb the wax that is applied in the dye resisting process. The fabrics must be of a high thread count (densely woven). It is important that cloth of high quality have this high thread count so that the intricate design qualities of batik can be maintained.

The cloth that is used for batik is washed and boiled in water many times prior to the application of wax so that all traces of starches, lime, chalk and other sizing materials are removed. Prior to the implementation of modern day techniques, the cloth would have been pounded with a wooden mallet or ironed to make it smooth and supple so it could best receive the wax design. With the finer machine-made cotton available today, the pounding or ironing processes can be omitted. Normally men did this step in the batik process.

Strict industry standards differentiate the different qualities of the cloth used today, which include Primissima (the best) and Prima. The cloth quality is often written on the edge of the design. A lesser quality cloth which is often used in Blaco.

Batik Design Tools

Although the art form of batik is very intricate, the tools that are used are still very simple. The *canting*, believed to be a purely Javanese invention, is a small thin wall spouted copper container (sometimes called a wax pen) that is connected to a short bamboo handle. Normally it is approximately 11 cm. in length. The copper container is filled with melted wax and the artisan then uses the *canting* to draw the design on the cloth.

Canting have different sizes of spouts (numbered to correspond to the size) to achieve varied design effects. The spout can vary from 1 mm in diameter for very fine detailed work to wider spouts used to fill in large design areas. Dots and parallel lines may be drawn with *canting* that have up to 9 spouts. Sometimes a wad of cotton is fastened over the mouth of the *canting* or attached to a stick that acts as a brush to fill in very large areas.

Wajan

The *wajan* is the container that holds the melted wax. It looks like a small wok. Normally it is made of iron or earthenware. The *wajan* is placed on a small brick charcoal stove or a spirit burner called an '*anglo*'. The wax is kept in a melted state while the artisan is applying the wax to the cloth.

Wax

Different kinds and qualities of wax are used in batik. Common waxes used for batik consist of a mixture of beeswax, used for its malleability, and paraffin, used for its friability. Resins can be added to increase adhesiveness and animal fats create greater liquidity.

The best waxes are from the Indonesian islands of Timor, Sumbawa and Sumatra; three types of petroleum-based paraffin (white, yellow and black) are used. The amounts mixed are measured in grams and vary according to the design. Wax recipes can be very closely guarded secrets. Varying colours of wax make it possible to disguise different parts of the pattern through the various dying stages. Larger areas of the pattern are filled in with wax that is cheaper quality and the higher quality wax is used on the more intricately detailed sections of the design.

The wax must be kept at the proper temperature. A wax that is too cool will clog the spout of the canting. A wax that is too hot will flow too quickly and be uncontrollable. The artisan will often blow into the spout of the canting before applying wax to the cloth in order to clear the canting of any obstructions.

Cap

Creating batik is a very time consuming craft. To meet growing demands and make the fabric more affordable to the masses, in the mid-19th century the . *cap.* (copper stamp - pronounced chop) was developed. This invention enabled a higher volume of batik production compared to the traditional method which entailed the tedious application of wax by hand with a *canting*.

Each *cap* is a copper block that makes up a design unit. *Cap* are made of 1.5 cm wide copper stripes that are bent into the shape of the design. Smaller pieces of wire are used for the dots. When complete, the pattern of copper strips is attached to the handle.

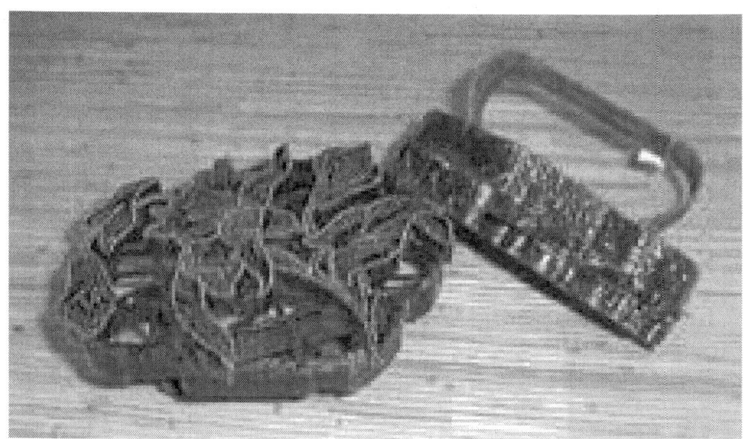

The *cap* must be precisely made. This is especially true if the pattern is to be stamped on both sides of the fabric. It is imperative that both sides of the *cap* are identical so that pattern will be consistent.

Sometimes *cap* are welded between two grids like pieces of copper that will make a base for the top and the bottom. The block is cut in half at the centre so the pattern on each half is identical. *Cap* vary in size and shape depending on the pattern they are needed for. It is seldom that a *cap* will exceed 24 cm in diameter, as this would make the handling too difficult.

Men usually handle the application of wax using *cap*. A piece of cloth that involves a complicated design could require as many as ten sets of *cap*. The usage of *cap*, as opposed to canting, to apply the wax has reduced the amount of time to make a cloth.

Today, batik quality is defined by *cap* or *tulis*, the second meaning hand-drawn designs which use a *canting*, or *kombinasi*, a combination of the two techniques.

Dyes

Traditional colours for Central Javanese batik were made from natural ingredients and consisted primarily of beige, blue, brown and black.

The oldest colour that was used in traditional batik making was blue. The colour was made from the leaves of the Indigo plant. The leaves were mixed with molasses sugar and lime and left to stand overnight. Sometimes sap from the Tinggi tree was added to act as a fixing agent. Lighter blue was achieved by leaving the cloth in the dye bath for short periods of time. For darker colours, the cloth would be left in the dye bath for days and may have been submerged up to 8 - 10 times a day.

In traditional batik, the second colour applied was a brown colour called *soga*. The colour could range from light yellow to a dark brown. The dye came from the bark of the Soga tree. Another colour that was traditionally used was a dark red colour called *mengkuda*. This dye was created from the leaves of the *Morinda Citrifolia*.

The final hue depended on how long the cloth was soaked in the dye bath and how often it was dipped. Skilled artisans can create many variations of these traditional colours. Aside from blue, green would be achieved by mixing blue with yellow; purple was obtained by mixing blue and red. The *soga* brown colour mixed with indigo would produce a dark blue-black colour.

Design Process

The outline of the pattern is blocked out onto the cloth, traditionally with charcoal or graphite. Traditional batik designs utilize patterns handed down over the generations. It is very seldom that an artisan is so skilled that he can work from memory and would not need to draw an outline of the pattern before applying the wax. Often designs are traced from stencils or patterns called *pola*. Another method of tracing a pattern onto a cloth is by laying the cloth on a glass table that is illuminated from below which casts a shadow of the pattern onto the cloth. The shadow is then traced with a pencil. In large batik factories today, men usually are in charge of drawing the patterns onto the cloth.

Waxing

Once the design is drawn out onto the cloth it is then ready to be waxed. Wax is applied to the cloth over the areas of the design that the artisan wishes to remain the original colour of the cloth. Normally this is white or cream.

Female workers sit on a low stool or on a mat to apply the wax with a canting. The fabric that they are working on is draped over light bamboo frames called *gawangan* to allow the freshly applied wax to cool and harden. The wax is heated in the *wajan* until it is of the desired consistency. The artisan then dips her canting into the wax to fill the bowl of the *canting*.

Artisans use the wax to retrace the pencil outline on the fabric. A small drop cloth is kept on the woman. slap to protect her from hot dripping wax. The stem of the *canting* is held with the right hand in a horizontal position to prevent any accidental spillage, which greatly reduces the value of the final cloth. The left hand is placed behind the fabric for support. The spout does not touch the fabric, but it held just above the area the artisan is working on. To ensure the pattern is well defined, batik is waxed on both sides. True *tulis* batik is reversible, as the pattern should be identical on both sides.

The most experienced artisans normally do first waxings. Filling in of large areas may be entrusted to less experienced artisans. Mistakes are very difficult to correct. If wax is accidentally spilt on the cloth, the artisan will try to remove the unwanted wax by sponging it with hot water. Then a heated iron rod with a curved end is used to try and lift off the remaining wax. Spilled wax can never be completely removed so it is imperative that the artisans are very careful.

If the cap method is utilized, this procedure is normally done by men. The *cap* are dipped into melted wax. Just under the surface of the melted wax is a folded cloth approximately 30 centimeters square. When this cloth is saturated with wax it acts like a stamp pad. The *cap* is pressed into the fabric until the design side of the cap is coated with wax. The saturated *cap* is then stamped onto the fabric, leaving the design of the *cap*. This process is repeated until the entire cloth is covered. Often *cap* and *canting* methods are combined on the same piece of cloth.

Better quality batik may be waxed utilizing canting in one part of Indonesia and then sent to another part of Indonesia where the *cap* part of the process is completed. On better quality *cap* fabric great care is taken to match the pattern exactly. Lower grade batik is characterized by overlapping lines or lightened coloured lines indicating the *cap* was not applied correctly.

Dyeing

After the initial wax has been applied, the fabric is ready for the first dye bath. Traditionally dying was done in earthenware tubs. Today most batik factories use large concrete vats. Above the vats are ropes with pulleys that the fabric is draped over after it has been dipped into the dye bath.

The waxed fabric is immersed in the dye bath of the first colour. The amount of time it is left in the bath determines the hue of the colour; darker colours require longer periods or numerous immersions. The fabric is then put into a cold water bath to harden the wax.

When the desired colour has been achieved and the fabric has dried, wax is reapplied over the areas that the artisan wishes to maintain the first dye colour or another colour at a later stage in the dying process.

When an area that has been covered with wax previously needs to be exposed so that it can be dyed, the applied wax is scraped away with a small knife. The area is then sponged with hot water and resized with rice starch before it is re-immersed in the subsequent dye bath.

If a marble effect is desired, the wax is intentionally cracked before being placed in the dye bath. The dye seeps into the tiny cracks that create the fine lines that are characteristic of batik. Traditionally, cracks were a sign of inferior cloth especially on indigo colour batik. On brown batik, however, the marble effect was accepted.

The number of colours in batik represents how many times it was immersed in the dye bath and how many times wax had to be applied and removed. A multicoloured batik represents a lot more work that a single or two-colour piece. Numerous dye processes are usually reflected in the price of the cloth. Nowadays, chemical dyes have pretty much replaced traditional dyes, so colours are endless and much more liberally used.

Special Treatments to the Batik Cloth

Prada *or Gold Cloth*

For special occasions, batik was formerly decorated with gold lead or gold dust. This cloth is known as Prada cloth. Gold leaf was used in the Jogjakarta and Surakarta area. The Central Javanese used gold dust to decorate their Prada cloth. It was applied to the fabric using a handmade glue consisting of egg white or linseed oil and yellow earth. The gold would remain on the cloth even after it had been washed. The gold could follow the design of the cloth or could take on its own design. Older batiks could be given a new look by applying gold to them. Gold decorated cloth is still made today; however, gold paint has replaced gold dust and leaf.

Batik Designs

Although there are thousands of different batik designs, particular designs have traditionally been associated with traditional festivals and specific religious ceremonies. Previously, it was thought that certain cloth had mystical powers to ward off ill fortune, while other pieces could bring good luck.

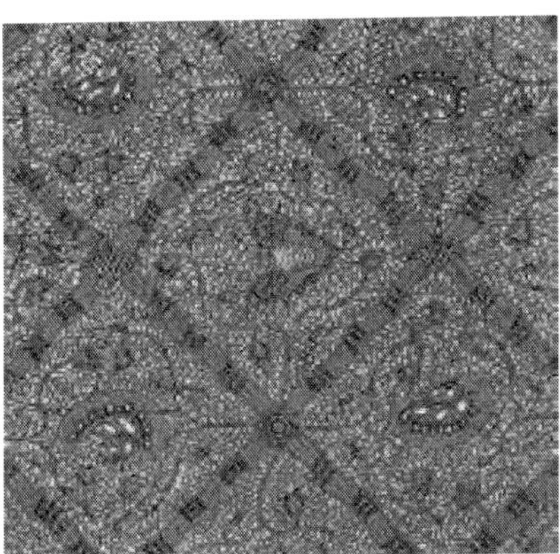

Certain batik designs are reserved for brides and bridegrooms as well as their families. Other designs are reserved for the Sultan and his family or their attendants. A person's rank could be determined by the pattern of the batik he/she wore.

In general, there are two categories of batik design: geometric motifs (which tend to be the earlier designs) and free form designs, which are based on stylized patterns of natural forms or imitations of a woven texture. *Nitik* is the most famous design illustrating this effect.

Certain areas are known for a predominance of certain designs. Central Javanese designs are influenced by traditional patterns and colours. Batik from the north coast of Java, near Pekalongan and Cirebon, have been greatly influenced by Chinese culture and effect brighter colours and more intricate flower and cloud designs.

High fashion designs drawn on silk are very popular with wealthy Indonesians. These exceptionally high-quality pieces can take months to create and costs hundreds of dollars.

Kawung

Kawung is another very old design consisting of intersecting circles, known in Java since at least the thirteenth century. This design has appeared carved into the walls of many temples throughout Java such as Prambanan near Jogjakarta and Kediri in East Java. For many years, this pattern was reserved for the royal court of the Sultan of Jogjakarta. The circles are sometimes embellished inside with two or more small crosses or other ornaments such as intersecting lines or dots. It has been suggested that the ovals might represent flora such as the fruit of the *kapok* (silk cotton) tree or the *aren* (sugar palm).

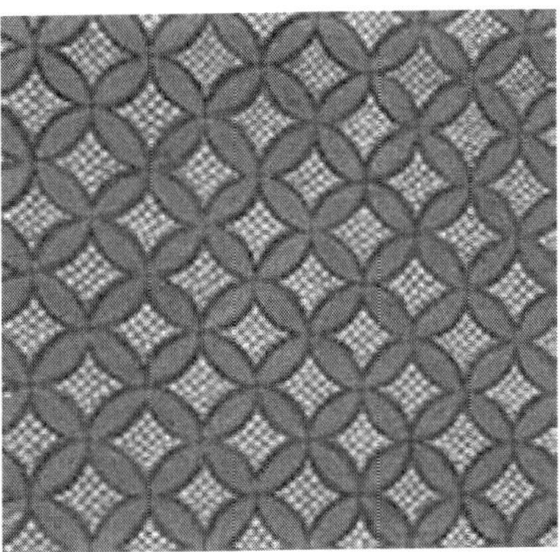

Ceplok

Ceplok is a general name for a whole series of geometric designs based on squares, rhombs, circles, stars, etc. Although fundamentally geometric, ceplok can also represent abstractions and stylization of flowers, buds, seeds and even animals. Variations in colour intensity can create illusions of depth and the overall effect is not unlike medallion patterns seen on Turkish tribal rugs. The Indonesian population is largely Muslim, a religion that forbids the portrayal of animal and human forms in a realistic manner. To get around this prohibition, the batik worker does not attempt to express this matter in a realistic form. A single element of the form is chosen and then that element is repeated again and again in the pattern.

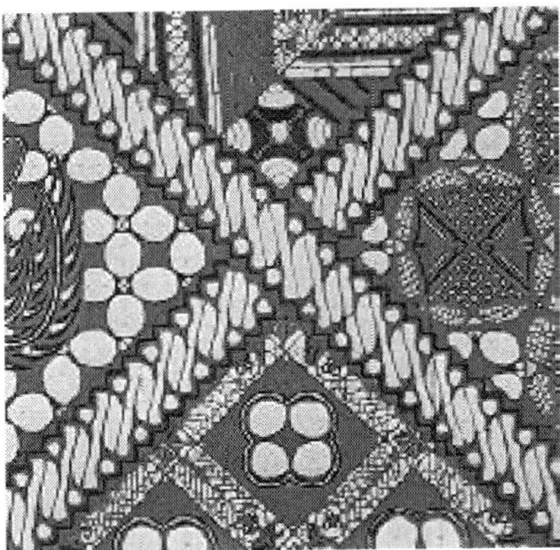

Parang

Parang was once used exclusively by the royal courts of Central Java. It has several suggested meanings such as 'rugged rock', 'knife pattern' or 'broken blade'. The Parang design consists of slanting rows of thick knife-like segments running in parallel diagonal bands. Parang usually alternated with narrower bands in a darker contrasting colour. These darker bands contain another design element, a line of lozenge-shaped motifs call mlinjon. There are many variations of this basic striped pattern with its elegant sweeping lines, with over forty parang designs recorded. The most famous is the *'Parang Rusak'* which in its most classical form consisting of rows of softly folded parang. This motif also appears in media other than batik, including woodcarving and as ornamentation on gamelan musical instruments.

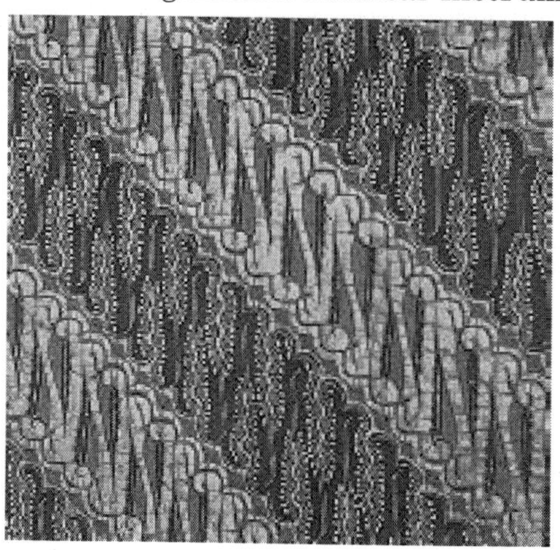

Washing Batik

Harsh chemical detergents, dryers and drying of fabrics in the sun may fade the colours in batik. Traditionally dyed batiks should be washed in soap for sensitive fabrics, such as Woolite, Silky or Halus. Fine batik in Indonesia is washed with the *lerak* fruit which can be purchased at most traditional markets. A bottled version of this detergent is also available at batik stores. Be sure to line dry batik in a shady area and not in direct sunlight.

Modern Batik

Modern batik, although having strong ties to traditional batik, utilizes linear treatment of leaves, flowers and birds. These batiks tend to be more dependent on the dictates of the designer rather than the stiff guidelines that have guided traditional craftsmen. This is also apparent in the use of colour that modern designers use. Artisans are no [* File contains invalid data | In-line.JPG *]longer dependent on traditional (natural) dyes, as chemical dyes can produce any colour that they wish to achieve. Modern batik still utilizes canting and cap to create intricate designs. Fashion designers such as Iwan Tirta have aggressively introduced batik into the world fashion scene. They have done much to promote the Indonesian art of batik dress, in its traditional and modern forms.

The horizon of batik is continuing to widen. While the design process has remained basically the same over the last century, the process shows great progress in recent decades. Traditionally, batik was sold in 2 1/4 metre lengths used for *kain panjang* or *sarong* in traditional dress. Now, not only is batik used as a material to clothe the human body, its uses also include furnishing fabrics, heavy canvas wall hangings, tablecloths and household accessories. Batik techniques are used by famous artists to create batik paintings which grace many homes and offices.

Fine quality handmade batik is very expensive and the production of such works is very limited. However, in a [* File contains invalid data | In-line.JPG *]world that is dominated by machines there is an increasing interest in materials that have been handmade. Batik is one of these materials.

During your stay in Indonesia, take advantage of your time here to learn more about the fascinating world of batik. Have a batik dress or men's business shirt made for you by a seamstress or tailor. Visit batik factories in Jogjakarta, Surakarta or Pekalongan to see for yourself how the intricate process is conducted or ask questions of batik artisans giving demonstrations in stores such as Sarinah or Pasaraya in Jakarta. You will come away with sense of wonder over the time, effort and patience put into the creation of each batik cloth. You too may soon grow to love the distinctive waxy smell of batik and your batik acquisitions will provide many memories of your stay in Indonesia. Your support of the batik industry will also ensure that this art form grows to even greater peaks.

Batik Home Furnishings

One of the distinct pleasures of living in (or visiting) Indonesia is the opportunity to purchase some truly magnificent home furnishings made of batik. As the fabric is truly unique to Indonesia, this is definitely the best place to purchase authentic batik! Batik factories can product batik to your order, with custom colours and designs in large rolls, ready to use for your home decoration projects. The 100% cotton fabric is usually preshrunk in the batik dying process and other fabrics are usually available with the batik design, should your design requirements warrant. Higher end shops also have design consultants who can help you with the layout of the room you are planning to design with your batik fabric and work with you on additional furnishings (pillows, bed covers, and cushions) to complete your colour scheme.

The Kebaya - An Indonesian Traditional Dress for Women

There is much speculation as to where the kebaya could have originated from. There are some who say that the kebaya originated in the Middle East, while others argue that it may have come from nearby China. Derived from the Arabic word *kaba* meaning "clothing" and introduced to Indonesia via the Portuguese language, the term *kebaya* has come to refer to a garment whose origins appear to be a blouse. It was first worn in Indonesia at some time during the 15th and 16th centuries. This garment is similar to what is described as a "long, fitted, flared *kebaya* known as *kebaya panjang6*, worn in the 16th century by Portuguese women arriving on the south-western coast of Malaysia, situated across the Malacca Straits from Sumatra, in northwestern Indonesia.

Many sources also cite Chinese influences on clothing of the time, one source comparing the *kebaya* to an open-fronted long-sleeved tunic worn by women of the Ming Dynasty. The introduction of this kind of dress were accredited to two major occurrences of this time; the emerging influence of Islam and the arrival of the Europeans to the archipelago. Whether it was Arabia or China that brought us the wonderful kebaya, there is no denying how quick the use of this garment was made uniquely Indonesian and spread from one island and ethnic group to another which its own regional variations. This quick diffusion of the use of the kebaya was also linked to the spice trade that was happening during this time in history.

Origins of the Kebaya

After Dutch colonization, the kebaya took on a new role as the formal dress for the European women in the country. During this time, the kebaya was made mostly from mori fabric. Modifications made to this traditional costume later introduced the use of silk and embroidery to add design and colour. The most dominant form of *kebaya* worn on the islands of Java and Bali today, can be visibly traced to the *kebaya* worn in Java and Sunda from the late 19th - early 20th century onwards.

Many of the easily recognizable features of today's *kebaya* – a tight fitting blouse that enhances the torso of the woman; the fold-back collarless neck and front opening; long sleeves; and the type of semi-transparent fabric – are evident in the *kebaya* of the past century. Traditional kebaya required the torso of the women to be wrapped with a long piece of cloth called a stagen. Women of higher social status would have help in wrapping their torso with the stagen however women who were not so fortunate to have help could dress themselves by tying the end of the stagen to a post and literally wrapping themselves into it.

The semi-transparent kebaya blouse was then worn overtop of the stagen. This blouse was fastened with a brooch rather than buttons and buttonholes. It was customary to combine the *kebaya* with *kain* – a length of unstitched cloth worn on the lower part of the body, often (and incorrectly) referred to in the English language as *sarong*. This kain was wrapped around the body with the pleats being placed at the front of the body. Traditinally this kain was dipped in a cornstach solution and then carefully folded by hand into pleats and pressed to produced the crisp look that was desired.

Indigenous Dress in the Making of a Nation

Considering the enormous historical – political and social – shifts that have occurred in Indonesia during the last century, the form of the *kebaya*, has remained relatively unchanged. Its function and meaning however, in contrast to its form, has seen major changes in colonial and post-colonial Indonesia, operating to meet different groups' political agendas, social needs and aspirations. The kebaya has come to symbolize the emancipation of women in Indonesia through a representation linking the *kebaya* to the 19th century "proto-feminist" figure of Raden A. Kartini.

During the 19th century, and prior to the Nationalist movement of the early 20th century, the *kebaya* had enjoyed a period of being worn by Indonesian, Eurasian, and European women alike, with slight style variations. During this time distinguishing class and status was important and produced variants of the basic costume. The kebaya of Javanese royalty were constructed of silk, velvet and brocade; Javanese women belonging to the commoner class wore figured cottons; the *kebaya* worn by Eurasian women was of white cotton trimmed with handmade European lace during the day, and of black silk in the evening; while the Dutch women preferred a shorter white *kebaya*. It was even possible for Dutch women planning to travel to the Dutch East Indies to purchase their *kebaya* in the Netherlands prior to leaving.

Bali's Kebaya

In Bali, the *kebaya* has a much more recent history. The Dutch, whose occupation of Bali began as late as 1849 in the north of the island, and whose direct rule did not begin until 1882, are believed to have enforced the wearing of the *kebaya*. At the time Balinese women's breasts were uncovered, except for formal and ceremonial occasions, during which a *sabuk* might be wound tightly around the upper torso, covering the breasts but leaving the shoulders and arms exposed. The women of Buleleng, the regency of northern Bali, therefore would have been some of the first to adopt the *kebaya*.

Other sources however, do not locate the *kebaya* being in use until the early 1920s by which time it was in full use in other areas of Indonesia. It is via the royalty and the palaces that the *kebaya* appears to have been disseminated out into the community. New dress codes adopted by members of the royalty returning to Bali from Java were passed down through the caste system. Yet despite the fact that clothing is often used to separate class, there seems to be no evidence of the time to indicate that there were any rules delineating styles of *kebaya* according to caste. Differences in *kebaya* cloth were more likely to be an outcome of differences in wealth.

Emerging as National Dress

By the 1920s however, and with the full emergence of the nationalist struggle in Indonesia, European women stopped wearing the *kebaya* because it was identified with typical Indonesian attire. For the European colonizers the Kebaya had become associated with Indonesian nationalism.

During the period of the Japanese occupation of Indonesia (1942-1945), educated Indonesian women prisoners-of-war chose to wear *kain-kebaya* rather than the western dress allocated to them as prison dress. A different set of political conditions produced a reversal of meaning. In this situation the women employed a cultural code (of traditional dress) to assert their political position, differentiating themselves from their European women that were also prisoners-of-war.

During the Proclamation of Independence by President Sukarno on August 17, 1945, the only woman in attendance, Ibu Trimutri was wearing kain kebaya. This image helped transform the *kebaya* from mere traditional dress, elevating it to the status of national dress for Indonesia women.

From the Palace to the Street - Popular and Traditional Images

While the *kebaya* is worn by a wide range of women from the former President Megawati to the *jamu* street vendor, the *kebaya* could never be claimed to operate as a social leveller. Women who sell *jamu* (traditional herbal medicine), from young to old, and right across the islands of Java and Bali are wearing *kebaya*. Today, in Indonesia the image of a woman wearing *kebaya* sells a variety of products from traditional herbs to Betadine to fried chicken. As an icon the women in her traditional clothing - *kebaya* - sells tradition and all the purity and goodness belonging to Indonesian cultural traditions. Perhaps she also evokes an element of nostalgia for urban consumers. Traditional as a way of life, is often less about the differences between rural and urban settings, than about socio-economic and class distinctions. For women 50 years and older, whose occupations and way of life come to distinguish them as traditional, traditional clothing of *kain-kebaya* is their choice of daily dress. These women, the majority of whom belong to the lower socio-economic group, often work in traditional settings such as markets, are employed as house servants or work in the agricultural sector.

Today's Kebaya

If we try to define what a kebaya is, it may prove to be difficult as it is constantly changing to reflect the changing times and fashions that Indonesia is experiencing. Nonetheless, it is possible to make some generalizations about the *kebaya*. Most Kebaya are made from a lace brocade. Most *kebaya* fabric uses a floral motif either printed or woven into the textile and its length can fall somewhere from above the waist to below the knee. It usually, but not always, has long sleeves. It is usually fastened at the front, and if not, then gives a semblance of doing so. Some variations of the kebaya will use a batik sash, which is coordinated with the kain, draped over the shoulder as an added accessory.

Although women in the market can be seen wearing kebaya, we can also see exquisite variations of them in government gatherings and parties and high society social functions. The beauty of this national dress is undeniable. Some of the most influential women in Indonesia are married in kebaya that can be described as "works of art" with their hand embroidered detailing and beading. Designers such as Ami Amianto have helped to promote the kebaya not only as a important part of Indonesian clothing history but as a very beautiful item of clothing that Indonesian women are proud to wear.

Textile Industry

The textile industry or apparel industry is primarily concerned with the production of yarn, and cloth and the subsequent design or manufacture of clothing and their distribution. The raw material may be natural, or synthetic using products of the chemical industry.

After the exclusion of global quota scheme, the textile industry is flourishing at high speed. The world is on a new corridor of industrial revolution. Analysts are anticipating more expansion with latest technologies in Textile Machineries. The textile machinery manufacturing hubs like China, Germany, Italy, Switzerland and India have already jumped in gigantic competition to craft and bid best technologies in textile machineries. Global Industry Analysts, Inc. (GIA) has declared that the global bazaar for textile machinery is estimated to reach US$22.9 billion by 2017.Demand for sophisticated machines that produce high quality cloth is increasing. Whatever is the technology, the purchasing decision is greatly influenced by the machines versatility, flexibility, and price offers. Key factors for dynamic growth in the textile machinery market contain economic revival post recession, rising demand for nonwoven disposable textile products, increasing demand from promising regions, especially Asia-Pacific, and going up demand for environmentally-friendly fibres. This article analyzes some of the world leading textile machinery manufacturing countries.

China Is Going High-Tech in Both Textile Machinery and Product

The Chinese textile manufacturers are developing some of the best answers in technical aspects of textile industry, along with very competitive prices. With the rapid expansion of textile industry, China s textile machinery industry also enjoys an occasion for development, and become the world s largest textile machinery manufacturer. China started industrialized machine virtually 80 years ago. At present, China-made textile machinery and equipment account for 80 percent of domestic textile machinery market. But, the industry is facing 50 percent less of sales share, and only 15 percent of gross margin, so loss coverage is high.

China is still the biggest machinery manufacturer in the global textile arena. Many countries in Asia are facing adjustment of product structure, so demand of high-end and complete sets of textile machinery are in demand. Chinese industry has obvious advantages compared with textile trade powers of India, Pakistan, Bangladesh, and Turkey, particularly in cotton spinning equipment, complete sets of polyester equipment and dyeing-printing equipment due to price.

As China is clearly emphasizing on high tech and high value added products, textile machinery would be a key area for the country to focus this year and onward. Ministry of Industry and Information Technology of China specifies that the percentage of high-tech products in sales should increase from original 40 percent to 60 percent and the proportion of research and development fund of high-tech products in total corporate sales should increase from original 2 percent to 5 percent each year.

China is not only exporter of textile machinery but also a potential importer of textile machinery. The potential import markets for textile machineries were Chinese provinces like Jiangsu, Zhejiang and Guangdong, which accounted for roughly 71% of the China s overall textile machinery imports. The last year machinery manufacturers experienced orders pouring in and the market witnessed attention of the world on Chinese machinery. Many leading machinery manufacturers around the world chose China for expanding their production base and established their manufacturing unit in China. Rapid industrialization and subsequent economic development in China over the last decade has contributed to a significant rise in Asian textile production. China Government initiatives such as China s 12th Five-Year Plan (2011-2015) which prioritizes technological advancement and improvement in craftsmanship and equipment on par with the international levels for textile and other industry sectors is expected to turnmomentous growth in the Asian market.

China is clearly focusing more on technical textiles and use of high tech automation in textile manufacturing, hence machineries for those industries will move towards China. Recently Shanghai has become one of the most fashion conscious cities in Asia. As China is producing fabric and apparels and look for value addition, they are moving for fast fashion products hence investments would take place for those production lines.

India Looks Forward To Improve In Technology

Indian textile machinery industry is more than 50 years old and the industry is increasing day by day. About 750 machinery and equipment manufacturing units are in India, of which over 250 units produce complete machines, and the rest produce parts and accessories. Textile machinery manufacturing sector at present is meeting 45-50 per cent of the overall demand of the domestic textile industry, whose main constituent is ginning, spinning, weaving and processing. The country is very good in manufacturing accessories, machine mountings & consumable parts but still the sector needs further development producing weaving machinery (shuttleless looms) and some high- tech processing machinery.

India s machinery exporters, though, have been employing various strategies to make sure that they remain competitive in the liberalized trading environment of 2013 and beyond. Many manufacturers are taking action for improving production efficiency through advanced automatic system, re-engineering of manufacturing systems, merging separate production units and Scheme for modernisation, technology upgradation and productivity advancement in anticipation of enhanced demand in 2013 and beyond among other manufacturer are seeking changes through Encouragement to the old used technology even for modernization under the subsidy scheme, encouragement to the decentralized power loom sector to expand its capacity with obsolete technology and some of are planning to raise added value by setting up joint ventures with foreign firms, to take benefit of their technical, design and marketing proficiency. Others are making relationships with foreign importers to increase their marketing capability.

As a textile product manufacturer, India faced some export decay during global economic slump during 2009-10, but then they recovered and remained slightly above the target during 2010-11. In the 2011-12 fiscal year the country has fulfilled the target of export of textiles and garments to around USD 28-30 billion. The US and EU, account for about two third of India s textiles exports. The other major export destinations are Canada, UAE, Japan, Saudi Arabia, Republic of Korea, Bangladesh and Turkey.

India is not only exporter of textile machinery but also importer of the textile machinery. Textile machinery import has risen from US$ 0.92billion during 2010-2011 to US$1.38billion (estimated) during 2011-2012. Exports during 2011-2012 were estimated at US$ 147 million as against US$ 168 million achieved during 2010-2011.The gloomy global market is responsible for lower exports.

Italian Textile Machinery Industry Grows Strongly

Italian textile machinery industrial sector is one of the foremost machinery manufacturers comprising around 300 companies (employing roughly 12,400 people) and producing machinery for an overall value of US$ 3.41 billion per year, with exports amounting to 80% of total sales. The quality of Italian textile technology is evidenced by the high number of countries in which Italian machinery is sold: around 130 countries worldwide.

Exports were always the driving force behind the sector s growth in Italy. The enthusiasm of major textile markets, combined with the capability of Italian machinery manufacturers to assert them on a global scale, contributed to sustained growth in exports. Almost 25 per cent of the sector s sales abroad are directed to China, with Asian markets generally accounting for 50 per cent of all foreign sales.

During the fourth quarter of 2012, the orders index for textile machinery rose by 22 per cent compared to the previous quarter. Even more significant was the increase with respect to the same period of the previous year (+46 per cent).

Overall orders also benefitted from a positive trend on the domestic market, for which a 47 per cent increase was actually recorded compared to the three previous months. Growth on foreign markets was slightly more contained at +20 per cent. Whereas the value of Italian textile machinery production for 2011 registered a 9 per cent increase compared to 2010, from US$ 3.072 to US$ 3.328 billion. A similar increase was recorded for exports (+10 per cent), valued at just over US$ 2.688 billion.

In contrast, Demand has remained especially weak from the domestic market. In Italy, as throughout the European Union in general, current economic uncertainty is hindering a recovery in investments, even in the textile industry. In spite of the growth experienced in 2012, Italian machinery manufacturers remain extremely cautious for the current year.

Spain Tries To Increase Its Capacity In Textile Machine Manufacturing

Spanish textile machinery industry has thrived with the arrangement of small and medium sized companies with the strength of less than 50 employees. These companies are still looking very hard competition with the world leaders to attain the international standards of price, design, quality and service. Weaving machine spare parts, knitting, sewing, accessories and spinning are the different categories integrated under the textile machinery sector of Spain. About 80 machinery companies gain fiscal credit value 260 million Euros in the Spain.

The exports in the countries like Latin America, North America and Middle East is also noteworthy. New destinations like USA,

Mexico, France, Turkey and India have new developing markets which are the motives for the go up in the demand of evolution.

Dyeing and finishing sector consists of 35 companies and is the leading sector of country. The other sector which follows it is a spinning machinery section with 25 companies. Both sub sectors has aneventual for new innovations in the machinery. The export of machinery in Spain is of 70% of its total production.

Germany Provides Reliable Technology In Machine Manufacturing

Germany has jumped out as acrucial manufacturer of textile machinery and has secured its place by the 5th rank worldwide in machinery export.The key strengths of German machinery manufacturers become obvious if one considers the entire life cycle of a machine. During the entire lifetime of a machine, the investment costs represent only about 10 to 50 per cent of the overall costs.

After two excellent years, the business climate in the global textile industry became more moderate in 2012. It was also reflected in the order intake of the German textile machinery industry that was below the figures of 2011, but still on a satisfying level. German textile machinery exports reached 1.82 billion Euro in the first half of 2012 (minus 2.7 per cent year-on-year). Based upon weak fiscal conditions within the most important markets, the industry had to go through a difficult year.

Asia is the biggest market as it absorbed 40% of the German textile machinery exports. India is thesingle largest client in Asia in the last year. Between January and July 2012, German textile machinery worth 111 million Euros was shipped to India. The second popular for German textile machine is USA. The 10 largest export markets for German textile machines and accessories areIndia, China (including Hong Kong), Turkey, US,Italy, Czech Republic, Brazil, Saudi Arabia and Pakistan.

German textile machinery is characterized by its high quality and customer-specific production. The trend setting players in the German Textile machinery industry have never stopped to explore new application fields which provide them with great opportunities.

Belgium Focuses On Its Textile Machinery Industry

The Belgian machinery industry, counting its textile machinery, is the best ever growing industrial sector measured by employment in Belgium. In the past 5 years ayearly growth rate of 4.5% was achieved in this sector, while its world market share rose with 10%.

Avital driver for that performance was the doubling of investments in the machining industry over the 1998-2008periods. Since 2012, investments have picked up again and Belgian machinery companies are altering themselves to accelerate their product development rate and flexibility. Now the Belgian machinery industry is the nation s 3th exporter.

Belgian machinery always focus of R&D, as 7% of added value of these industries has been endowed in R&D and employs over 10% of the total Belgian research head count. The industry strongly accelerated its research efforts on energy efficiency.

The Belgian textile machinery industry counts 30 companies, has a turnover of 1 Billion euro and a headcount of 4000. Its companies are active in machinery for indoor textiles (carpet, upholstery, velvet, table - bed linen), garment textiles, technical textiles and textile finishing. Belgium produces the fastest air jet weaving machines in the world. The Belgian textile machinery companies pursue technological leadership strategies.

France Emphasizes On Waste Recycling Technologies

It may be noted that the French textile machinery industry is a dynamic sector, play a particularly important role in the historical development of the textile industry. In particular, think about the illustrious name of Jacquard, the French inventor of the most sophisticated weaving technology. French has 35 textile machine manufacturing -companies, with a global turnover of 1.5 billion Euros, exports 91 per cent of their products to 115 customer countries.

The French industry strategy now is to differentiate standard from mass products, modernize equipment and technology, and to innovate and move to products with higher added value. The specific sectors covered are long fibre spinning machinery; textile waste recovery machines; systems for yarn treatment and production of technical textiles; nonwovens manufacturing lines; additional equipment for weaving (dobbies and jacquard heads); finishing machines for bleaching, dyeing, yarn finishing, finishing lines for knitted goods and textile hydro-extractors; and air-conditioning equipment for textile factories. In the new sectors of the textile industry like nonwoven processes, the French machinery is also at the pinpoint of innovation.

Recycling the textile materials at the end of their life cycle and transform them into new products, being environmentally friendly, is also an issue on which the French machinery manufacturers are among world leaders.

Turkey Moving Well With Both Textile Goods and Machinery Manufacturing

Textile is one of the key sectors in the Turkish economy in terms of GDP, employment and export. Textile accounts for 10 % of the Turkish GDP and 20% of employment in manufacturing sector. The value of textiles and clothing industry production is around US$ 30 billion and exported US$ 19,3 billion worth of textile and clothing per year. With this amount, it had a share of 19 % in total exports of Turkey The strong textile industry in Turkey kicked off the expansion of the textile machinery industry. Until 1980 nearly all textile machinery was imported. However, starting in 1980 some local production of small and medium sized low-tech machinery began. At present, the line of products manufactured by the companies varies substantially from highly automated equipment to basic models, and local producers are able to compete with foreign companies in most machinery categories, such as atmospheric jet dyeing (overflow) or blow dyeing machinery.

Textile machinery exports have an upward trend between 2002 and 2008. Turkish textile machinery exports were US$ 271 million in 2008, and decreased to US$ 263 million in 2009 with a share of 3.2 % in total machinery exports. During 2010 the export market was a growth of 266 million dollars. At present, the Turkish textile machinery industry is the most modern in the Middle East, North Africa, Balkans, Baltic and Central Asia and produces machinery and equipment required for the textile industry and all parts and accessories. The sector exports are directed to about 135 countries and major export markets in order of rank are Egypt, Ethiopia, India, Uzbekistan and Bangladesh, almost all textile manufacturing countries. High engineering skills, product flexibility, continuous product development and adaptation, and efficient after sales services enable Turkey to export Turkish made textile machinery all over the world at anrising rate.

Bangladeshi Import Is Going Down

As per recent Bangladesh Bank data import of capital machinery fell drastically by 26 per cent during the July-April period of the current fiscal year from the same period last year due to slow growth of both local and foreign investments. BB data shows LCs opening for import of capital machinery was only $ 1.797 billion during the first ten months of the current fiscal year compared to $ 2.421 billion during corresponding period of last year. Textile industry is the number one manufacturing industry of the country hence the lion share of the above mentioned capital machinery would be for this industry. But due to unavailability of data it could not summed up that textile & RMG industry capital machinery import has reduced or not. But it is definitely the trend that Bangladesh is suffering lack of machinery investment as a whole in this fiscal year which can be a result of banking sector, gas electricity & political turbulences going through the year. But we have seen in February issue cover story that before this fiscal year Bangladesh was having a robust growth in textile machinery import through the years 2006 to 2011 and before that from 2000 to 2005 textile machinery import growth was drastically increasing year on year.

Textile machinery manufacturing is an essential sector for the production chain. The range of textile machinery used in the sector is, therefore, large. More than 80 tariff lines cover the international trade of textile machinery and spare parts which are used directly in manufacturing of textiles and clothing products. Investment in this sector needs to be encouraged to decrease dependence on imports and ultimately lead to export of not only textiles and clothing products but machinery and spares parts as well.Price, flexibility and versatility comprise the determining factors for new equipment purchases. As such, the market is witnessing emergence of more efficient machines, at competitive prices, thanks to rapid technological advances in the textile machinery industry. End-users are increasingly seeking complete automation solutions with enhanced flexibility that can be availed at reasonable costs.

Textile Industry in India

The Textile industry in India traditionally, after agriculture, is the only industry that has generated huge employment for both skilled and unskilled labour in textiles. The textile industry continues to be the second largest employment generating sector in India. It offers direct employment to over 35 million in the country. The share of textiles in total exports was 11.04% during April–July 2010, as per the Ministry of Textiles. During 2009-2010, Indian textiles industry was pegged at US$55 billion, 64% of which services domestic demand. In 2010, there were 2,500 textile weaving factories and 4,135 textile finishing factories in all of India.

The archaeological surveys and studies have found that the people of Harappan civilization knew weaving and the spinning of cotton four thousand years ago. Reference to weaving and spinning materials is found in the Vedic Literature also.

There was textile trade in India during the early centuries. A block printed and resist-dyed fabrics, whose origin is from Gujarat is found in tombs of Fostat, Egypt. This proves that Indian export of cotton textiles to the Egypt or the Nile Civilization in medieval times were to a large extent. Large quantity of north Indian silk were traded through the silk route in China to the western countries. The Indian silk were often exchanged with the western countries for their spices in the barter system. During the late 17th and 18th century there were large export of the Indian cotton to the western countries to meet the need of the European industries during industrial revolution. Consequently there was development of nationalist movement like the famous Swadeshi movement which was headed by the Aurobindo Ghosh.

There was also export of Indian silk, Muslin cloth of Bengal, Bihar and Orissa to other countries by the East Indian company. Bhilwara is known as textile city.

Production

India is the second largest producer of fibre in the world and the major fibre produced is cotton. Other fibres produced in India include silk, jute, wool, and man-made fibres. 60% of the Indian textile Industry is cotton based.

The strong domestic demand and the revival of the Economic markets by 2009 has led to huge growth of the Indian textile industry. In December 2010, the domestic cotton price was up by 50% as compared to the December 2009 prices. The causes behind high cotton price are due to the floods in Pakistan and China.India projected a high production of textile (325 lakh bales for 2010 -11). There has been increase in India's share of global textile trading to seven percent in five years. The rising prices are the major concern of the domestic producers of the country.

- Man Made Fibres: These includes manufacturing of clothes using fibre or filament synthetic yarns. It is produced in the large power loom factories. They account for the largest sector of the textile production in India.This sector has a share of 62% of the India's total production and provides employment to about 4.8 million people.
- The Cotton Sector: It is the second most developed sector in the Indian Textile industries. It provides employment to huge

amount of people but its productions and employment is seasonal depending upon the seasonal nature of the production.

- The Handloom Sector: It is well developed and is mainly dependent on the SHGs for their funds. Its market share is 13%. of the total cloth produced in India.
- The Woolen Sector: India is the 7th largest producer. of the wool in the world. India also produces 1.8% of the world's total wool.
- The Jute Sector: The jute or the golden fibre in India is mainly produced in the Eastern states of India like Assam and West Bengal. India is the largest producer of jute in the world.
- The Sericulture and Silk Sector: India is the 2nd largest producer of silk in the world. India produces 18% of the world's total silk. Mulberry, Eri, Tasar, and Muga are the main types of silk produced in the country. It is a labour-intensive sector.

8

Design Elements and Principles

Design elements and principles describe fundamental ideas about the practice of good visual design. As William Lidwell stated in *Universal Principles of Design*: The best designers sometimes disregard the principles of design. When they do so, however, there is usually some compensating merit attained at the cost of the violation. Unless you are certain of doing as well, it is best to abide by the principles.

Art Elements

Design elements are the basic units of a painting, drawing, design or other visual piece and include:

Line

A line is a fundamental mark or stroke used in drawing in which the length is longer than the width. Two connected points form a line and every line has a length, width, and direction if it is straight.

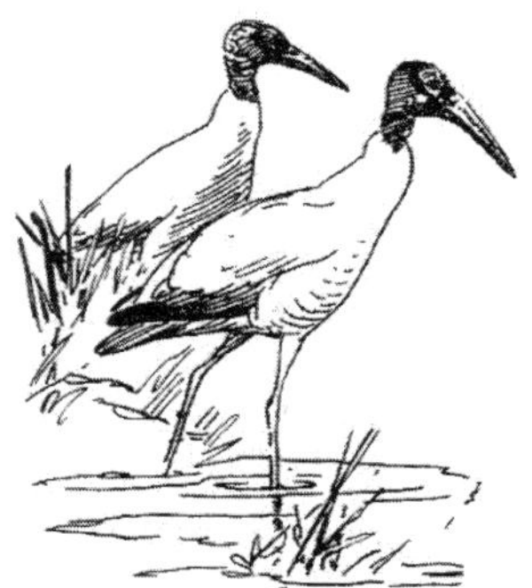

Figure: *This image contains contour lines (the outline of the birds) and decoration lines (hatching).*

Uses

- A line that defines or bounds an edge, but not always the outside edge, could represent a fold or colour change.
- A line that defines the edge of space can also be created by a gap of negative space. Many uses include to separate columns, rows of type, or to show a change in document type.
- Lines are used in linear shapes and patterns to decorate many different substrates, and can be used to create shadows representing tonal value, called hatching.

Colour

Colour can play a large role in the elements of design with the colour wheel being used as a tool, and colour theory providing a body of practical guidance to colour mixing and the visual impacts of specific colour combination.

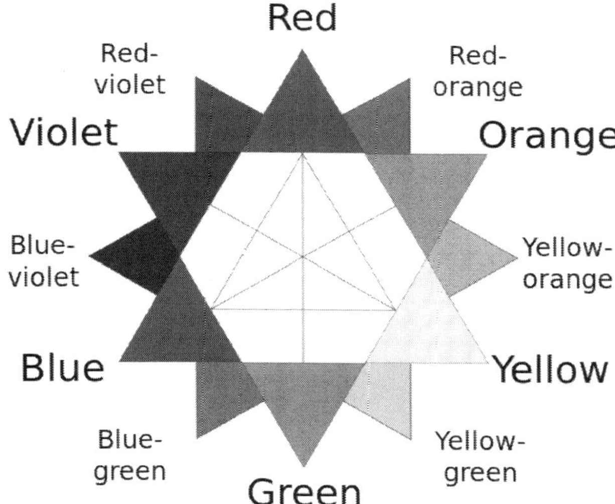

Figure: *Colour star containing primary, secondary, and tertiary colours.*

Uses

- Colour can aid organization so develop a colour strategy and stay consistent with those colours.
- It can give emphasis to create a hierarchy

Hue

Hue is one of the main properties of a colour, defined technically (in the CIECAM02 model), as "the degree to which a stimulus can be described as similar to or different from stimuli that are described as red, green, blue, and yellow," (the unique hues). The other main correlatives of colour appearance are colourfulness, chroma, saturation, lightness, and brightness.

Usually, colours with the same hue are distinguished with adjectives referring to their lightness and/or colourfulness, such as with "light blue", "pastel blue", "vivid blue". Exceptions include brown, which is a dark orange, and pink, a light red with reduced chroma.

In painting colour theory, a hue refers to a *pure* colour—one without tint or shade (added white or black pigment, respectively). A hue is an element of the colour wheel. Hues are first processed in the brain in areas in the extended V4 called globs.

Computing Hue

In opponent colour spaces in which two of the axes are perceptually orthogonal to lightness, such as the CIE 1976 (L^*, a^*, b^*) (CIELAB) and 1976 (L^*, u^*, v^*) (CIELUV) colour spaces, hue may be computed together with chroma by converting these coordinates from rectangular form to polar form. Hue is the angular component of the polar representation, while chroma is the radial component.

Specifically, in CIELAB:

$$h_{ab} = \text{atan2}(b^*, a^*)$$

while, analogously, in CIELUV:

$$h_{uv} = \text{atan2}(v^*, u^*) = \text{atan2}(v', u')$$

Where, atan2 is a two-argument inverse tangent.

Computing Hue from RGB

Preucil describes a colour hexagon, similar to a trilinear plot described by Evans, Hanson, and Brewer, which may be used to compute hue from RGB. To place red at 0°, green at 120°, and blue at 240°.

$$h_{rgb} = \text{atan2}\left(\sqrt{3}\cdot(G - B), 2\cdot R - G - B\right)$$

Equivalently, one may solve:

$$\tan(h_{rgb}) = \frac{\sqrt{3}\cdot(G - B)}{2\cdot R - G - B}$$

Preucil used a polar plot, which he termed a colour circle. Using R, G, and B, one may compute hue angle using the following scheme:

determine which of the six possible orderings of R, G, and B prevail, then apply the formula given in the table below.

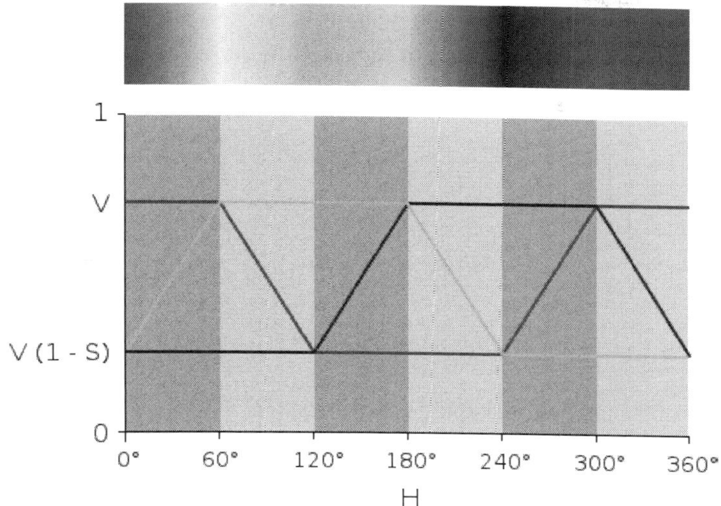

Figure: *An illustration of the relationship between the "hue" of colours with maximal saturation in HSV and HSL with their corresponding RGB coordinates.*

Ordering	*Hue Region*	*Formula*
$R \geq G \geq B$	Red-Yellow	$h_{Preucil\ circle} = 60^\circ \cdot \frac{G-B}{R-B}$
$G > R \geq B$	Yellow-Green	$h_{Preucil\ circle} = 60^\circ \cdot \left(2 - \frac{R-B}{G-B}\right)$
$G \geq B > R$	Green-Cyan	$h_{Preucil\ circle} = 60^\circ \cdot \left(2 + \frac{B-R}{G-R}\right)$
$B > G > R$	Cyan-Blue	$h_{Preucil\ circle} = 60^\circ \cdot \left(4 - \frac{G-R}{B-R}\right)$
$B > R \geq G$	Blue-Magenta	$h_{Preucil\ circle} = 60^\circ \cdot \left(4 + \frac{R-G}{B-G}\right)$
$R \geq B > G$	Magenta-Red	$h_{Preucil\ circle} = 60^\circ \cdot \left(6 - \frac{B-G}{R-G}\right)$

Note that in each case the formula contains the fraction $\frac{M-L}{H-L}$, where H is the highest of R, G, and B; L is the lowest, and M is the mid one between the other two. This is referred to as the Preucil Hue

Error, and was used in the computation of mask strength in photomechanical colour reproduction.

Hue angles computed for the Preucil circle agree with the hue angle computed for the Preucil Hexagon at integer multiples of 30 degrees (red, yellow, green, cyan, blue, magenta, and the colours midway between contiguous pairs) and differ by approximately 1.2 degrees at odd integer multiples of 15 degrees (based on the circle formula), the maximum divergence between the two.

The process of converting an RGB colour into an HSL colour space or HSV colour space is usually based on a 6-piece piecewise mapping, treating the HSV cone as a hexacone, or the HSL double cone as a double hexacone. The formulae used are those in the table above.

Specialized Hues

The hues exhibited by caramel colourings and beers are fairly limited in range. The Linner hue index is used to quantify the hue of such products.

Usage in Art

Manufacturers of pigments use the word hue e.g. 'Cadmium Yellow (hue)' to indicate that the original pigmentation ingredient, often toxic, has been replaced by safer (or cheaper) alternatives whilst retaining the hue of the original. Replacements are often used for chromium, cadmium and alizarin.

Hue vs. Dominant Wavelength

Dominant wavelength (or sometimes equivalent wavelength) is a physical analog to the perceptual attribute hue. On a chromaticity diagram, a line is drawn from a white point through the coordinates of the colour in question, until it intersects the spectral locus. The wavelength at which the line intersects the spectrum locus is identified as the colour's dominant wavelength if the point is on the same side of the white point as the spectral locus, and as the colour's complementary wavelength if the point is on the opposite side.

Hue Difference: Δh or ΔH^*?

There are two main ways in which hue difference is quantified. The first is the simple difference between the two hue angles. The symbol for this expression of hue difference is Δh_{ab} in CIELAB and Δh_{uv} in CIELUV. The other is computed as the residual total colour difference after Lightness and Chroma differences have been accounted for; its symbol is ΔH^*_{ab} in CIELAB and ΔH^*_{uv} in CIELUV.

- Values and tints and shades of colours that are created by adding black to a colour for a shade and white for a tint. Creating a tint or shade of a colour reduces the saturation.

In colour theory, a tint is the mixture of a colour with white, which increases lightness, and a shade is the mixture of a colour with black, which reduces lightness. A tone is produced either by mixing with gray, or by both tinting and shading. Mixing a colour with any neutral colour, including black and white, reduces the chroma, or colourfulness, while the hue remains unchanged.

When mixing coloured light (additive colour models), the achromatic mixture of spectrally balanced red, green and blue (RGB) is always white, not gray or black. When we mix colourants, such as the pigments in paint mixtures, a colour is produced which is always darker and lower in chroma, or saturation, than the parent colours. This moves the mixed colour toward a neutral colour—a gray or near-black. Lights are made brighter or dimmer by adjusting their brightness, or energy level; in painting, lightness is adjusted through mixture with white, black or a colour's complement.

It is common among some artistic painters to darken a paint colour by adding black paint—producing colours called *shades*—or to lighten a colour by adding white—producing colours called *tints*. However, this is not always the best way for representational painting, since an unfortunate result is for colours to also shift in their hues. For instance, darkening a colour by adding black can cause colours such as yellows, reds and oranges, to shift toward the greenish or bluish part of the spectrum. Lightening a colour by adding white can cause a shift towards blue when mixed with reds and oranges. Another practice when darkening a colour is to use its opposite, or complementary, colour (e.g. violet-purple added to yellowish-green) in order to neutralize it without a shift in hue, and darken it if the additive colour is darker than the parent colour. When lightening a colour this hue shift can be corrected with the addition of a small amount of an adjacent colour to bring the hue of the mixture back in line with the parent colour (e.g. adding a small amount of orange to a mixture of red and white will correct the tendency of this mixture to shift slightly towards the blue end of the spectrum).

Colourfulness

In colourimetry and colour theory, colourfulness, chroma, and saturation are related but distinct concepts referring to the perceived intensity of a specific colour. *Colourfulness* is the degree of difference between a colour and gray. *Chroma* is the colourfulness relative to the brightness of another colour that appears white under similar viewing conditions. Saturation is the colourfulness of a colour relative to its own brightness. Though this general concept is intuitive, terms such as *chroma, saturation, purity*, and *intensity* are often used without great precision, and even when well-defined depend greatly on the specific colour model in use.

A highly colourful stimulus is vivid and intense, while a less colourful stimulus appears more muted, closer to gray. With no colourfulness at all, a colour is a "neutral" gray (an image with no colourfulness in any of its colours is called *grayscale*). With three attributes—colourfulness (or chroma or saturation), lightness (or brightness), and hue—any colour can be described.

Shape

A shape is defined as an area that stands out from the space next to or around it due to a defined or implied boundary, or because of differences of value, colour, or texture. All objects are composed of shapes and all other 'Elements of Design' are shapes in some way.

Categories

- Mechanical Shapes or Geometric Shapes are the shapes that can be drawn using a ruler or compass. Mechanical shapes, whether simple or complex, produce a feeling of control or order.
- Organic Shapes are freehand drawn shapes that are complex and normally found in nature. Organic shapes produce a natural feel.

Texture

Meaning the way a surface feels or is perceived to feel. Texture can be added to attract or repel interest to an element, depending on the pleasantness of the texture.

Types of Texture

- Tactile texture is the actual three-dimension feel of a surface that can be touched. Painter can use impasto to build peaks and create texture.
- Visual texture is the illusion of the surfaces peaks and valleys, like the tree pictured. Any texture shown in a photo is a visual texture, meaning the paper is smooth no matter how rough the image perceives it to be.

Most textures have a natural feel but still seem to repeat a motif in some way. Regularly repeating a motif will result in a texture appearing as a pattern.

Space

In design, space is concerned with the area deep within the moment of designated design, the design will take place on. For a two-dimensional design space concerns creating the illusion of a third dimension on a flat surface:

- Overlap is the effect where objects appear to be on top of each other. This illusion makes the top element look closer to the observer. There is no way to determine the depth of the space, only the order of closeness.
- Shading adds gradation marks to make an object of a two-dimensional surface seem three-dimensional.
- Highlight, Transitional Light, Core of the Shadow, Reflected Light, and Cast Shadow give an object a three-dimensional look.
- Linear Perspective is the concept relating to how an object seems smaller the farther away it gets.
- Atmospheric Perspective is based on how air acts as a filter to change the appearance of distance objects.

Form

Form is any three dimensional object. Form can be measured, from top to bottom (height), side to side (width), and from back to front (depth). Form is also defined by light and dark. There are two types of form, geometric (man-made) and natural (organic form). Form may be created by the combining of two or more shapes. It may be enhanced by tone, texture and colour. It can be illustrated or constructed.

Principles of Design

Principles applied to the elements of design that bring them together into one design. How one applies these principles determines how successful a design may be.

Unity/Harmony

According to Alex White, author of *The Elements of Graphic Design*, to achieve visual unity is a main goal of graphic design. When all elements are in agreement, a design is considered unified. No individual part is viewed as more important than the whole design.

A good balance between unity and variety must be established to avoid a chaotic or a lifeless design.

Methods

- Proximity
- Similarity
- Continuation
- Repetition
- Rhythm is achieved when recurring position, size, colour, and use of a graphic element has a focal point interruption.
- Altering the basic theme achieves unity and helps keep interest.

Balance

It is a state of equalized tension and equilibrium, which may not always be calm.

Types

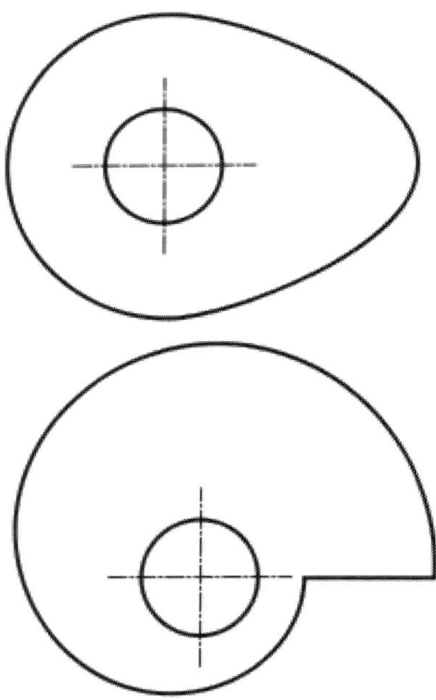

Figure: *The top image has symmetrical balance and the bottom image has asymmetrical balance*

- Symmetry
- Asymmetrical produces an informal balance that is attention attracting and dynamic.

- Radial balance is arranged around a central element. The elements placed in a radial balance seem to 'radiate' out from a central point in a circular fashion.
- Overall is a mosaic form of balance which normally arises from too many elements being put on a page. Due to the lack of hierarchy and contrast, this form of balance can look noisy.

Hierarchy

A good design contains elements that lead the reader through each element in order of its significance. The type and images should be expressed starting from most important to the least.

Scale/proportion

Using the relative size of elements against each other can attract attention to a focal point. When elements are designed larger than life, scale is being used to show drama.

Dominance/emphasis

Dominance is created by contrasting size, positioning, colour, style, or shape. The focal point should dominate the design with scale and contrast without sacrificing the unity of the whole.

Similarity and Contrast

Planning a consistent and similar design is an important aspect of a designers work to make their focal point visible. Too much similarity is boring but without similarity important elements will not exist and an image without contrast is uneventful so the key is to find the balance between similarity and contrast.

Similar Environment

There are several ways to develop a similar environment:

- Build a unique internal organization structure.
- Manipulate shapes of images and text to correlate together.
- Express continuity from page to page in publications. Items to watch include headers, themes, borders, and spaces.
- Develop a style manual and stick with the format.

Contrasts

- Space
  - Filled / Empty
  - Near / Far
  - 2-D / 3-D

- Position
  - Left / Right
  - Isolated / Grouped
  - Centred / Off-Centre
- Form
  - Simple / Complex
  - Beauty / Ugly
  - Whole / Broken
- Direction
  - Stability / Movement
- Structure
  - Organized / Chaotic
  - Mechanical / Hand-Drawn
- Size
  - Large / Small
  - Deep / Shallow
  - Fat / Thin
- Colour
  - Grayscale / Colour
  - Light / Dark
- Texture
  - Fine / Coarse
  - Smooth / Rough
  - Sharp / Dull
- Density
  - Transparent / Opaque
  - Thick / Thin
  - Liquid / Solid
- Gravity
  - Light / Heavy
  - Stable / Unstable

Movement is the path the viewer's eye takes through the artwork, often to focal areas. Such movement can be directed along lines edges, shape and colour within the artwork.

Composition (Visual Arts)

The term composition means 'putting together,' and can apply to any work of art, from music to writing to photography, that is arranged or put together using conscious thought. In the visual arts, composition is often used interchangeably with various terms such as *design, form, visual ordering,* or *formal structure,* depending on the context. In graphic design for press and desktop publishing composition is commonly referred to as page layout.

These paintings all show the same *subject*, the *Raising of Lazarus*, and essentially the same figures, but have very different compositions:

Geometry and Symmetry

Related to the rule of odds is the observation that triangles are an aesthetically pleasing implied shape within an image. In a canonically attractive face, the mouth and eyes fall within the corners of the area of an equilateral triangle. Paul Cézanne successfully used triangles in his compositions of still lifes.

Other Techniques

- There should be a centre of interest or focus in the work, to prevent it becoming a pattern in itself;
- The direction followed by the viewer's eye should lead the viewer's gaze around all elements in the work before leading out of the picture;
- The subject should not be facing out of the image;
- A moving subject should have space in front;
- Exact bisections of the picture space should be avoided;
- Small, high contrast, elements have as much impact as larger, duller elements;
- The prominent subject should be off-centre, unless a symmetrical or formal composition is desired, and can be balanced by smaller satellite elements
- the horizon line should not divide the art work in two equal parts but be positioned to emphasize either the sky or ground; showing more sky if painting is of clouds, sun rise/set, and more ground if a landscape

These principles *can* be means of a good composition yet they *cannot* be applied separately but should act together to form a good composition.

Pattern Language

A pattern language, a term coined by architect Christopher Alexander and popularized by his book *A Pattern Language*, is a structured method of describing good design practices within a field of expertise. Advocates of this design approach claim that ordinary people can use it to successfully solve very large, complex design problems.

Like all languages, a pattern language has vocabulary, syntax, and grammar—but a pattern language applies to some complex activity other than communication. In pattern languages for design, the parts break down in this way:

- The language description—the vocabulary—is a collection of named, described solutions to problems in a field of interest. These are called "design patterns." So, for example, the language for architecture describes items like: settlements, buildings, rooms, windows, latches, etc.
- Each solution includes "syntax," a description that shows where the solution fits in a larger, more comprehensive or more abstract design. This automatically links the solution into a web of other needed solutions. For example, rooms have ways to get light, and ways to get people in and out.
- The solution includes "grammar" that describes how the solution solves a problem or produces a benefit. So, if the benefit is unneeded, the solution is not used. Perhaps that part of the design can be left empty to save money or other resources; if people do not need to wait to enter a room, a simple doorway can replace a waiting room.
- In the language description, grammar and syntax cross index (often with a literal alphabetic index of pattern names) to other named solutions, so the designer can quickly think from one solution to related, needed solutions, and document them in a logical way. In Alexander's book, the patterns are in decreasing order by size, with a separate alphabetic index.
- The web of relationships in the index of the language provides many paths through the design process.

This simplifies the design work, because designers can start the process from any part of the problem they understand, and work toward the unknown parts. At the same time, if the pattern language has worked well for many projects, there is reason to believe that even a designer who does not completely understand the design problem at first will complete the design process, and the result will be usable. For example, skiers coming inside must shed snow and store equipment. The messy snow and boot cleaners should stay outside. The equipment needs care, so the racks should be inside. etc.

- It really is a language: There is even an analogy to spelling or phonology, in the documentation standards for the designs and patterns. Without these, the people building the design won't be able to read the design.

What is a Pattern?

When a designer designs something—whether a house, computer programme, or lamp—they must make many decisions about how to solve problems. A single problem is documented with its typical place (the syntax), and use (the grammar) with the most common and recognized good solution seen in the wild, like the examples seen in dictionaries. Each such entry is a single design pattern. Each pattern has a name, a descriptive entry, and some cross-references, much like a dictionary entry. A documented pattern should explain why that solution is good in the pattern's contexts.

Many Patterns form a Language

Just as words must have grammatical and semantic relationships to each other in order to make a spoken language useful, design patterns must be related to each other in position and utility order to form a pattern language. Alexander's work describes a process of decomposition, in which the designer has a problem (perhaps a commercial assignment), selects a solution, then discovers new, smaller problems resulting from the larger solution. Occasionally, the smaller problems have no solution, and a different larger solution must be selected. Eventually all of the remaining design problems are small enough or routine enough to be solved by improvisation by the builders, and the "design" is done.

The actual organizational structure (hierarchical, iterative, etc.) is left to the discretion of the designer, depending on the problem. This explicitly lets a designer explore a design, starting from some small part. When this happens, it's common for a designer to realize that the problem is actually part of a larger solution. At this point, the design almost always becomes a better design.

In the language, therefore, each pattern has to indicate its relationships to other patterns and to the language as a whole. This gives the designer using the language a great deal of guidance about the related problems that must be solved.

The most difficult part of having an outside expert apply a pattern language is in fact to get a reliable, complete list of the problems to be solved. Of course, the people most familiar with the problems are the people that need a design. So, Alexander famously advocated on-site improvisation by concerned, empowered users, as a powerful way to form very workable large-scale initial solutions, maximizing the utility of a design, and minimizing the design rework. The desire to empower users of architecture was, in fact, what led Alexander to undertake a pattern language project for architecture in the first place.

Design Problems in a Context

An important aspect of design patterns is to identify and document the key ideas that make a good system different from a poor system (that may be a house, a computer programme or an object of daily use), and to assist in the design of future systems. The idea expressed in a pattern should be general enough to be applied in very different systems within its context, but still specific enough to give constructive guidance.

The range of situations in which the problems and solutions addressed in a pattern apply is called its context. An important part in each pattern is to describe this context. Examples can further illustrate how the pattern applies to very different situation.

For instance, Alexander's pattern "A PLACE TO WAIT" addresses bus stops in the same way as waiting rooms in a surgery, while still proposing helpful and constructive solutions. The "Gang-of-Four" book by Gamma et al. proposes solutions that are independent of the programming language, and the programme's application domain.

Still, the problems and solutions described in a pattern can vary in their level of abstraction and generality on the one side, and specificity on the other side. In the end this depends on the author's preferences. However, even a very abstract pattern will usually contain examples that are, by nature, absolutely concrete and specific.

Patterns can also vary in how far they are proven in the real world. Alexander gives each pattern a rating by zero, one or two stars, indicating how well they are proven in real-world examples. It is generally claimed that all patterns need at least some existing real-world examples. It is, however, conceivable to document yet unimplemented ideas in a pattern-like format.

The patterns in Alexander's book also vary in their level of scale - some describing how to build a town or neighbourhood, others dealing with individual buildings and the interior of rooms. Alexander sees the low-scale artifacts as constructive elements of the large-scale world, so they can be connected to a hierarchic network.

Balancing of Forces

A pattern must characterize the problems that it is meant to solve, the context or situation where these problems arise, and the conditions under which the proposed solutions can be recommended.

Often these problems arise from a conflict of different interests or "forces". A pattern emerges as a dialogue that will then help to balance the forces and finally make a decision.

For instance, there could be a pattern suggesting a wireless telephone. The forces would be the need to communicate, and the need to get other things done at the same time (cooking, inspecting the bookshelf). A very specific pattern would be just "WIRELESS TELEPHONE". More general patterns would be "WIRELESS DEVICE" or "SECONDARY ACTIVITY", suggesting that a secondary activity (such as talking on the phone, or inspecting the pockets of your jeans) should not interfere with other activities.

Though quite unspecific in its context, the forces in the "SECONDARY ACTIVITY" pattern are very similar to those in "WIRELESS TELEPHONE". Thus, the competing forces can be seen as part of the essence of a design concept expressed in a pattern.

Patterns Contain Their Own Rationale

Usually a pattern contains a rationale referring to some given values. For Christopher Alexander, it is most important to think about the people who will come in contact with a piece of architecture. One of his key values is making these people feel more alive. He talks about the "quality without a name" (QWAN).

More generally, we could say that a good system should be accepted, welcomed and happily embraced as an enrichment of daily life by those who are meant to use it, or - even better - by all people it affects. For instance, when discussing a street café, Alexander discusses the possible desires of a guest, but also mentions people who just walk by.

The same thinking can be applied to technical devices such as telephones and cars, to social structures like a team working on a project, or to the user interface of a computer programme. The qualities of a software system, for instance, could be rated by observing whether users spend their time enjoying or struggling with the system.

Another possible value is the efficiency of a system, regarding a specific task. Here the happiness of the participants is less important, as long as they do their job. In software engineering, design patterns usually help to create object-oriented code that is easy to read, maintain, modify and reuse.

By focusing on the impacts on human life, we can identify patterns that are independent from changing technology, and thus find "timeless quality" (Alexander).

Generic Structure and Layout

Usually the author of a pattern language or collection chooses a generic structure for all the patterns it contains, breaking each into generic sections like context, problem statement, solution etc.

Alexander's patterns, for instance, each consist of a short name, a rating (up to two '*' symbols), a sensitizing picture, the context description, the problem statement, a longer part of text with examples and explanations, a solution statement, a sketch and further references. This structure and layout is sometimes referred to as the "Alexandrian form".

Alexander uses a special text layout to mark the different sections of his patterns. For instance, the problem statement and the solution statement are printed in bold font, the latter is always preceded by the "Therefore:" keyword. Some authors instead use explicit labels, which creates some degree of redundancy.

Meaningful Names

When design is done by a team, pattern names will form a vocabulary they can share. This makes it necessary for pattern names to be easy to remember and highly descriptive. Some examples from Alexander's works are WINDOW PLACE (helps define where windows should go in a room) and A PLACE TO WAIT (helps define the characteristics of bus stops and hospital waiting rooms, for example).

Aggregation in an Associative Network ("Pattern Language")

A pattern language, as thought by Alexander, contains links from one pattern to another, so when trying to apply one pattern in a project, a designer is pushed to other patterns that are considered helpful in its context.

In Alexander's book, such links are collected in the "references" part, and echoed in the linked pattern's "context" part - thus the overall structure is a directed graph. A pattern that is linked to in the "references" usually addresses a problem of lower scale, that is suggested as a part of the higher-scale problem. For instance, the "PUBLIC OUTDOOR ROOM" pattern has a reference to "STAIR SEATS".

Even without the pattern description, these links, along with meaningful names, carry a message: When building a place outside where people can spend time ("PUBLIC OUTDOOR ROOM"), consider to surround it by stairs where people can sit ("STAIR SEATS"). If you are planning an office ("WORKSHOPS AND OFFICES"), consider to arrange workspaces in small groups ("SMALL WORKING GROUPS"). Alexander argues that the connections in the network can be considered even more meaningful than the text of the patterns themselves.

The links in Alexander's book clearly result in a hierarchic network. Alexander draws a parallel to the hierarchy of a grammar - that is one argument for him to speak of a pattern *language*.

The idea of linking is generally accepted among pattern authors, though the semantic rationale behind the links may vary. Some authors, however, like Gamma et al. in Design Patterns, make only little use of pattern linking - possibly because it did not make that much sense for their collection of patterns. In such a case we would speak of a *pattern catalogue* rather than a *pattern language*.

Usage

Alexander encouraged people who used his system to expand his language with patterns of their own. In order to enable this, his books do not focus strictly on architecture or civil engineering; he also explains the general method of pattern languages. Consequently, his methods have been used to document expertise in diverse fields. Some examples are architectural patterns, computer science patterns, human computer interaction patterns, and educational patterns. Alexander's specifications for using pattern languages as well as creating new ones remain influential, and his books are referenced for style by experts in unrelated fields.

It is important to note that notations such as UML or the flowchart symbol collection are not pattern languages. They could more closely be compared to an alphabet: their symbols could be used to document a pattern language, but they are not a language by themselves. A recipe or other sequential set of steps to be followed, with only one correct path from start to finish, is also not a pattern language. However, the process of designing a new recipe might benefit from the use of a pattern language.

Simple Example of a Pattern

Name: ChocolateChipRatio

Context: You are baking chocolate chip cookies in small batches for family and friends

Consider These Patterns First: SugarRatio, FlourRatio, Egg Ratio.

Problem: Determine the optimum ratio of chocolate chips to cookie dough.

Solution: Observe that most people consider chocolate to be the best part of the chocolate chip cookie. Also observe that too much chocolate may prevent the cookie from holding together, decreasing its appeal. Since you are cooking in small batches, cost is not a consideration. Therefore, use the maximum amount of chocolate chips that results in a really sturdy cookie.

Consider Next: NutRatio or CookingTime or FreezingMethod

Origin

Christopher Alexander, an architect and author, coined the term pattern language. He used it to refer to common problems of the design and construction of buildings and towns and how they should be solved. The solutions proposed in the book include suggestions ranging from how cities and towns should be structured to where windows should be placed in a room.

The framework and philosophy of the "pattern language" approach was initially popularized in the book *A Pattern Language* that was written by Christopher Alexander and five colleagues at the Centre for Environmental Structure in Berkeley, California in the late 1970s. While *A Pattern Language* contains 253 "patterns" from the first pattern, "Independent Regions" (the most general) to the last, "Things from Your Life", Alexander's book *The Timeless Way of Building* goes into more depth about the motivation and purpose of the work. The following definitions of "pattern" and "pattern language" are paraphrased from "A Pattern Language":

"A *pattern* is a careful description of a perennial solution to a recurring problem within a building context, describing one of the configurations that brings life to a building. Each pattern describes a problem that occurs over and over again in our environment, and then describes the core solution to that problem, in such a way that you can use the solution a million times over, without ever doing it the same way twice."

A *pattern language* is a network of patterns that call upon one another. Patterns help us remember insights and knowledge about design and can be used in combination to create solutions.

Since the original publications, thinking in terms of patterns and pattern languages has been applied to other fields, including software design, user interface design, classroom curriculum, and social change.

Application Domains

Christopher Alexander's idea has been adopted in other disciplines, often much more heavily than the original application to architecture as depicted the book *A Pattern Language.* Recent examples include in software engineering and, more generally, to computer science, as well as in interaction designs. Pedagogical patterns are used to document good practices in teaching. The book "Liberating Voices: A Pattern Language for Communication Revolution," containing 136 patterns for using information and communication to promote sustainability, democracy and positive social change, was published in 2008. Recently, patterns were also introduced into Systems architecture design. Chess strategy and tactics involve many patterns from opening to checkmate.

Principles of Art

The principles of visual art are the rules, tools and/or guidelines that artists use to organize the elements of art in an artwork. When successfully combined with the elements of art they aid in creating an aesthetically pleasing or interesting work of art. Some principles of art that have been identified are movement, unity, harmony, variety, balance, rhythm, emphasis, contrast, proportion, and pattern. This list may vary, according to the art educator, but encompasses the generally accepted principles. Rhythm and pattern are often combined in art education.

Movement

Movement shows actions, or alternatively, the path the viewer's eye follows throughout an artwork. Movement is caused by using elements under the rules of the principles in picture to give the feeling of motion and to guide the viewer's eyes throughout the artwork. In movement an art should flow, because the artist has the ability to control the viewer's eye. The artists control what the viewers see and how they see it, like a path leading across the page to the item the artist wants the viewer's attention focused on.

Techniques such as scale and proportion can be used to create an effect of movement in a visual artwork. For instance, an element that is further into the background is smaller in scale and lighter in value. The same element repeated in different places within the same image can also demonstrate the passing of time or movement.

Unity

Unity is the concept behind the artwork. An analogy would be the way in which a conductor directs a wide variety of instruments in an orchestra to produce a symphony that is recognized as a single comprehensible piece. Unity is how well different parts of an artwork build on each other.

Harmony

Harmony is achieved in a body of work by using similar elements throughout the work, harmony gives an uncomplicated look to a piece of artwork or sculpture.

Colour harmony or colour theory is also considered a principle through the application of the design element of colour.

Variety

Variety is the quality or state of having different forms or types, notable use of contrast, emphasis, difference in size and colour.

Balance

Balance is arranging elements so that no one part of a work overpowers, or seems heavier than any other part. The three different kinds of balance are symmetrical, asymmetrical, and radial. Symmetrical (or formal) balance is the most stable, in a visual sense. When both sides of an artwork on either side of the horizontal or vertical axis of the picture plane are exactly (or nearly exactly) the same the work is said to exhibit this type of balance.

Contrast

Contrast is created by using elements that conflict with one another. Often, contrast is created using complementary colours or extremely light and dark values. Contrast creates interest in a piece and often draws the eye to certain areas. It is used to make a painting more visually interesting.

Proportion

Proportion is a measurement of the size and quantity of elements within a composition. In ancient arts, proportions of forms were enlarged to show importance. This is why Egyptian gods and political figures appear so much larger than common people. The ancient Greeks found fame with their accurately-proportioned sculptures of the human form. Beginning with the Renaissance, artists recognized the connection between proportion and the illusion of 3-dimensional space.

Pattern and Rhythm

Pattern and rhythm is showing consistency with colours or lines. Putting a red spiral at the bottom left and top right, for example, will cause the eye to move from one spiral, to the other, and everything in between. It is indicating movement by the repetition of elements. Rhythm can make an artwork seem active.

9

Colour Theory

In the visual arts, colour theory is a body of practical guidance to colour mixing and the visual effects of specific colour combination. There are also definitions (or categories) of colours based on the colour wheel: primary colour, secondary colour and tertiary colour. Although colour theory principles first appeared in the writings of Leone Battista Alberti (c.1435) and the notebooks of Leonardo da Vinci (c.1490), a tradition of "coloury theory" began in the 18th century, initially within a partisan controversy around Isaac Newton's theory of colour (*Opticks*, 1704) and the nature of so-called primary colours. From there it developed as an independent artistic tradition with only superficial reference to colorimetry and vision science.

Colour Abstractions

The foundations of pre-20th-century colour theory were built around "pure" or ideal colours, characterized by sensory experiences rather than attributes of the physical world. This has led to a number of inaccuracies in traditional colour theory principles that are not always remedied in modern formulations.

The most important problem has been a confusion between the behaviour of light mixtures, called additive colour, and the behaviour of paint or ink or dye or pigment mixtures, called subtractive colour. This problem arises because the absorption of light by material substances follows different rules from the perception of light by the eye.

A second problem has been the failure to describe the very important effects of strong luminance (lightness) contrasts in the appearance of colours reflected from a surface (such as paints or inks) as opposed to colours of light; "colours" such as browns or ochres cannot appear in mixtures of light. Thus, a strong lightness contrast between a mid-valued yellow paint and a surrounding bright white makes the yellow appear to be green or brown, while a strong brightness contrast between a rainbow and the surrounding sky makes the yellow in a rainbow appear to be a fainter yellow, or white.

A third problem has been the tendency to describe colour effects holistically or categorically, for example as a contrast between "yellow" and "blue" conceived as generic colours, when most colour effects are due to contrasts on three relative attributes that define all colours:

1. lightness (light vs. dark, or white vs. black),
2. saturation (intense vs. dull), and
3. hue (e.g., red, orange, yellow, green, blue or purple).

Thus, the visual impact of "yellow" vs. "blue" hues in visual design depends on the relative lightness and intensity of the hues.

These confusions are partly historical, and arose in scientific uncertainty about colour perception that was not resolved until the late 19th century, when the artistic notions were already entrenched. However, they also arise from the attempt to describe the highly contextual and flexible behaviour of colour perception in terms of abstract colour sensations that can be generated equivalently by any visual media.

Many historical "colour theorists" have assumed that three "pure" primary colours can mix *all possible colours*, and that any failure of specific paints or inks to match this ideal performance is due to the impurity or imperfection of the colorants. In reality, only imaginary "primary colours" used in colorimetry can "mix" or quantify all visible (perceptually possible) colours; but to do this, these imaginary primaries are defined as lying outside the range of visible colours; i.e., they cannot be seen. Any three real "primary" colours of light, paint or ink can mix only a limited range of colours, called a gamut, which is always smaller (contains fewer colours) than the full range of colours humans can perceive.

Historical Background

Colour theory was originally formulated in terms of three "primary" or "primitive" colours—red, yellow and blue (RYB)—because these colours were believed capable of mixing all other colours. This colour mixing behaviour had long been known to printers, dyers and painters, but these trades preferred pure pigments to primary colour mixtures, because the mixtures were too dull (unsaturated). The RYB primary colours became the foundation of 18th century theories of colour vision, as the fundamental sensory qualities that are blended in the perception of all physical colours and equally in the physical mixture of pigments or dyes. These theories were enhanced by 18th-century investigations of a variety of purely psychological colour effects, in particular the contrast between "complementary" or opposing hues that are produced by colour afterimages and in the contrasting shadows in coloured light. These ideas and many personal colour observations were summarized in two founding documents in colour theory: the *Theory of Colours* (1810) by the German poet and government minister Johann Wolfgang von Goethe, and *The Law of Simultaneous Colour Contrast* (1839) by the French industrial chemist Michel Eugène Chevreul.

Subsequently, German and English scientists established in the late 19th century that colour perception is best described in terms of a different set of primary colours—red, green and blue violet (RGB)—modelled through the additive mixture of three monochromatic lights. Subsequent research anchored these primary colours in the differing responses to light by three types of colour receptors or *cones* in the retina (trichromacy). On this basis the quantitative description of colour mixture or colorimetry developed in the early 20th century, along with a series of increasingly sophisticated models of colour space and colour perception, such as the opponent process theory.

Across the same period, industrial chemistry radically expanded the colour range of lightfast synthetic pigments, allowing for substantially improved saturation in colour mixtures of dyes, paints and inks. It also created the dyes and chemical processes necessary for colour photography. As a result three-colour printing became aesthetically and economically feasible in mass printed media, and the artists' colour theory was adapted to primary colours most effective in inks or photographic dyes: cyan, magenta, and yellow (CMY). (In printing, dark colours are supplemented by a black ink, known as the CMYK system; in both printing and photography, white is provided by the colour of the paper.) These CMY primary colours were reconciled with the RGB primaries, and subtractive colour mixing with additive colour mixing, by defining the CMY primaries as substances that *absorbed* only one of the retinal primary colours: cyan absorbs only red ("R+G+B), magenta only green (+R"G+B), and yellow only blue violet (+R+G"B). It is important to add that the CMYK, or process, colour printing is meant as an economical way of producing a wide range of colours for printing, but is deficient in reproducing certain colours, notably orange and slightly deficient in reproducing purples. A wider range of colour can be obtained with the addition of other colours to the printing process, such as in Pantone's Hexachrome printing ink system (six colours), among others.

For much of the 19th century artistic colour theory either lagged behind scientific understanding or was augmented by science books written for the lay public, in particular *Modern Chromatics* (1879) by the American physicist Ogden Rood, and early colour atlases developed by Albert Munsell and Wilhelm Ostwald (Colour Atlas, 1919). Major advances were made in the early 20th century by artists teaching or associated with the German Bauhaus, in particular Wassily Kandinsky, Johannes Itten, Faber Birren and Josef Albers, whose writings mix speculation with an empirical or demonstration-based study of colour design principles.

Contemporary colour theory must address the expanded range of media created by digital media and print management systems, which substantially expand the range of imaging systems and viewing contexts in which colour can be used. These applications are areas of intensive research, much of it proprietary; artistic colour theory has little to say about these complex new opportunities.

Traditional Colour Theory

Complementary Colours: For the mixing of coloured light, Newton's colour wheel is often used to describe complementary colours, which are colours which cancel each other's hue to produce an achromatic (white, gray or black) light mixture. Newton offered as a conjecture that colours exactly opposite one another on the hue circle cancel out each other's hue; this concept was demonstrated more thoroughly in the 19th century.

A key assumption in Newton's hue circle was that the "fiery" or maximum saturated hues are located on the outer circumference of the circle, while achromatic white is at the centre. Then the saturation of the mixture of two spectral hues was predicted by the straight line between them; the mixture of three colours was predicted by the "centre of gravity" or centroid of three triangle points, and so on.

According to traditional colour theory based on subtractive primary colours and the RYB colour model, which is derived from paint mixtures, yellow mixed with violet, orange mixed with blue, or red mixed with green produces an equivalent gray and are the painter's complementary colours. These contrasts form the basis of Chevreul's law of colour contrast: colours that appear together will be altered as if mixed with the complementary colour of the other colour. Thus, a piece of yellow fabric placed on a blue background will appear tinted orange, because orange is the complementary colour to blue.

However, when complementary colours are chosen based on definition by light mixture, they are not the same of the artists' primary colours. This discrepancy becomes important when colour theory is applied across media. Digital colour management uses a hue circle defined around the additive primary colours (the RGB colour model), as the colours in a computer monitor are additive mixtures of light, not subtractive mixtures of paints.

One reason the artist's primary colours work at all is that the imperfect pigments being used have sloped absorption curves, and thus change colour with concentration. A pigment that is pure red at high concentrations can behave more like magenta at low concentrations. This allows it to make purples that would otherwise be impossible. Likewise, a blue that is ultramarine at high concentrations appears cyan at low concentrations, allowing it to be used to mix green. Chromium red pigments can appear orange, and then yellow, as the concentration is reduced. It is even possible to mix very low concentrations of the blue mentioned and the chromium red to get a greenish colour. This works much better with oil colours than it does with watercolours and dyes.

So the old primaries depend on sloped absorption curves and pigment leakages to work, while newer scientifically derived ones depend solely on controlling the amount of absorption in certain parts of the spectrum.

Another reason the correct primary colours were not used by early artists is that they were not available as durable pigments. Modern methods in chemistry were needed to produce them.

Warm vs. Cool Colours

The distinction between 'warm' and 'cool' colours has been important since at least the late 18th century. It is generally not remarked in modern colour science or colorimetry in reference to painting, but is still used in design practices today. The contrast, as traced by etymologies in the Oxford English Dictionary, seems related to the observed contrast in landscape light, between the "warm" colours associated with daylight or sunset and the "cool" colours associated with a gray or overcast day. Warm colours are often said to be hues from red through yellow, browns and tans included; cool colours are often said to be the hues from blue green through blue violet, most grays included. There is historical disagreement about the colours that anchor the polarity, but 19th-century sources put the peak contrast between red orange and greenish blue.

Colour theory has described perceptual and psychological effects to this contrast. Warm colours are said to advance or appear more active in a painting, while cool colours tend to recede; used in interior design or fashion, warm colours are said to arouse or stimulate the viewer, while cool colours calm and relax. Most of these effects, to the extent they are real, can be attributed to the higher saturation and lighter value of warm pigments in contrast to cool pigments. Thus, brown is a dark, unsaturated warm colour that few people think of as visually active or psychologically arousing.

Contrast the traditional warm–cool association of colour with the colour temperature of a theoretical radiating black body, where the association of colour with temperature is reversed. For instance, the hottest stars radiate blue light (i.e., with shorter wavelength and higher frequency) and the coolest radiate red.

Achromatic Colours

Any colour that lacks strong chromatic content is said to be *unsaturated, achromatic*, or near *neutral*. Pure achromatic colours include black, white and all grays; near neutrals include browns, tans, pastels and darker colours. Near neutrals can be of any hue or lightness.

Neutrals are obtained by mixing pure colours with white, black or grey, or by mixing two complementary colours. In colour theory, neutral colours are colours easily modified by adjacent more saturated colours and they appear to take on the hue complementary to the saturated colour. Next to a bright red couch, a gray wall will appear distinctly greenish.

Black and white have long been known to combine well with almost any other colours; black decreases the apparent *saturation* or *brightness* of colours paired with it, and white shows off all hues to equal effect.

Tints and Shades

When mixing coloured light (additive colour models), the achromatic mixture of spectrally balanced red, green and blue (RGB) is always white, not gray or black. When we mix colorants, such as the pigments in paint mixtures, a colour is produced which is always darker and lower in chroma, or saturation, than the parent colours. This moves the mixed colour toward a neutral colour—a gray or near-black. Lights are made brighter or dimmer by adjusting their brightness, or energy level; in painting, lightness is adjusted through mixture with white, black or a colour's complement.

It is common among some painters to darken a paint colour by adding black paint—producing colours called *shades*—or lighten a colour by adding white—producing colours called *tints*. However it is not always the best way for representational painting, as an unfortunate result is for colours to also shift in hue. For instance, darkening a colour by adding black can cause colours such as yellows, reds and oranges, to shift toward the greenish or bluish part of the spectrum. Lightening a colour by adding white can cause a shift towards blue when mixed with reds and oranges. Another practice when darkening a colour is to use its opposite, or complementary, colour (e.g. purplish-red added to yellowish-green) in order to neutralize it without a shift in hue, and darken it if the additive colour is darker than the parent colour. When lightening a colour this hue shift can be corrected with the addition of a small amount of an adjacent colour to bring the hue of the mixture back in line with the parent colour (e.g. adding a small amount of orange to a mixture of red and white will correct the tendency of this mixture to shift slightly towards the blue end of the spectrum).

Split Primary Colours

In painting and other visual arts, two-dimensional colour wheels or three-dimensional colour solids are used as tools to teach beginners the essential relationships between colours. The organization of colours in a particular colour model depends on the purpose of that model: some models show relationships based on human colour perception, whereas others are based on the colour mixing properties of a particular medium such as a computer display or set of paints.

This system is still popular among contemporary painters, as it is basically a simplified version of Newton's geometrical rule that colours closer together on the hue circle will produce more vibrant mixtures. However, with the range of contemporary paints available, many artists simply add more paints to their palette as desired for a variety of practical reasons. For example, they may add a scarlet, purple and/or green paint to expand the mixable gamut; and they include one or more dark colours (especially "earth" colours such as yellow ochre or burnt sienna) simply because they are convenient to have premixed. Printers commonly augment a CYMK palette with spot (trademark specific) ink colours.

Colour Harmony

It has been suggested that "Colours seen together to produce a pleasing affective response are said to be in harmony". However, colour harmony is a complex notion because human responses to colour is both affective and cognitive, involving emotional response and judgement. Hence, our responses to colour and the notion of colour harmony is open to the influence of a range of different factors. These factors include individual differences (such as age, gender, personal preference, affective state, etc.) as well as cultural, sub-cultural and socially-based differences which gives rise to conditioning and learned responses about colour. In addition, context always has an influence on responses about colour and the notion of colour harmony, and this concept is also influenced by temporal factors (such as changing trends) and perceptual factors (such as simultaneous contrast) which may impinge on human response to colour. The following conceptual model illustrates this 21st century approach to colour harmony:

$$\text{Color harmony} = f(\text{Col}1, 2, 3, \ldots, n) \cdot (ID + CE + CX + P + T)$$

Wherein colour harmony is a function (*f*) of the interaction between colour/s (Col 1, 2, 3, ..., *n*) and the factors that influence positive aesthetic response to colour: individual differences (*ID*) such as age, gender, personality and affective state; cultural experiences (*CE*), the prevailing context (*CX*) which includes setting and ambient lighting; intervening perceptual effects (*P*) and the effects of time (*T*) in terms of prevailing social trends.

In addition, given that humans can perceive over 2.8 million different hues, it has been suggested that the number of possible colour combinations is virtually infinite thereby implying that predictive colour harmony formulae are fundamentally unsound. Despite this, many colour theorists have devised formulae, principles or guidelines for colour combination with the aim being to predict or specify positive aesthetic response or "colour harmony". Colour wheel models have often been used as a basis for colour combination principles or guidelines and for defining relationships between colours. Some theorists and artists believe juxtapositions of complementary colour will produce strong contrast, a sense of visual tension as well as "colour harmony"; while others believe juxtapositions of analogous colours will elicit positive aesthetic response. Colour combination guidelines suggest that colours next to each other on the colour wheel model (analogous colours) tend to produce a single-hued or monochromatic colour experience and some theorists also refer to these as "simple harmonies". In addition, split complementary colour schemes usually depict a modified complimentary pair, with instead of the "true" second colour being chosen, a range of analogous hues around it are chosen, i.e. the split compliments of red are blue-green and yellow-green. A triadic colour scheme adopts any three colours approximately equidistant around a colour wheel model. Feisner and Mahnke are among a number of authors who provide colour combination guidelines in greater detail.

Colour combination formulae and principles may provide some guidance but have limited practical application. This is because of the influence of contextual, perceptual and temporal factors which will influence how colour/s are perceived in any given situation, setting or context. Such formulae and principles may be useful in fashion, interior and graphic design, but much depends on the tastes, lifestyle and cultural norms of the viewer or consumer.

As early as the ancient Greek philosophers, many theorists have devised colour associations and linked particular connotative meanings to specific colours. However, connotative colour associations and colour symbolism tends to be culture-bound and may also vary across different contexts and circumstances. For example, red has many different connotative and symbolic meanings from exciting, arousing, sensual, romantic and feminine; to a symbol of good luck; and also acts as a signal of danger. Such colour associations tend to be learned and do not necessarily hold irrespective of individual and cultural differences or contextual, temporal or perceptual factors. It is important to note that while colour symbolism and colour associations exist, their existence does not provide evidential support for colour psychology or claims that colour has therapeutic properties.

Current Status

Colour theory has not developed an explicit explanation of how specific media affect colour appearance: colours have always been defined in the abstract, and whether the colours were inks or paints, oils or watercolours, transparencies or reflecting prints, computer displays or movie theaters, was not considered especially relevant. source insertJosef Albers investigated the effects of relative contrast and colour saturation on the illusion of transparency, but this is an exception to the rule. Known for his colour theory paintings of the 1970s, Frederick Spratt created diptychs consisting of flat rectangular panels of two different monochrome colours.

Rendering

Rendering is the process of generating an image from a model (or models in what collectively could be called a *scene* file), by means of computer programmes. Also, the results of such a model can be called a rendering. A scene file contains objects in a strictly defined language or data structure; it would contain geometry, viewpoint, texture, lighting, and shading information as a description of the virtual scene. The data contained in the scene file is then passed to a rendering programme to be processed and output to a digital image or raster graphics image file. The term "rendering" may be by analogy with an "artist's rendering" of a scene. Though the technical details of rendering methods vary, the general challenges to overcome in producing a 2D image from a 3D representation stored in a scene file are outlined as the graphics pipeline along a rendering device, such as a GPU. A GPU is a purpose-built device able to assist a CPU in performing complex rendering calculations. If a scene is to look relatively realistic and predictable under virtual lighting, the rendering software should solve the rendering equation. The rendering equation doesn't account for all lighting phenomena, but is a general lighting model for computer-generated imagery. 'Rendering' is also used to describe the process of calculating effects in a video editing programme to produce final video output.

Rendering is one of the major sub-topics of 3D computer graphics, and in practice is always connected to the others. In the graphics pipeline, it is the last major step, giving the final appearance to the models and animation. With the increasing sophistication of computer graphics since the 1970s, it has become a more distinct subject.

Rendering has uses in architecture, video games, simulators, movie or TV visual effects, and design visualization, each employing a different balance of features and techniques. As a product, a wide variety of renderers are available. Some are integrated into larger modelling and animation packages, some are stand-alone, some are free open-source projects. On the inside, a renderer is a carefully engineered programme, based on a selective mixture of disciplines related to: light physics, visual perception, mathematics and software development.

In the case of 3D graphics, rendering may be done slowly, as in pre-rendering, or in real time. Pre-rendering is a computationally intensive process that is typically used for movie creation, while real-time rendering is often done for 3D video games which rely on the use of graphics cards with 3D hardware accelerators.

Usage

When the pre-image (a wireframe sketch usually) is complete, rendering is used, which adds in bitmap textures or procedural textures, lights, bump mapping and relative position to other objects. The result is a completed image the consumer or intended viewer sees.

For movie animations, several images (frames) must be rendered, and stitched together in a programme capable of making an animation of this sort. Most 3D image editing programmes can do this.

Features

A rendered image can be understood in terms of a number of visible features. Rendering research and development has been largely motivated by finding ways to simulate these efficiently. Some relate directly to particular algorithms and techniques, while others are produced together.

- shading — how the colour and brightness of a surface varies with lighting
- texture-mapping — a method of applying detail to surfaces
- bump-mapping — a method of simulating small-scale bumpiness on surfaces
- fogging/participating medium — how light dims when passing through non-clear atmosphere or air
- shadows — the effect of obstructing light
- soft shadows — varying darkness caused by partially obscured light sources
- reflection — mirror-like or highly glossy reflection
- transparency (optics), transparency (graphic) or opacity — sharp transmission of light through solid objects
- translucency — highly scattered transmission of light through solid objects
- refraction — bending of light associated with transparency
- diffraction — bending, spreading and interference of light passing by an object or aperture that disrupts the ray
- indirect illumination — surfaces illuminated by light reflected off other surfaces, rather than directly from a light source (also known as global illumination)

- caustics (a form of indirect illumination) — reflection of light off a shiny object, or focusing of light through a transparent object, to produce bright highlights on another object
- depth of field — objects appear blurry or out of focus when too far in front of or behind the object in focus
- motion blur — objects appear blurry due to high-speed motion, or the motion of the camera
- non-photorealistic rendering — rendering of scenes in an artistic style, intended to look like a painting or drawing

Techniques

Many rendering algorithms have been researched, and software used for rendering may employ a number of different techniques to obtain a final image.

Tracing every particle of light in a scene is nearly always completely impractical and would take a stupendous amount of time. Even tracing a portion large enough to produce an image takes an inordinate amount of time if the sampling is not intelligently restricted.

Therefore, four loose families of more-efficient light transport modelling techniques have emerged: rasterization, including scanline rendering, geometrically projects objects in the scene to an image plane, without advanced optical effects; ray casting considers the scene as observed from a specific point-of-view, calculating the observed image based only on geometry and very basic optical laws of reflection intensity, and perhaps using Monte Carlo techniques to reduce artifacts; and ray tracing is similar to ray casting, but employs more advanced optical simulation, and usually uses Monte Carlo techniques to obtain more realistic results at a speed that is often orders of magnitude slower. The fourth type of light transport technique, radiosity is not usually implemented as a rendering technique, but instead calculates the passage of light as it leaves the light source and illuminates surfaces. These surfaces are usually rendered to the display using one of the other three techniques.

Most advanced software combines two or more of the techniques to obtain good-enough results at reasonable cost.

Another distinction is between image order algorithms, which iterate over pixels of the image plane, and object order algorithms, which iterate over objects in the scene. Generally object order is more efficient, as there are usually fewer objects in a scene than pixels.

Scanline Rendering and Rasterisation

A high-level representation of an image necessarily contains elements in a different domain from pixels. These elements are referred to as primitives. In a schematic drawing, for instance, line segments and curves might be primitives. In a graphical user interface, windows and buttons might be the primitives. In rendering of 3D models, triangles and polygons in space might be primitives.

If a pixel-by-pixel (image order) approach to rendering is impractical or too slow for some task, then a primitive-by-primitive (object order) approach to rendering may prove useful. Here, one loops through each of the primitives, determines which pixels in the image it affects, and modifies those pixels accordingly. This is called rasterization, and is the rendering method used by all current graphics cards.

Rasterization is frequently faster than pixel-by-pixel rendering. First, large areas of the image may be empty of primitives; rasterization will ignore these areas, but pixel-by-pixel rendering must pass through them. Second, rasterization can improve cache coherency and reduce redundant work by taking advantage of the fact that the pixels occupied by a single primitive tend to be contiguous in the image. For these reasons, rasterization is usually the approach of choice when interactive rendering is required; however, the pixel-by-pixel approach can often produce higher-quality images and is more versatile because it does not depend on as many assumptions about the image as rasterization.

The older form of rasterization is characterized by rendering an entire face (primitive) as a single colour. Alternatively, rasterization can be done in a more complicated manner by first rendering the vertices of a face and then rendering the pixels of that face as a blending of the vertex colours. This version of rasterization has overtaken the old method as it allows the graphics to flow without complicated textures (a rasterized image when used face by face tends to have a very block-like effect if not covered in complex textures; the faces are not smooth because there is no gradual colour change from one primitive to the next). This newer method of rasterization utilizes the graphics card's more taxing shading functions and still achieves better performance because the simpler textures stored in memory use less space. Sometimes designers will use one rasterization method on some faces and the other method on others based on the angle at which that face meets other joined faces, thus increasing speed and not hurting the overall effect.

Ray Casting

In ray casting the geometry which has been modelled is parsed pixel by pixel, line by line, from the point of view outward, as if casting rays out from the point of view. Where an object is intersected, the colour value at the point may be evaluated using several methods. In the simplest, the colour value of the object at the point of intersection becomes the value of that pixel. The colour may be determined from a texture-map. A more sophisticated method is to modify the colour value by an illumination factor, but without calculating the relationship to a simulated light source. To reduce artifacts, a number of rays in slightly different directions may be averaged.

Rough simulations of optical properties may be additionally employed: a simple calculation of the ray from the object to the point of view is made. Another calculation is made of the angle of incidence of light rays from the light source(s), and from these as well as the specified intensities of the light sources, the value of the pixel is calculated. Another simulation uses illumination plotted from a radiosity algorithm, or a combination of these two.

Raycasting is primarily used for realtime simulations, such as those used in 3D computer games and cartoon animations, where detail is not important, or where it is more efficient to manually fake the details in order to obtain better performance in the computational stage. This is usually the case when a large number of frames need to be animated. The resulting surfaces have a characteristic 'flat' appearance when no additional tricks are used, as if objects in the scene were all painted with matte finish.

Ray Tracing

Ray tracing aims to simulate the natural flow of light, interpreted as particles. Often, ray tracing methods are utilized to approximate the solution to the rendering equation by applying Monte Carlo methods to it. Some of the most used methods are Path Tracing, Bidirectional Path Tracing, or Metropolis light transport, but also semi realistic methods are in use, like Whitted Style Ray Tracing, or hybrids. While most implementations let light propagate on straight lines, applications exist to simulate relativistic spacetime effects.

In a final, production quality rendering of a ray traced work, multiple rays are generally shot for each pixel, and traced not just to the first object of intersection, but rather, through a number of sequential 'bounces', using the known laws of optics such as "angle of incidence equals angle of reflection" and more advanced laws that deal with refraction and surface roughness.

Once the ray either encounters a light source, or more probably once a set limiting number of bounces has been evaluated, then the surface illumination at that final point is evaluated using techniques described above, and the changes along the way through the various bounces evaluated to estimate a value observed at the point of view. This is all repeated for each sample, for each pixel.

In distribution ray tracing, at each point of intersection, multiple rays may be spawned. In path tracing, however, only a single ray or none is fired at each intersection, utilizing the statistical nature of Monte Carlo experiments.

As a brute-force method, ray tracing has been too slow to consider for real-time, and until recently too slow even to consider for short films of any degree of quality, although it has been used for special effects sequences, and in advertising, where a short portion of high quality (perhaps even photorealistic) footage is required.

However, efforts at optimizing to reduce the number of calculations needed in portions of a work where detail is not high or does not depend on ray tracing features have led to a realistic possibility of wider use of ray tracing. There is now some hardware accelerated ray tracing equipment, at least in prototype phase, and some game demos which show use of real-time software or hardware ray tracing.

Radiosity

Radiosity is a method which attempts to simulate the way in which directly illuminated surfaces act as indirect light sources that illuminate other surfaces. This produces more realistic shading and seems to better capture the 'ambience' of an indoor scene. A classic example is the way that shadows 'hug' the corners of rooms.

The optical basis of the simulation is that some diffused light from a given point on a given surface is reflected in a large spectrum of directions and illuminates the area around it.

The simulation technique may vary in complexity. Many renderings have a very rough estimate of radiosity, simply illuminating an entire scene very slightly with a factor known as ambiance. However, when advanced radiosity estimation is coupled with a high quality ray tracing algorithim, images may exhibit convincing realism, particularly for indoor scenes. In advanced radiosity simulation, recursive, finite-element algorithms 'bounce' light back and forth between surfaces in the model, until some recursion limit is reached. The colouring of one surface in this way influences the colouring of a neighbouring surface, and vice versa. The resulting values of illumination throughout the model (sometimes including for empty spaces) are stored and used as additional inputs when performing calculations in a ray-casting or ray-tracing model.

Due to the iterative/recursive nature of the technique, complex objects are particularly slow to emulate. Prior to the standardization of rapid radiosity calculation, some graphic artists used a technique referred to loosely as false radiosity by darkening areas of texture maps corresponding to corners, joints and recesses, and applying them via self-illumination or diffuse mapping for scanline rendering. Even now, advanced radiosity calculations may be reserved for calculating the ambiance of the room, from the light reflecting off walls, floor and ceiling, without examining the contribution that complex objects make to the radiosity—or complex objects may be replaced in the radiosity calculation with simpler objects of similar size and texture.

Radiosity calculations are viewpoint independent which increases the computations involved, but makes them useful for all viewpoints. If there is little rearrangement of radiosity objects in the scene, the same radiosity data may be reused for a number of frames, making radiosity an effective way to improve on the flatness of ray casting, without seriously impacting the overall rendering time-per-frame.

Because of this, radiosity is a prime component of leading real-time rendering methods, and has been used from beginning-to-end to create a large number of well-known recent feature-length animated 3D-cartoon films.

Sampling and Filtering

One problem that any rendering system must deal with, no matter which approach it takes, is the sampling problem. Essentially, the rendering process tries to depict a continuous function from image space to colours by using a finite number of pixels. As a consequence of the Nyquist–Shannon sampling theorem (or Kotelnikov theorem), any spatial waveform that can be displayed must consist of at least two pixels, which is proportional to image resolution. In simpler terms, this expresses the idea that an image cannot display details, peaks or troughs in colour or intensity, that are smaller than one pixel.

If a naive rendering algorithm is used without any filtering, high frequencies in the image function will cause ugly aliasing to be present in the final image. Aliasing typically manifests itself as jaggies, or jagged edges on objects where the pixel grid is visible. In order to remove aliasing, all rendering algorithms (if they are to produce good-looking images) must use some kind of low-pass filter on the image function to remove high frequencies, a process called antialiasing.

Optimization

Optimizations used by an artist when a scene is being developed:

Due to the large number of calculations, a work in progress is usually only rendered in detail appropriate to the portion of the work being developed at a given time, so in the initial stages of modelling, wireframe and ray casting may be used, even where the target output is ray tracing with radiosity. It is also common to render only parts of the scene at high detail, and to remove objects that are not important to what is currently being developed.

Common Optimizations for Real Time Rendering

For real-time, it is appropriate to simplify one or more common approximations, and tune to the exact parameters of the scenery in question, which is also tuned to the agreed parameters to get the most 'bang for the buck'.

Academic Core

The implementation of a realistic renderer always has some basic element of physical simulation or emulation — some computation which resembles or abstracts a real physical process.

The term "*physically based*" indicates the use of physical models and approximations that are more general and widely accepted outside rendering. A particular set of related techniques have gradually become established in the rendering community.

The basic concepts are moderately straightforward, but intractable to calculate; and a single elegant algorithm or approach has been elusive for more general purpose renderers. In order to meet demands of robustness, accuracy and practicality, an implementation will be a complex combination of different techniques.

Rendering research is concerned with both the adaptation of scientific models and their efficient application.

The Rendering Equation

This is the key academic/theoretical concept in rendering. It serves as the most abstract formal expression of the non-perceptual aspect of rendering. All more complete algorithms can be seen as solutions to particular formulations of this equation.

$$L_o(x,\vec{w}) = L_e(x,\vec{w}) + \int_{\Omega} f_r(x,\vec{w}',\vec{w})L_i(x,\vec{w}')(\vec{w}'\cdot\vec{n})\mathrm{d}\vec{w}'$$

Meaning: at a particular position and direction, the outgoing light (L_o) is the sum of the emitted light (L_e) and the reflected light. The reflected light being the sum of the incoming light (L_i) from all directions, multiplied by the surface reflection and incoming angle. By connecting outward light to inward light, via an interaction point, this equation stands for the whole 'light transport' — all the movement of light — in a scene.

The Bidirectional Reflectance Distribution Function

The bidirectional reflectance distribution function (BRDF) expresses a simple model of light interaction with a surface as follows:

$$f_r(x,\vec{w}',\vec{w}) = \frac{\mathrm{d}L_r(x,\vec{w})}{L_i(x,\vec{w}')(\vec{w}'\cdot\vec{n})\mathrm{d}\vec{w}'}$$

Light interaction is often approximated by the even simpler models: diffuse reflection and specular reflection, although both can ALSO be BRDFs.

Geometric Optics

Rendering is practically exclusively concerned with the particle aspect of light physics — known as geometric optics. Treating light, at its basic level, as particles bouncing around is a simplification, but appropriate: the wave aspects of light are negligible in most scenes, and are significantly more difficult to simulate. Notable wave aspect phenomena include diffraction and polarisation. Both types of effect, if needed, are made by appearance-oriented adjustment of the reflection model.

Visual Perception

Though it receives less attention, an understanding of human visual perception is valuable to rendering. This is mainly because image displays and human perception have restricted ranges. A renderer can simulate an almost infinite range of light brightness and colour, but current displays — movie screen, computer monitor, etc. — cannot handle so much, and something must be discarded or compressed. Human perception also has limits, and so does not need to be given large-range images to create realism. This can help solve the problem of fitting images into displays, and, furthermore, suggest what short-cuts could be used in the rendering simulation, since certain subtleties won't be noticeable. This related subject is tone mapping.

Mathematics used in rendering includes: linear algebra, calculus, numerical mathematics, signal processing, and Monte Carlo methods.

Rendering for movies often takes place on a network of tightly connected computers known as a render farm.

The current state of the art in 3-D image description for movie creation is the mental ray scene description language designed at mental images and the RenderMan shading language designed at Pixar. (compare with simpler 3D fileformats such as VRML or APIs such as OpenGL and DirectX tailored for 3D hardware accelerators).

Other renderers (including proprietary ones) can and are sometimes used, but most other renderers tend to miss one or more of the often needed features like good texture filtering, texture caching, programmable shaders, highend geometry types like hair, subdivision or nurbs surfaces with tesselation on demand, geometry caching, raytracing with geometry caching, high quality shadow mapping, speed or patent-free implementations. Other highly sought features these days may include IPR and hardware rendering/shading.

Monte Carlo Method

Monte Carlo methods (or Monte Carlo experiments) are a broad class of computational algorithms that rely on repeated random sampling to obtain numerical results; i.e., by running simulations many times over in order to calculate those same probabilities heuristically just like actually playing and recording your results in a real casino situation: hence the name. They are often used in physical and mathematical problems and are most suited to be applied when it is impossible to obtain a closed-form expression or infeasible to apply a deterministic algorithm. Monte Carlo methods are mainly used in three distinct problems: optimization, numerical integration and generation of samples from a probability distribution.

Monte Carlo methods are especially useful for simulating systems with many coupled degrees of freedom, such as fluids, disordered materials, strongly coupled solids, and cellular structures. They are used to model phenomena with significant uncertainty in inputs, such as the calculation of risk in business. They are widely used in mathematics, for example to evaluate multidimensional definite integrals with complicated boundary conditions. When Monte Carlo simulations have been applied in space exploration and oil exploration, their predictions of failures, cost overruns and schedule overruns are routinely better than human intuition or alternative "soft" methods.

The modern version of the Monte Carlo method was invented in the late 1940s by Stanislaw Ulam, while he was working on nuclear weapon projects at the Los Alamos National Laboratory. It was named by Nicholas Metropolis, after the Monte Carlo Casino, where Ulam's uncle often gambled. Immediately after Ulam's breakthrough, John von Neumann understood its importance and programmed the ENIAC computer to carry out Monte Carlo calculations.

Introduction

Monte Carlo methods vary, but tend to follow a particular pattern:

1. Define a domain of possible inputs.
2. Generate inputs randomly from a probability distribution over the domain.
3. Perform a deterministic computation on the inputs.
4. Aggregate the results.

For example, consider a circle inscribed in a unit square. Given that the circle and the square have a ratio of areas that is $\pi/4$, the value of ð can be approximated using a Monte Carlo method:

1. Draw a square on the ground, then inscribe a circle within it.
2. Uniformly scatter some objects of uniform size (grains of rice or sand) over the square.
3. Count the number of objects inside the circle and the total number of objects.
4. The ratio of the two counts is an estimate of the ratio of the two areas, which is $\pi/4$. Multiply the result by 4 to estimate π.

In this procedure the domain of inputs is the square that circumscribes our circle. We generate random inputs by scattering grains over the square then perform a computation on each input (test whether it falls within the circle). Finally, we aggregate the results to obtain our final result, the approximation of π.

If the grains are not uniformly distributed, then our approximation will be poor. Secondly, there should be a large number of inputs. The approximation is generally poor if only a few grains are randomly dropped into the whole square. On average, the approximation improves as more grains are dropped.

History

Before the Monte Carlo method was developed, simulations tested a previously understood deterministic problem and statistical sampling was used to estimate uncertainties in the simulations. Monte Carlo simulations invert this approach, solving deterministic problems using a probabilistic analog.

An early variant of the Monte Carlo method can be seen in the Buffon's needle experiment, in which π can be estimated by dropping needles on a floor made of parallel strips of wood. In the 1930s, Enrico Fermi first experimented with the Monte Carlo method while studying neutron diffusion, but did not publish anything on it.

In 1946, physicists at Los Alamos Scientific Laboratory were investigating radiation shielding and the distance that neutrons would likely travel through various materials. Despite having most of the necessary data, such as the average distance a neutron would travel in a substance before it collided with an atomic nucleus, and how much energy the neutron was likely to give off following a collision, the Los Alamos physicists were unable to solve the problem using conventional, deterministic mathematical methods. Stanislaw Ulam had the idea of using random experiments. He recounts his inspiration as follows:

The first thoughts and attempts I made to practice [the Monte Carlo Method] were suggested by a question which occurred to me in 1946 as I was convalescing from an illness and playing solitaires. The question was what are the chances that a Canfield solitaire laid out with 52 cards will come out successfully? After spending a lot of time trying to estimate them by pure combinatorial calculations, I wondered whether a more practical method than "abstract thinking" might not be to lay it out say one hundred times and simply observe and count the number of successful plays. This was already possible to envisage with the beginning of the new era of fast computers, and I immediately thought of problems of neutron diffusion and other questions of mathematical physics, and more generally how to change processes described by certain differential equations into an equivalent form interpretable as a succession of random operations. Later [in 1946], I described the idea to John von Neumann, and we began to plan actual calculations.

–Stanislaw Ulam

Being secret, the work of von Neumann and Ulam required a code name. Von Neumann chose the name *Monte Carlo*. The name refers to the Monte Carlo Casino in Monaco where Ulam's uncle would borrow money to gamble. Using lists of "truly random" random numbers was extremely slow, but von Neumann developed a way to calculate pseudorandom numbers, using the middle-square method. Though this method has been criticized as crude, von Neumann was aware of this: he justified it as being faster than any other method at his disposal, and also noted that when it went awry it did so obviously, unlike methods that could be subtly incorrect.

Monte Carlo methods were central to the simulations required for the Manhattan Project, though severely limited by the computational tools at the time. In the 1950s they were used at Los Alamos for early work relating to the development of the hydrogen bomb, and became popularized in the fields of physics, physical chemistry, and operations research. The Rand Corporation and the U.S. Air Force were two of the major organizations responsible for funding and disseminating information on Monte Carlo methods during this time, and they began to find a wide application in many different fields.

Uses of Monte Carlo methods require large amounts of random numbers, and it was their use that spurred the development of pseudorandom number generators, which were far quicker to use than the tables of random numbers that had been previously used for statistical sampling.

Definitions

There is no consensus on how *Monte Carlo* should be defined. For example, Ripley defines most probabilistic modelling as *stochastic simulation*, with *Monte Carlo* being reserved for Monte Carlo integration and Monte Carlo statistical tests. Sawilowsky distinguishes between a simulation, a Monte Carlo method, and a Monte Carlo simulation: a simulation is a fictitious representation of reality, a Monte Carlo method is a technique that can be used to solve a mathematical or statistical problem, and a Monte Carlo simulation uses repeated sampling to determine the properties of some phenomenon (or behaviour). Examples:

- Simulation: Drawing one pseudo-random uniform variable from the interval (0,1] can be used to simulate the tossing of a coin: If the value is less than or equal to 0.50 designate the outcome as heads, but if the value is greater than 0.50 designate the outcome as tails. This is a simulation, but not a Monte Carlo simulation.

- Monte Carlo method: The area of an irregular figure inscribed in a unit square can be determined by throwing darts at the square and computing the ratio of hits within the irregular figure to the total number of darts thrown. This is a Monte Carlo method of determining area, but not a simulation.
- Monte Carlo simulation: Drawing a large number of pseudo-random uniform variables from the interval (0, 1], and assigning values less than or equal to 0.50 as heads and greater than 0.50 as tails, is a Monte Carlo simulation of the behaviour of repeatedly tossing a coin.

Kalos and Whitlock point out that such distinctions are not always easy to maintain. For example, the emission of radiation from atoms is a natural stochastic process. It can be simulated directly, or its average behaviour can be described by stochastic equations that can themselves be solved using Monte Carlo methods. "Indeed, the same computer code can be viewed simultaneously as a 'natural simulation' or as a solution of the equations by natural sampling."

Monte Carlo and Random Numbers

Monte Carlo simulation methods do not always require truly random numbers to be useful — while for some applications, such as primality testing, unpredictability is vital. Many of the most useful techniques use deterministic, pseudorandom sequences, making it easy to test and re-run simulations. The only quality usually necessary to make good simulations is for the pseudo-random sequence to appear "random enough" in a certain sense.

What this means depends on the application, but typically they should pass a series of statistical tests. Testing that the numbers are uniformly distributed or follow another desired distribution when a large enough number of elements of the sequence are considered is one of the simplest, and most common ones. Weak correlations between successive samples is also often desirable/necessary.

Sawilowsky lists the characteristics of a high quality Monte Carlo simulation:

- the (pseudo-random) number generator has certain characteristics (*e.g.*, a long "period" before the sequence repeats)
- the (pseudo-random) number generator produces values that pass tests for randomness
- there are enough samples to ensure accurate results
- the proper sampling technique is used

- the algorithm used is valid for what is being modelled
- it simulates the phenomenon in question.

Pseudo-random number sampling algorithms are used to transform uniformly distributed pseudo-random numbers into numbers that are distributed according to a given probability distribution.

Low-discrepancy sequences are often used instead of random sampling from a space as they ensure even coverage and normally have a faster order of convergence than Monte Carlo simulations using random or pseudorandom sequences. Methods based on their use are called quasi-Monte Carlo methods.

Monte Carlo Simulation Versus "what if" Scenarios

There are ways of using probabilities that are definitely not Monte Carlo simulations — for example, deterministic modelling using single-point estimates. Each uncertain variable within a model is assigned a "best guess" estimate. Scenarios (such as best, worst, or most likely case) for each input variable are chosen and the results recorded.

By contrast, Monte Carlo simulations sample probability distribution for each variable to produce hundreds or thousands of possible outcomes. The results are analyzed to get probabilities of different outcomes occurring. For example, a comparison of a spreadsheet cost construction model run using traditional "what if" scenarios, and then run again with Monte Carlo simulation and Triangular probability distributions shows that the Monte Carlo analysis has a narrower range than the "what if" analysis. This is because the "what if" analysis gives equal weight to all scenarios, while Monte Carlo method hardly samples in the very low probability regions. The samples in such regions are called "rare events".

Applications

Monte Carlo methods are especially useful for simulating phenomena with significant uncertainty in inputs and systems with a large number of coupled degrees of freedom. Areas of application include:

Physical Sciences

Monte Carlo methods are very important in computational physics, physical chemistry, and related applied fields, and have diverse applications from complicated quantum chromodynamics calculations to designing heat shields and aerodynamic forms. In statistical physics

Monte Carlo molecular modelling is an alternative to computational molecular dynamics, and Monte Carlo methods are used to compute statistical field theories of simple particle and polymer systems. Quantum Monte Carlo methods solve the many-body problem for quantum systems. In experimental particle physics, Monte Carlo methods are used for designing detectors, understanding their behaviour and comparing experimental data to theory. In astrophysics, they are used in such diverse manners as to model both the evolution of galaxies and the transmission of microwave radiation through a rough planetary surface. Monte Carlo methods are also used in the ensemble models that form the basis of modern weather forecasting.

Engineering

Monte Carlo methods are widely used in engineering for sensitivity analysis and quantitative probabilistic analysis in process design. The need arises from the interactive, co-linear and non-linear behaviour of typical process simulations. For example,

- In microelectronics engineering, Monte Carlo methods are applied to analyze correlated and uncorrelated variations in analog and digital integrated circuits.
- In geostatistics and geometallurgy, Monte Carlo methods underpin the design of mineral processing flowsheets and contribute to quantitative risk analysis.
- In wind energy yield analysis, the predicted energy output of a wind farm during its lifetime is calculated giving different levels of uncertainty (P90, P50, etc.)
- impacts of pollution are simulated and diesel compared with petrol.
- In autonomous robotics, Monte Carlo localization can determine the position of a robot. It is often applied to stochastic filters such as the Kalman filter or Particle filter that forms the heart of the SLAM (Simultaneous Localization and Mapping) algorithm.
- In aerospace engineering, Monte Carlo methods are used to ensure that multiple parts of an assembly will fit into an engine component.
- In telecommunications, when planning a wireless network, design must be proved to work for a wide variety of scenarios that depend mainly on the number of users, their locations and the services they want to use. Monte Carlo methods are typically

used to generate these users and their states. The network performance is then evaluated and, if results are not satisfactory, the network design goes through an optimization process.

- In reliability engineering, one can use Monte Carlo simulation to generate mean time between failures and mean time to repair for components.

Computational Biology

Monte Carlo methods are used in computational biology, such for as Bayesian inference in phylogeny.

Biological systems such as proteins membranes, images of cancer, are being studied by means of computer simulations.

The systems can be studied in the coarse-grained or *ab initio* frameworks depending on the desired accuracy. Computer simulations allow us to monitor the local environment of a particular molecule to see if some chemical reaction is happening for instance. We can also conduct thought experiments when the physical experiments are not feasible, for instance breaking bonds, introducing impurities at specific sites, changing the local/global structure, or introducing external fields.

Computer Graphics

Path Tracing, occasionally referred to as Monte Carlo Ray Tracing, renders a 3D scene by randomly tracing samples of possible light paths. Repeated sampling of any given pixel will eventually cause the average of the samples to converge on the correct solution of the rendering equation, making it one of the most physically accurate 3D graphics rendering methods in existence.

Applied Statistics

In applied statistics, Monte Carlo methods are generally used for two purposes:

1. To compare competing statistics for small samples under realistic data conditions. Although Type I error and power properties of statistics can be calculated for data drawn from classical theoretical distributions (*e.g.*, normal curve, Cauchy distribution) for asymptotic conditions (*i. e*, infinite sample size and infinitesimally small treatment effect), real data often do not have such distributions.

2. To provide implementations of hypothesis tests that are more efficient than exact tests such as permutation tests (which are often impossible to compute) while being more accurate than critical values for asymptotic distributions.

Monte Carlo methods are also a compromise between approximate randomization and permutation tests. An approximate randomization test is based on a specified subset of all permutations (which entails potentially enormous housekeeping of which permutations have been considered). The Monte Carlo approach is based on a specified number of randomly drawn permutations (exchanging a minor loss in precision if a permutation is drawn twice – or more frequently—for the efficiency of not having to track which permutations have already been selected).

Artificial Intelligence for Games

Monte Carlo methods have been developed into a technique called Monte Carlo tree search that is useful for searching for the best move in a game. Possible moves are organized in a search tree and a large number of random simulations are used to estimate the long-term potential of each move. A black box simulator represents the opponent's moves.

The Monte Carlo Tree Search (MCTS) method has four steps:

1. Starting at root node of the tree, select optimal child nodes until a leaf node is reached.
2. Expand the leaf node and choose one of its children.
3. Play a simulated game starting with that node.
4. Use the results of that simulated game to update the node and its ancestors.

The net effect, over the course of many simulated games, is that the value of a node representing a move will go up or down, hopefully corresponding to whether or not that node represents a good move.

Monte Carlo Tree Search has been used successfully to play games such as Go, Tantrix, Battleship, Havannah, and Arimaa.

Design and Visuals

Monte Carlo methods are also efficient in solving coupled integral differential equations of radiation fields and energy transport, and thus these methods have been used in global illumination computations that produce photo-realistic images of virtual 3D models, with applications in video games, architecture, design, computer generated films, and cinematic special effects.

Finance and Business

Monte Carlo methods in finance are often used to evaluate investments in projects at a business unit or corporate level, or to evaluate financial derivatives. They can be used to model project schedules, where simulations aggregate estimates for worst-case, best-case, and most likely durations for each task to determine outcomes for the overall project.

Use in Mathematics

In general, Monte Carlo methods are used in mathematics to solve various problems by generating suitable random numbers and observing that fraction of the numbers that obeys some property or properties. The method is useful for obtaining numerical solutions to problems too complicated to solve analytically. The most common application of the Monte Carlo method is Monte Carlo integration.

Integration

Deterministic numerical integration algorithms work well in a small number of dimensions, but encounter two problems when the functions have many variables. First, the number of function evaluations needed increases rapidly with the number of dimensions. For example, if 10 evaluations provide adequate accuracy in one dimension, then 10^{100} points are needed for 100 dimensions—far too many to be computed. This is called the curse of dimensionality. Second, the boundary of a multidimensional region may be very complicated, so it may not be feasible to reduce the problem to a series of nested one-dimensional integrals. 100 dimensions is by no means unusual, since in many physical problems, a "dimension" is equivalent to a degree of freedom.

Monte Carlo methods provide a way out of this exponential increase in computation time. As long as the function in question is reasonably well-behaved, it can be estimated by randomly selecting points in 100-dimensional space, and taking some kind of average of the function values at these points. By the central limit theorem, this method displays $1/\sqrt{N}$ convergence—i.e., quadrupling the number of sampled points halves the error, regardless of the number of dimensions.

A refinement of this method, known as importance sampling in statistics, involves sampling the points randomly, but more frequently where the integrand is large. To do this precisely one would have to already know the integral, but one can approximate the integral by an integral of a similar function or use adaptive routines such as stratified sampling, recursive stratified sampling, adaptive umbrella sampling or the VEGAS algorithm.

A similar approach, the quasi-Monte Carlo method, uses low-discrepancy sequences. These sequences "fill" the area better and sample the most important points more frequently, so quasi-Monte Carlo methods can often converge on the integral more quickly.

Another class of methods for sampling points in a volume is to simulate random walks over it (Markov chain Monte Carlo). Such methods include the Metropolis-Hastings algorithm, Gibbs sampling and the Wang and Landau algorithm.

Simulation and Optimization

Another powerful and very popular application for random numbers in numerical simulation is in numerical optimization. The problem is to minimize (or maximize) functions of some vector that often has a large number of dimensions. Many problems can be phrased in this way: for example, a computer chess programme could be seen as trying to find the set of, say, 10 moves that produces the best evaluation function at the end. In the travelling salesman problem the goal is to minimize distance travelled. There are also applications to engineering design, such as multidisciplinary design optimization.

The travelling salesman problem is what is called a conventional optimization problem. That is, all the facts (distances between each destination point) needed to determine the optimal path to follow are known with certainty and the goal is to run through the possible travel choices to come up with the one with the lowest total distance. However, let's assume that instead of wanting to minimize the total distance travelled to visit each desired destination, we wanted to minimize the total time needed to reach each destination. This goes beyond conventional optimization since travel time is inherently uncertain (traffic jams, time of day, etc.). As a result, to determine our optimal path we would want to use simulation - optimization to first understand the range of potential times it could take to go from one point to another (represented by a probability distribution in this case rather than a specific distance) and then optimize our travel decisions to identify the best path to follow taking that uncertainty into account.

Simulating industry problems using spreadsheet software is a powerful application of Monte Carlo simulation. With a basic spreadsheet tool and some formulas built into the sheet, industry can often attain good solutions without having to procure expensive simulation software.

Inverse Problems

Probabilistic formulation of inverse problems leads to the definition of a probability distribution in the model space. This probability distribution combines prior information with new information obtained by measuring some observable parameters (data). As, in the general case, the theory linking data with model parameters is nonlinear, the posterior probability in the model space may not be easy to describe (it may be multimodal, some moments may not be defined, etc.).

When analyzing an inverse problem, obtaining a maximum likelihood model is usually not sufficient, as we normally also wish to have information on the resolution power of the data. In the general case we may have a large number of model parameters, and an inspection of the marginal probability densities of interest may be impractical, or even useless. But it is possible to pseudorandomly generate a large collection of models according to the posterior probability distribution and to analyze and display the models in such a way that information on the relative likelihoods of model properties is conveyed to the spectator. This can be accomplished by means of an efficient Monte Carlo method, even in cases where no explicit formula for the *a priori* distribution is available.

The best-known importance sampling method, the Metropolis algorithm, can be generalized, and this gives a method that allows analysis of (possibly highly nonlinear) inverse problems with complex *a priori* information and data with an arbitrary noise distribution.

Computational Mathematics

Monte Carlo methods are useful in many areas of computational mathematics, where a "lucky choice" can find the correct result. A classic example is Rabin's algorithm for primality testing: for any n that is not prime, a random x has at least a 75% chance of proving that n is not prime. Hence, if n is not prime, but x says that it might be, we have observed at most a 1-in-4 event. If 10 different random x say that "n is probably prime" when it is not, we have observed a one-in-a-million event. In general a Monte Carlo algorithm of this kind produces one correct answer with a guarantee n is composite, and x proves it so, but another one without, but with a guarantee of not getting this answer when it is wrong too often—in this case at most 25% of the time.

Path tracing

Path tracing is a computer graphics method of rendering images of three dimensional scenes such that the global illumination is faithful to reality. Fundamentally, the algorithm is integrating over all the illuminance arriving to a single point on the surface of an object. This illuminance is then reduced by a surface reflectance function to determine how much of it will go towards the viewpoint camera. This integration procedure is repeated for every pixel in the output image. When combined with physically accurate models of surfaces, accurate models of real light sources (light bulbs), and optically-correct cameras, path tracing can produce still images that are indistinguishable from photographs.

Path tracing naturally simulates many effects that have to be specifically added to other methods (conventional ray tracing or scanline rendering), such as soft shadows, depth of field, motion blur, caustics, ambient occlusion, and indirect lighting. Implementation of a renderer including these effects is correspondingly simpler.

Due to its accuracy and unbiased nature, path tracing is used to generate reference images when testing the quality of other rendering algorithms. In order to get high quality images from path tracing, a large number of rays must be traced to avoid visible noisy artifacts.

The rendering equation and its use in computer graphics was presented by James Kajiya in 1986. Path Tracing was introduced then as an algorithm to find a numerical solution to the integral of the rendering equation. A decade later, Lafortune suggested many refinements, including bidirectional path tracing.

Metropolis light transport, a method of perturbing previously found paths in order to increase performance for difficult scenes, was introduced in 1997 by Eric Veach and Leonidas J. Guibas.

More recently, CPUs and GPUs have become powerful enough to render images more quickly, causing more widespread interest in path tracing algorithms. Tim Purcell first presented a global illumination algorithm running on a GPU in 2002. In February 2009 Austin Robison of Nvidia demonstrated the first commercial implementation of a path tracer running on a GPU , and other implementations have followed, such as that of Vladimir Koylazov in August 2009. This was aided by the maturing of GPGPU programming toolkits such as CUDA and OpenCL and GPU ray tracing SDKs such as OptiX.

Description

The rendering equation of Kajiya adheres to three particular principles of optics; the Principle of global illumination, the Principle of Equivalence (reflected light is equivalent to emitted light), and the Principle of Direction (reflected light and scattered light have a direction).

In the real world, objects and surfaces are visible due to the fact that they are reflecting light. This reflected light then illuminates other objects in turn. From that simple observation, two principles follow.

I. For a given indoor scene, every object in the room must contribute illumination to every other object.

II. Second, there is no distinction to be made between illumination emitted from a light source and illumination reflected from a surface.

Invented in 1984, a rather different method called radiosity was faithful to both principles. However, radiosity equivocates the illuminance falling on a surface with the luminance that leaves the surface. This forced all surfaces to be Lambertian, or “perfectly diffuse”. While radiosity received a lot of attention at its invocation, perfectly diffuse surfaces do not exist in the real world. The realization that illumination scattering throughout a scene must also scatter with a direction was the focus of research throughout the 1990s, since accounting for direction always exacted a price of steep increases in calculation times on desktop computers. Principle III follows.

III. The illumination coming from surfaces must scatter in a particular direction that is some function of the incoming direction of the arriving illumination, and the outgoing direction being sampled.

Kajiya’s equation is a complete summary of these three principles, and path tracing, which approximates a solution to the equation, remains faithful to them in its implementation. There are other principles of optics which are not the focus of Kajiya’s equation, and therefore are often difficult or incorrectly simulated by the algorithm. Path Tracing is confounded by optical phenomena not contained in the three principles. For example,

- Bright, sharp caustics; radiance scales by the density of illuminance in space.
- Subsurface scattering; a violation of principle III above.
- Chromatic aberration. fluorescence. iridescence. Light is a spectrum of frequencies.

Bidirectional Path Tracing

Sampling the integral for a point can be done by solely gathering from the surface, or by solely shooting rays from light sources. (1) Shooting rays from the light sources and creating paths in the scene. The path is cut off at a random number of bouncing steps and the resulting light is sent through the projected pixel on the output image. During rendering, billions of paths are created, and the output image is the mean of every pixel that received some contribution. (2) Gathering rays from a point on a surface. A ray is projected from the surface to the scene in a bouncing path that terminates when a light source is intersected. The light is then sent backwards through the path and to the output pixel. The creation of a single path is called a "sample". For a single point on a surface, approximately 800 samples (up to as many as 3 thousand samples) are taken. The final output of the pixel is the arithmetic mean of all those samples, not the sum.

Bidirectional Path Tracing combines both *Shooting* and *Gathering* in the same algorithm to obtain faster convergence of the integral. A shooting path and a gathering path are traced independently, and then the head of the shooting path is connected to the tail of the gathering path. The light is then attenuated at every bounce and back out into the pixel. This technique at first seems paradoxically slower, since for every gathering sample we additionally trace a whole shooting path. In practice however, the extra speed of convergence far outweighs any performance loss from the extra ray casts on the shooting side.

The following pseudocode is a procedure for performing naive path tracing. This function calculates a single sample of a pixel, where only the Gathering Path is considered.

```
Color TracePath(Ray r, depth) {
  if (depth == MaxDepth) {
    return Black;  // Bounced enough times.
  }
  r.FindNearestObject();
  if (r.hitSomething == false) {
    return Black;  // Nothing was hit.
  }
  Material m = r.thingHit->material;
  Color emittance = m.emittance;
  // Pick a random direction from here and keep going.
  Ray newRay;
  newRay.origin = r.pointWhereObjWasHit;
  newRay.direction = RandomUnitVectorInHemisphereOf(r.normalWhereObjWasHit);
// This is NOT a cosine-weighted distribution!
  // Compute the BRDF for this ray (assuming Lambertian reflection)
  float cos_theta = DotProduct(newRay.direction, r.normalWhereObjWasHit);
  Color BDRF = 2 * m.reflectance * cos_theta;
  Color reflected = TracePath(newRay, depth + 1);
  // Apply the Rendering Equation here.
  return emittance + (BDRF * reflected);
}
```

All these samples must then be averaged to obtain the output colour. Note this method of always sampling a random ray in the normal's hemisphere only works well for perfectly diffuse surfaces. For other materials, one generally has to use importance-sampling, i.e. probabilistically select a new ray according to the BRDF's distribution. For instance, a perfectly specular (mirror) material would not work with the method above, as the probability of the new ray being the correct reflected ray - which is the only ray through which any radiance will be reflected - is zero. In these situations, one must divide the reflectance by the probability density function of the sampling scheme, as per Monte-Carlo integration (in the naive case above, there is no particular sampling scheme, so the PDF turns out to be 1).

There are other considerations to take into account to ensure conservation of energy. In particular, in the naive case, the reflectance of a diffuse BRDF must not exceed $\frac{1}{\pi}$ or the object will reflect more light than it receives (this however depends on the sampling scheme used, and can be difficult to get right).

Performance

A path tracer continuously samples pixels of an image. The image starts to become recognisable after only a few samples per pixel, perhaps 100. However, for the image to "converge" and reduce noise to acceptable levels usually takes around 5000 samples for most images, and many more for pathological cases. Noise is particularly a problem for animations, giving them a normally-unwanted "film-grain" quality of random speckling.

The central performance bottleneck in Path Tracing is the complex geometrical calculation of casting a ray. Importance Sampling is a technique which is motivated to cast less rays through the scene while still converging correctly to outgoing luminance on the surface point. This is done by casting more rays in directions in which the luminance would have been greater anyway. If the density of rays cast in certain directions matches the strength of contributions in those directions, the result is identical, but far less rays were actually cast. Importance Sampling is used to match ray density to Lambert's Cosine law, and also used to match BRDFs.

Metropolis light transport can result in a lower-noise image with fewer samples. This algorithm was created in order to get faster convergence in scenes in which the light must pass through odd corridors or small holes in order to reach the part of the scene that the camera is viewing. It is also shown promise on correctly rendering pathological situations with caustics. Instead of generating random paths, new sampling paths are created as slight mutations of existing ones. In this sense, the algorithm "remembers" the successful paths from light sources to the camera.

Scattering Distribution Functions

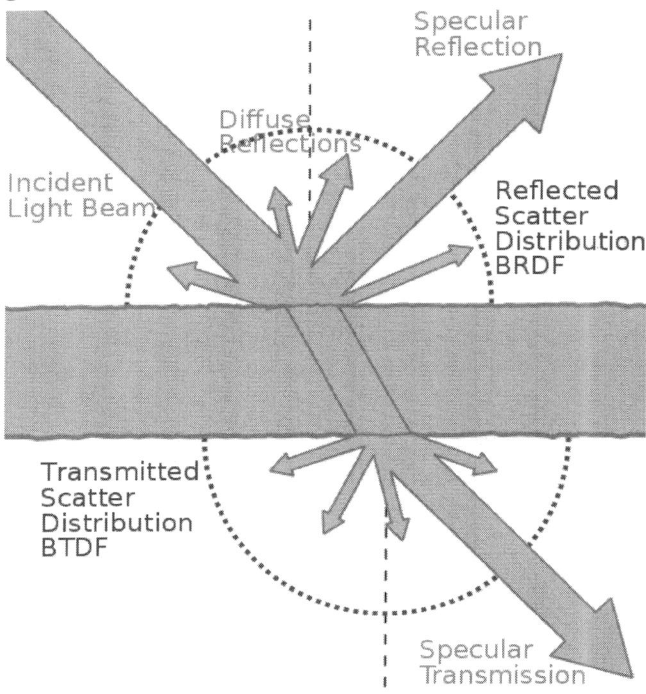

Figure: *Scattering distribution functions*

The reflective properties (amount, direction and colour) of surfaces are modelled using BRDFs. The equivalent for transmitted light (light that goes through the object) are BSDFs. A path tracer can take full advantage of complex, carefully modelled or measured distribution functions, which controls the appearance ("material", "texture" or "shading" in computer graphics terms) of an object.

In Real Time

An example of advanced path-tracing engine capable of real-time graphic is Brigade by Jacco Bikker. The first version of this highly-optimized game-oriented engine was released on January 26th, 2012.

It's the successor of the Arauna real-time ray-tracing engine, made by the same author, and it requires the CUDA architecture (by Nvidia) to run.

Arnold (Software)

Arnold is an unbiased, physically based, path tracing 3D rendering application created by the company Solid Angle. Notable films that have used Arnold include Cloudy with a Chance of Meatballs, Thor, Captain America, The Avengers, Alice in Wonderland, X-Men: First Class, Red Tails, Underworld: Awakening and Gravity.

History

Marcos Fajardo is the chief architect of Arnold. The beginnings of what is now Arnold emerged in 1997 when Fajardo decided to write his own renderer. That year, he attended Siggraph, where his interest in stochastic ray tracing (a foundational part of Arnold's rendering technology) was piqued in discussions with friends attending the conference.

Early versions of Fajardo's renderer were called RenderAPI. The name Arnold emerged when one of Fajardo's friends suggested it after mocking an Arnold Schwarzenegger film they saw in a theater.

Blender (Software)

Blender is a free and open-source 3D computer graphics software product used for creating animated films, visual effects, art, 3D printed models, interactive 3D applications and video games. Blender's features include 3D modelling, UV unwrapping, texturing, rigging and skinning, fluid and smoke simulation, particle simulation, soft body simulation, sculpting, animating, match moving, camera tracking, rendering, video editing and compositing. It also features a built-in game engine.

The Dutch animation studio Neo Geo and Not a Number Technologies (NaN) developed Blender as an in-house application. The primary author was Ton Roosendaal, who previously wrote a ray tracer called Traces for Amiga in 1989. The name *Blender* was inspired by a song by Yello, from the album *Baby*.

Roosendaal founded NaN in June 1998 to further develop and distribute the programme. They initially distributed the programme as shareware until NaN went bankrupt in 2002.

The creditors agreed to release Blender under the GNU General Public License, for a one-time payment of €100,000 (US$100,670 at the time). On July 18, 2002, Roosendaal started a Blender funding campaign to collect donations, and on September 7, 2002, announced that they had collected enough funds and would release the Blender source code. Today, Blender is free, open-source software and is—apart from the Blender Institute's two half-time and two full-time employees—developed by the community.

The Blender Foundation initially reserved the right to use dual licensing, so that, in addition to GNU GPL, Blender would have been available also under the *Blender License* that did not require disclosing source code but required payments to the Blender Foundation. However, they never exercised this option and suspended it indefinitely in 2005. Currently, Blender is solely available under GNU GPL.

Suzanne

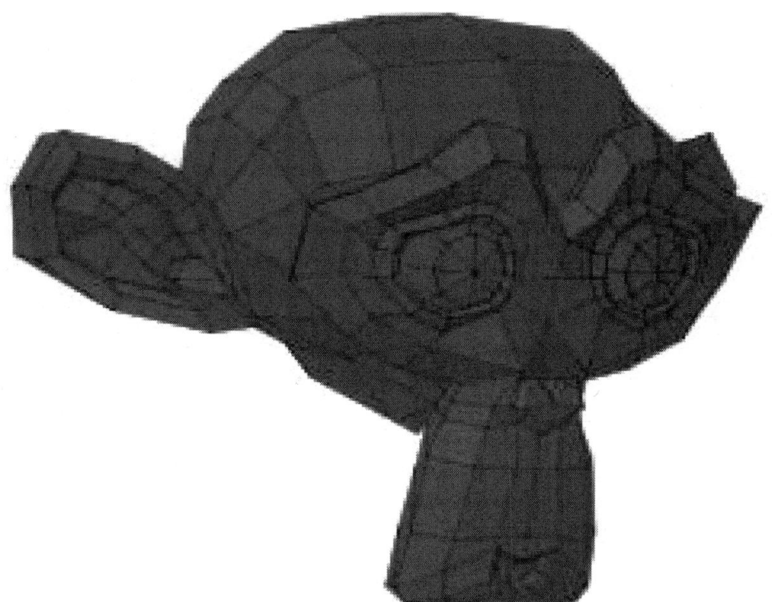

Figure: *Suzanne*

In January–February 2002 it was clear that NaN could not survive, and would close the doors in March. Nevertheless, they put out one more release: 2.25. As a sort-of easter egg, a last personal tag, the artists and developers decided to add a 3D model of a chimpanzee. It was created by Willem-Paul van Overbruggen (SLiD3), who named it Suzanne after the orangutan in the Kevin Smith film *Jay and Silent Bob Strike Back.*

Suzanne is Blender's alternative to more common test models such as the Utah Teapot and the Stanford Bunny. A low-polygon model with only 500 faces, Suzanne is often used as a quick and easy way to test material, animation, rigs, texture, and lighting setups, and is also frequently used in joke images. Suzanne is still included in Blender. The largest Blender contest gives out an award called the Suzanne Awards.

Features

Blender has a relatively small installation size, of about 70 megabytes for builds and 115 megabytes for official releases. Official versions of the software are released for Linux, Mac OS X, Microsoft Windows, and FreeBSD in both 32 and 64 bits. Though it is often distributed without extensive example scenes found in some other programmes, the software contains features that are characteristic of high-end 3D software. Among its capabilities are:

- Support for a variety of geometric primitives, including polygon meshes, fast subdivision surface modelling, Bezier curves, NURBS surfaces, metaballs, multi-res digital sculpting (including maps baking, remeshing, resymetrize, decimation..), outline font, and a new n-gon modelling system called B-mesh.
- Internal render engine with scanline ray tracing, indirect lighting, and ambient occlusion that can export in a wide variety of formats.
- A pathtracer render engine called Cycles, which can take advantage of the GPU for rendering. Cycles supports the Open Shading Language since blender 2.65.
- Integration with a number of external render engines through plugins.
- Keyframed animation tools including inverse kinematics, armature (skeletal), hook, curve and lattice-based deformations, shape keys (morphing), non-linear animation, constraints, and vertex weighting.
- Simulation tools for Soft body dynamics including mesh collision detection, LBM fluid dynamics, smoke simulation, Bullet rigid body dynamics, ocean generator with waves.
- A particle system that includes support for particle-based hair.
- Modifiers to apply non-destructive effects.

- Python scripting for tool creation and prototyping, game logic, importing and/or exporting from other formats, task automation and custom tools.
- Basic non-linear video/audio editing.
- The Blender Game Engine, a sub-project, offers interactivity features such as collision detection, dynamics engine, and programmable logic. It also allows the creation of stand-alone, real-time applications ranging from architectural visualization to video game construction.
- A fully integrated node-based compositor within the rendering pipeline accelerated with OpenCL.
- Procedural and node-based textures, as well as texture painting, projective painting, vertex painting, weight painting and dynamic painting.

User Interface

Blender has had a reputation of being difficult to learn for users accustomed to other 3D graphics software. Nearly every function has a direct keyboard shortcut and there can be several different shortcuts per key. Since Blender became free software, there has been effort to add comprehensive contextual menus as well as make the tool usage more logical and streamlined. There have also been efforts to visually enhance the user interface, with the introduction of colour themes, transparent floating widgets, a new and improved object tree overview, and other small improvements (such as a colour picker widget). Blender's user interface incorporates the following concepts:

Editing Modes

The two primary modes of work are *Object Mode* and *Edit Mode*, which are toggled with the Tab key. Object mode is used to manipulate individual objects as a unit, while Edit mode is used to manipulate the actual object data. For example, Object Mode can be used to move, scale, and rotate entire polygon meshes, and Edit Mode can be used to manipulate the individual vertices of a single mesh. There are also several other modes, such as Vertex Paint, Weight Paint, and Sculpt Mode. The 2.45 release also had the UV Mapping Mode, but it was merged with the Edit Mode in 2.46 Release Candidate 1.

Hotkey Utilization

Most of the commands are accessible via hotkeys. Until the 2.x and especially the 2.3x versions, this was in fact the only way to give commands, and this was largely responsible for creating Blender's reputation as a difficult-to-learn programme. The new versions have more comprehensive GUI menus.

Numeric Input

Numeric buttons can be "dragged" to change their value directly without the need to aim at a particular widget, thus saving screen real estate and time. Both sliders and number buttons can be constrained to various step sizes with modifiers like the Ctrl and Shift keys. Python expressions can also be typed directly into number entry fields, allowing mathematical expressions to specify values.

Workspace Management

The Blender GUI builds its own tiled (non-overlapping) windowing system on top of one or multiple windows provided by the underlying platform. One platform window (often sized to fill the screen) is divided into sections and subsections that can be of any type of Blender's views or window-types. The user can define multiple layouts of such Blender windows, called *screens*, and switch quickly between them by selecting from a menu or with keyboard shortcuts. Each window-type's own GUI elements can be controlled with the same tools that manipulate 3D view. For example, one can zoom in and out of GUI-buttons using similar controls one zooms in and out in the 3D viewport. The GUI viewport and screen layout is fully user-customizable. It is possible to set up the interface for specific tasks such as video editing or UV mapping or texturing by hiding features not utilized for the task.

Hardware Requirements

Blender has very low hardware requirements compared to other 3D suites. However, for advanced effects and working with complex scenes, a more powerful system is needed.

Blender hardware requirements			
Hardware	***Minimum***	***Recommended***	***Production-standard***
Processor	2 GHz, Dual Core	Quad Core	Dual 8-Core
Memory	2 GB RAM	8 GB	16 GB
Graphics card	OpenGL card with 256 MB Video RAM	OpenGL card with 1 GB Video RAM (CUDA or OpenCL for GPU rendering)	Dual OpenGL cards with 3 GB RAM, ATI FireGL or Nvidia Quadro
Display	1280×768 pixels, 24-bit color	1920×1080 pixels, 24-bit color	2x 1920×1080 pixels, 24-bit color
Input	Two-button mouse	Three-button mouse	Three-button mouse and a graphics tablet

File Format

Blender features an internal file system that allows one to pack multiple scenes into a single file (called a ".blend" file).

- All of Blender's ".blend" files are forward, backward, and cross-platform compatible with other versions of Blender, with the following exceptions:
  - o Loading animations stored in post-2.5 files in Blender pre-2.5. This is due to the reworked animation subsystem introduced in Blender 2.5 being inherently incompatible with older versions.
  - o Loading meshes stored in post 2.63. This is due to the introduction of BMesh, a more versatile/featureful mesh format.
- Snapshot ".blend" files can be auto-saved periodically by the programme, making it easier to survive a programme crash.
- All scenes, objects, materials, textures, sounds, images, post-production effects for an entire animation can be stored in a single ".blend" file. Data loaded from external sources, such as images and sounds, can also be stored externally and referenced through either an absolute or relative pathname. Likewise, ".blend" files themselves can also be used as libraries of Blender assets.
- Interface configurations are retained in the ".blend" files, such that what you save is what you get upon load. This file can be stored as "user defaults" so this screen configuration, as well as all the objects stored in it, is used every time you load Blender.

The actual ".blend" file is similar to the EA Interchange File Format, starting with its own header (for example BLENDER_v248) that specifies the version, endianness and pointer size, followed by the file's DNA (a full specification of the data format used) and, finally, a collection of binary blocks storing actual data. Presence of the DNA block in .blend files means the format is self-descriptive and any software able to decode the DNA can read any .blend file, even if some fields or data block types must be ignored.

Although it is relatively difficult to read and convert a ".blend" file to another format using external tools, there are several software packages able to do this, for example readblend. A wide variety of import/export scripts that extend Blender capabilities (accessing the object data via an internal API) make it possible to inter-operate with other 3D tools. CAD software uses surface description models that are significantly different from the ones used in Blender because Blender is not designed for CAD. Therefore, the direct import or export of CAD files is not possible.

Jeroen Bakker documented the Blender file format to allow inter-operation with other tooling. The document can be found at the *The mystery of the blend* website. A DNA structure browser is also available on this site.

Blender organizes data as various kinds of "data blocks", such as Objects, Meshes, Lamps, Scenes, Materials, Images and so on. An object in Blender consists of multiple data blocks – for example, what the user would describe as a polygon mesh consists of at least an Object and a Mesh data block, and usually also a Material and many more, linked together. This allows various data blocks to refer to each other. There may be, for example, multiple Objects that refer to the same Mesh, allowing Blender to keep a single copy of the mesh data in memory, and making subsequent editing of the shared mesh result in shape changes in all Objects using this Mesh. This data-sharing approach is fundamental to Blender's philosophy and its user interface and can be applied to multiple data types. Objects, meshes, materials, textures etc. can also be linked to from other .blend files, allowing the use of .blend files as reusable resource libraries.

Comparison with Other 3D Software

A 2007 article stated that Blender's interface was not up to industry standards, but was nevertheless suited to fast workflow and was sometimes more intuitive. Poor documentation was also criticized.

Blender is a dominant open-source product with a range of features comparable to mid- to high-range commercial, proprietary software. In 2010, CGenie rated Blender as a fledgling product with the majority of its users being "hobbyists" rather than students or professionals but with its high standards rising yearly. They also reported that users thought Blender needed more development and required more compatibility with other programmes. Blender is also used by scientific groups all over the world in tandem with applications such as MatLab.

In 2011, Blender 2.5 was released. Featuring a completely redesigned user interface, it aims to improve work flow and ease of use. During beta-testing, the Sintel animators considered Blender

2.5's animation system as good as, or better than, some commercial packages.

Development

Since the opening of the source, Blender has experienced significant refactoring of the initial codebase and major additions to its feature set.

Improvements include an animation system refresh; a stack-based modifier system; an updated particle system (which can also be used to simulate hair and fur); fluid dynamics; soft-body dynamics; GLSL shaders support in the game engine; advanced UV unwrapping; a fully recoded render pipeline, allowing separate render passes and "render to texture"; node-based material editing and compositing; Projection painting.

Part of these developments were fostered by Google's Summer of Code programme, in which the Blender Foundation has participated since 2005.

Blender has come a long way since then. The current stable release version is 2.68a (as of 24 July 2013), a bugfix release to the previous version 2.68 that was released on July 18, 2013.

Version 2.68 included many enhancements to its existing platform, but was mostly bugfixes over 2.67. It was released with the addition of Texture Atlas for baking shadows and lightmaps for an entire scene, and the Edit Linked Library, for quick editing of linked assets.

The enhancements include the following but is not limited to:

- Improved weight painting tools
- Mask modifier for sequencer strips
- Improvement for 2D image paint more consistent with 3D painting
- Better key shortcuts display
- Quick enabling and disabling of multiple layers
- Auto indent for multi-line Python statements
- Motion Tracking marker positions
- Auto keyframe selection
- Ray visibility for all light versions in Cycles
- Mist render pass for Cycles

- Improved smoke simulation to avoid blockiness
- Multiple modelling improvements (on existing features)

A Python Security protocol was included as well. This disabled python scripting on .blend file start-up to prevent malicious actions on load. This feature is accessible in the User Preferences and can be turned off or on.

Shading

Shading is a process used in drawing for depicting levels of darkness on paper by applying media more densely or with a darker shade for darker areas, and less densely or with a lighter shade for lighter areas. There are various techniques of shading including cross hatching where perpendicular lines of varying closeness are drawn in a grid pattern to shade an area. The closer the lines are together, the darker the area appears. Likewise, the farther apart the lines are, the lighter the area appears.

Light patterns, such as objects having light and shaded areas, help when creating the illusion of depth on paper.

Computer Graphics

In computer graphics, shading refers to the process of altering the colour of an object/surface/polygon in the 3D scene, based on its angle to lights and its distance from lights to create a photorealistic effect. Shading is performed during the rendering process by a programme called a shader.

Angle to Light Source

Shading alters the colours of faces in a 3D model based on the angle of the surface to a light source or light sources.

The first image below has the faces of the box rendered, but all in the same colour. Edge lines have been rendered here as well which makes the image easier to see.

The second image is the same model rendered without edge lines. It is difficult to tell where one face of the box ends and the next begins.

The third image has shading enabled, which makes the image more realistic and makes it easier to see which face is which.

Lighting

Shading is also dependant on the lighting used. Usually, upon rendering a scene a number of different lighting techniques will be used to make the rendering look more realistic. Different types of light sources are used to give different effects.

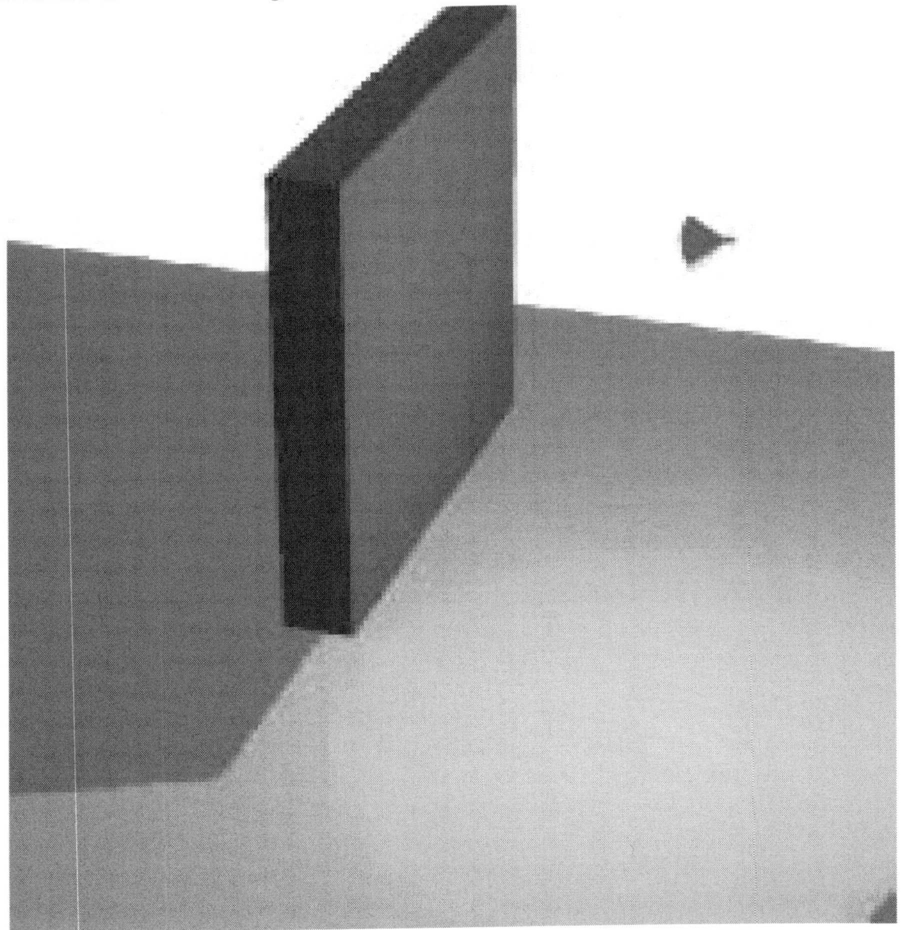

Figure: *Shading effects from floodlight.*

Ambient Lighting

An ambient light source represents a fixed-intensity and fixed-colour light source that affects all objects in the scene equally. Upon rendering, all objects in the scene are brightened with the specified intensity and colour. This type of light source is mainly used to provide the scene with a basic view of the different objects in it. This is the simplest type of lighting to implement and models how light can be scattered or reflected many times producing a uniform effect.

Directional Lighting

A directional light source illuminates all objects equally from a given direction, like an area light of infinite size and infinite distance from the scene; there is shading, but cannot be any distance falloff.

Point Lighting

Light originates from a single point, and spreads outward in all directions.

Spotlight Lighting

Models a Spotlight. Light originates from a single point, and spreads outward in a cone.

Area Lighting

Light originates from a small area on a single plane. A more accurate model than a point light source.

Volumetric Lighting

Light originating from a small volume, an enclosed space lighting objects within that space.

Shading is interpolated based on how the angle of these light sources reach the objects within a scene. Of course, these light sources can be and often are combined in a scene. The renderer then interpolates how these lights must be combined, and produces a 2d image to be displayed on the screen accordingly.

Distance Falloff

Theoretically, two surfaces which are parallel, are illuminated the same amount from a distant light source, such as the sun. Even though one surface is further away, your eye sees more of it in the same space, so the illumination appears the same.

Notice in the first image that the colour on the front faces of the two boxes is exactly the same. It appears that there is a slight difference where the two faces meet, but this is an optical illusion because of the vertical edge below where the two faces meet.

Notice in the second image that the surfaces on the boxes are bright on the front box and darker on the back box. Also the floor goes from light to dark as it gets farther away.

This distance falloff effect produces images which appear more realistic without having to add additional lights to achieve the same effect.

Distance falloff can be calculated in a number of ways:

- *None* - The light intensity received is the same regardless of the distance between the point and the light source.
- *Linear* - For a given point at a distance x from the light source, the light intensity received is proportional to $1/x$.
- *Quadratic* - This is how light intensity decreases in reality if the light has a free path (i.e. no fog or any other thing in the air that can absorb or scatter the light). For a given point at a distance x from the light source, the light intensity received is proportional to $1/x^2$.
- *Factor of n* - For a given point at a distance x from the light source, the light intensity received is proportional to $1/x^n$.
- Any number of other mathematical functions may also be used.

Flat Shading

Flat shading is a lighting technique used in 3D computer graphics to shade each polygon of an object based on the angle between the polygon's surface normal and the direction of the light source, their respective colours and the intensity of the light source. It is usually used for high speed rendering where more advanced shading techniques are too computationally expensive. As a result of flat shading all of the polygon's vertices are coloured with one colour, allowing differentiation between adjacent polygons. Specular highlights are rendered poorly with flat shading: If there happens to be a large specular component at the representative vertex, that brightness is drawn uniformly over the entire face. If a specular highlight doesn't fall on the representative point, it is missed entirely. Consequently, the specular reflection component is usually not included in flat shading computation.

Smooth Shading

In contrast to flat shading with smooth shading the colour changes from pixel to pixel. It assumes that the surfaces are curved and uses interpolation techniques to calculate the values of pixels between the vertices of the polygons.

Types of smooth shading include:

- Gouraud shading
- Phong shading

Gouraud Shading

1. Determine the normal at each polygon vertex
2. Apply an illumination model to each vertex to calculate the vertex intensity
3. Linearly interpolate the vertex intensities over the surface polygon

Data Structures

- Sometimes vertex normals can be computed directly (e.g. height field with uniform mesh)
- More generally, need data structure for mesh
- Key: which polygons meet at each vertex

Advantages

- Polygons, more complex than triangles, can also have different colours specified for each vertex. In these instances, the underlying logic for shading can become more intricate.

Problems

- Even the smoothness introduced by Gouraud shading may not prevent the appearance of the shading differences between adjacent polygons.
- Gouraud shading is more CPU intensive and can become a problem when rendering real time environments with many polygons.
- T-Junctions with adjoining polygons can sometimes result in visual anomalies. In general, T-Junctions should be avoided.

Phong Shading

Phong shading, is similar to Gouraud shading except that the Normals are interpolated. Thus, the specular highlights are computed much more precisely than in the Gouraud shading model:

1. Compute a normal N for each vertex of the polygon.
2. From bi-linear interpolation compute a normal, Ni for each pixel. (This must be renormalized each time)
3. From Ni compute an intensity Ii for each pixel of the polygon.
4. Paint pixel to shade corresponding to Ii.

Flat vs. Smooth Shading

Flat	*Smooth*
Uses the same color for every pixel in a face - usually the color of the first vertex.	Smooth shading uses linear interpolation of colors between vertices
Edges appear more pronounced than they would on a real object because of a phenomenon in the eye known as lateral inhibition	The edges disappear with this technique
Same color for any point of the face	Each point of the face has its own color
Individual faces are visualized	Visualize underlying surface
Not suitable for smooth objects	Suitable for any objects
Less expensive	More expensive

10

Texture

In the visual arts, texture is the perceived surface quality of a work of art. It is an element of two-dimensional and three-dimensional design and is distinguished by its perceived visual and physical properties. Use of *texture*, along with other elements of design, can convey a variety of messages and emotions.

Two Varieties of Texture

Physical Texture

Physical texture, also known as *actual texture* or *tactile texture*, are the actual variations upon a surface. This can include, but is not limited to, fur, wood grain, sand, smooth surface of canvas or metal, glass, and leather. It differentiates itself from visual texture by having a physical quality that can be felt by touch. Specific use of a texture can affect the smoothness that an artwork conveys. For instance, use of *rough surfaces* can be visually active, whilst *smooth surfaces* can be visually restful. The use of both can give a sense of personality to a design, or utilized to create emphasis, rhythm, contrast, etc.

Light is an important factor for physical artwork, because it can affect how a surface is viewed. Strong lights on a smooth surface can obscure the readability of a drawing or photograph, whilst they can create strong contrasts in a highly textural surface such as moose or pigs.

Visual Texture

Visual texture is the illusion of having physical texture. Every material and every support surface has its own visual texture and needs to be taken into consideration before creating a composition. As such, materials such as canvas and watercolour paper are considerably rougher than, for example, photo-quality computer paper and may not be best suited to creating a flat, smooth texture. Photography, drawings and paintings use visual texture both to portray their subject matter realistically and with interpretation. Texture in these media are generally created by the repetition of shape and line.

Hypertexture

Hypertexture can be defined as both the "realistic simulated surface texture produced by adding small distortions across the surface of an object" (as pioneered by Ken Perlin) and a new avenue for describing the fluid morphic nature of texture in the realm of cyber graphics and the tranversally responsive works created in the field of visual arts therein (as described by Lee Klein).

Texture Mapping

Texture mapping is a method for adding detail, surface texture (a bitmap or raster image), or colour to a computer-generated graphic or 3D model. Its application to 3D graphics was pioneered by Edwin Catmull in 1974.

A texture map is applied (mapped) to the surface of a shape or polygon. This process is akin to applying patterned paper to a plain white box. Every vertex in a polygon is assigned a texture coordinate (which in the 2d case is also known as a UV coordinate) either via explicit assignment or by procedural definition. Image sampling locations are then interpolated across the face of a polygon to produce a visual result that seems to have more richness than could otherwise be achieved with a limited number of polygons. Multitexturing is the use of more than one texture at a time on a polygon. For instance, a light map texture may be used to light a surface as an alternative to recalculating that lighting every time the surface is rendered. Another multitexture technique is bump mapping, which allows a texture to directly control the facing direction of a surface for the purposes of its lighting calculations; it can give a very good appearance of a complex surface, such as tree bark or rough concrete, that takes on lighting detail in addition to the usual detailed colouring. Bump mapping has become popular in recent video games as graphics hardware has become powerful enough to accommodate it in real-time.

The way the resulting pixels on the screen are calculated from the texels (texture pixels) is governed by texture filtering. The fastest method is to use the nearest-neighbour interpolation, but bilinear interpolation or trilinear interpolation between mipmaps are two commonly used alternatives which reduce aliasing or jaggies. In the event of a texture coordinate being outside the texture, it is either clamped or wrapped.

Perspective Correctness

Texture coordinates are specified at each vertex of a given triangle, and these coordinates are interpolated using an extended Bresenham's line algorithm. If these texture coordinates are linearly interpolated across the screen, the result is affine texture mapping. This is a fast calculation, but there can be a noticeable discontinuity between adjacent triangles when these triangles are at an angle to the plane of the screen.

Perspective correct texturing accounts for the vertices' positions in 3D space, rather than simply interpolating a 2D triangle. This achieves the correct visual effect, but it is slower to calculate. Instead of interpolating the texture coordinates directly, the coordinates are divided by their depth (relative to the viewer), and the reciprocal of the depth value is also interpolated and used to recover the perspective-correct coordinate. This correction makes it so that in parts of the polygon that are closer to the viewer the difference from pixel to pixel between texture coordinates is smaller (stretching the texture wider), and in parts that are farther away this difference is larger (compressing the texture).

Affine texture mapping directly interpolates a texture coordinate u_α between two endpoints u_0 and u_1 :

$$u_\alpha = (1-\alpha)u_0 + \alpha u_1 \text{ where } 0 \leq \alpha \leq 1$$

Perspective correct mapping interpolates after dividing by depth z, then uses its interpolated reciprocal to recover the correct coordinate:

$$u_\alpha = \frac{(1-\alpha)\frac{u_0}{z_0} + \alpha\frac{u_1}{z_1}}{(1-\alpha)\frac{1}{z_0} + \alpha\frac{1}{z_1}}$$

All modern 3D graphics hardware implements perspective correct texturing.

Bump Mapping

Bump mapping is very much like Texture Mapping. However, where Texture Mapping added colour to a polygon, Bump Mapping adds, what appears to be surface roughness. This can have a dramatic effect on the look of a polygonal object. Bump Mapping can add minute detail to an object which would otherwise require a large number of polygons. Note that the polygon is still physically flat, but appears to a be bumpy.

Take a look at the cube on the left. If you look closely, you can see lots of detail on it. It looks as if it must have been made from millions of tiny polygons, but is made from just 6. You might ask how this differs from Texture Mapping. The difference is that a Bump Map is a Texture Map that responds to the direction of the light.

The Theory Behind Bump Mapping

Take a close look at a rough surface. From a distance, the only way you know it is rough is by the fact that it's brightness changes up and down across it's surface. Your brain can pick out these bright and dark patterns and interpret them as bumps on the surface.

The little picture on the left illustrates this. You see what looks like an embossed surface. Some rectangles and letters have been pressed into it, but if you touch it, it just feels like the glass of your monitor. Nothing more has been done than change the brightness if the image in just the right places, your brain does the rest. This technique can be used to add real feeling to a polygon.

So how did we know which bits to make bright, and which to make dark? It's easy. Most people spend their lives in an environment where the main light source is above them (except us spods of course, whose main light source comes from the monitor). So surfaces angled upwards tend to be brightly lit, and downward inclined surfaces tend to be darker. Therefore it follows that if your eyes see light and dark areas on an object, they will interpret them as bumps; lighter bits it takes as up-facing, and darker bits it takes as down-facing. So, I just coloured the lines on the image accordingly.

As if you needed any more evidence, here is exactly the same image, but rotated 180 degrees. It appears to be the inverse of the previous one. Those areas that appeared to be pushed in, now seem to have popped out, and vice-versa.

Now, your brain is not entirely stupid. If you had visual evidence that the inverted image was lit from underneath, your brain would again interpret it as the first image. Infact, if you stare, and think hard enough about a light source comming from the bottom right, you can make that happen.

What is a Bump Map

A bump map is very much like a texture map. However, rather than containing colours, it contains bumps. The most common way to represent bumps is by the height field method. A greyscaled texture map is used, where the brightness of each pixel represents how much it sticks out from the surface. This is a very convenient way to store a bump map, and it's simple to make. How this information is used by the renderer will become apparent later.

Of course, you needn't limit yourself to such simple patterns. You can have wood, stone, peeling paint, anything you want.

So How's it Done

Bump mapping is an extension of the Phong Shading technique. In Phong Shading, the surface normal was interpolated over the polygon, and that vector was used to calculate the brightness of that pixel. When you add bump mapping, you are altering the normal vector slightly, based on information in the bump map. Adjusting the normal vector causes changes in the brightness of the pixels in the polygon. Simple.

Now, there are several ways of acheving this.

We need a method for converting the height information on the bump map into vector adjustment information for the phong shader. This is not so hard to do, but it might be tricky to explain.

Now you'll need a way to convert the bumps on the bumpmap into little vectors, one vector for each pixel. Take a look at the zoomed-in view of a bumpmap on the left. The lighter pixels stick out more than the darker ones. Get the picture? Now, for each pixel, a vector must be computed. These vectors represent the incline of the surface at that pixel. The picture on the right represents this. The little red vectors point in the 'downhill' direction.

There are many ways to calculate these vectors. Some are more accurate than others, but it depends exactly what you mean by accurate. One of the most common methods is to calculate the X and Y gradient at that pixel:

```
x_gradient = pixel(x-1, y) - pixel(x+1, y)
y_gradient = pixel(x, y-1) - pixel(x, y+1)
```

With these two gradients, you will now need to adjust the normal vector of the polygon at that point.

Here is the polygon, with it's origional normal vector, n. Also shown are the two vectors which are going to be used to adjust the normal vector for this pixel. The two vectors must be aligned with the bumpmap for the polygon to be rendered correctly. I.E. the vectors are parallel to the axes of the bumpmap.

On the right are the bump map, and the polygon. Both pictures show the U and V vectors.

Now you can see the new Normal vector after adjustment. The adjustment is simply:

New_Normal = Normal + (U * x_gradient) + (V * y_gradient)

With this New_Normal vector, you can procede to calculate the brightness of the polygon at that point, using the usual phong shading technique.

Reflection

Reflection is most commonly used in high-level virtual machine programming languages like Smalltalk and scripting languages and also in manifestly typed or statically typed programming languages such as Java, ML, Haskell, C#, Go and Scala.

The earliest computers were programmed in their native assembly language, which were inherently reflective as these original architectures could be programmed by defining instructions as data and using self-modifying code. As programming moved to higher level languages such as C, this reflective ability disappeared (outside of malware) until programming languages with reflection built into their type systems appeared.

Brian Cantwell Smith's 1982 doctoral dissertation introduced the notion of computational reflection in programming languages, and the notion of the meta-circular interpreter as a component of 3-Lisp.

Uses

Reflection can be used for observing and/or modifying programme execution at runtime. A reflection-oriented programme component can monitor the execution of an enclosure of code and can modify itself according to a desired goal related to that enclosure. This is typically accomplished by dynamically assigning programme code at runtime.

In object oriented programming languages such as Java, reflection allows inspection of classes, interfaces, fields and methods at runtime without knowing the names of the interfaces, fields, methods at compile time. It also allows instantiation of new objects and invocation of methods.

Reflection can also be used to adapt a given programme to different situations dynamically. For example, consider an application that uses two different classes X and Y interchangeably to perform similar operations. Without reflection-oriented programming, the application might be hard-coded to call method names of class X and class Y. However, using the reflection-oriented programming paradigm, the application could be designed and written to utilize reflection in order to invoke methods in classes X and Y without hard-coding method names. Reflection-oriented programming almost always requires additional knowledge, framework, relational mapping, and object relevance in order to take advantage of more generic code execution. Hard-coding can be avoided to the extent that reflection-oriented programming is used.

Reflection is often used as part of software testing, such as for the runtime creation/instantiation of mock objects.

Reflection is also a key strategy for metaprogramming.

Implementation

A language supporting reflection provides a number of features available at runtime that would otherwise be very obscure to accomplish in a lower-level language. Some of these features are the abilities to:

- Discover and modify source code constructions (such as code blocks, classes, methods, protocols, etc.) as a first-class object at runtime.
- Convert a string matching the symbolic name of a class or function into a reference to or invocation of that class or function.
- Evaluate a string as if it were a source code statement at runtime.
- Create a new interpreter for the language's bytecode to give a new meaning or purpose for a programming construct.

These features can be implemented in different ways. In MOO, reflection forms a natural part of everyday programming idiom. When verbs (methods) are called, various variables such as *verb* (the name of the verb being called) and *this* (the object on which the verb is called) are populated to give the context of the call. Security is typically managed by accessing the caller stack programmatically: Since *callers()* is a list of the methods by which the current verb was eventually called, performing tests on callers (the command invoked by the original user) allows the verb to protect itself against unauthorised use.

Compiled languages rely on their runtime system to provide information about the source code. A compiled Objective-C executable, for example, records the names of all methods in a block of the executable, providing a table to correspond these with the underlying methods (or selectors for these methods) compiled into the programme. In a compiled language that supports runtime creation of functions, such as Common Lisp, the runtime environment must include a compiler or an interpreter.

Reflection can be implemented for languages not having built-in reflection facilities by using a programme transformation system to define automated source code changes.

Examples

The following code snippets create an instance foo of class Foo, and invoke its method hello. For each programming language, normal and reflection-based call sequences are shown.

ECMAScript

The following is an example in ECMAScript, and therefore also applies to JavaScript and ActionScript:

```
// Without reflection
new Foo().hello()
// With reflection
// assuming that Foo resides in this
new this['Foo']()['hello']()
// or without assumption
new (eval('Foo'))()['hello']()
// or simply
eval('new Foo().hello()')
```

PHP

The following is an example in PHP:

```
// without reflection
$foo = new Foo();
$foo->hello();
```

```
// with reflection
$reflector = new ReflectionClass('Foo');
$foo = $reflector->newInstance();
$hello = $reflector->getMethod('hello');
$hello->invoke($foo);
// using callback
$foo = new Foo();
call_user_func(array($foo, 'hello'));
// using variable variables syntax
$className = 'Foo';
$foo = new $className();
$method = 'hello';
$foo->$method();
```

Objective-C

The following is an example in Objective-C—implying either the OpenStep or Foundation Kit framework is used:

```
// Foo class.
@interface Foo : NSObject
- (void)hello;
@end
// Sending "hello" to a Foo instance without reflection.
Foo *obj = [[Foo alloc] init];
[obj hello];
// Sending "hello" to a Foo instance with reflection.
id obj = [[NSClassFromString(@"Foo") alloc] init];
[obj performSelector: @selector(hello)];
```

R

The following is an example in R:

```
# Without reflection, assuming foo() returns a list or S3-type object
foo()$hello()
# With reflection
eval(parse(text = "foo()$hello()"))
```

Ruby

The following is an example in Ruby:

```
# without reflection
obj = Foo.new
obj.hello
# with reflection
class_name = "Foo"
method = :hello
obj = Kernel.const_get(class_name).new
obj.send method
# with eval
eval "Foo.new.hello"
```

Python

The following is an example in Python:

```
# without reflection
obj = Foo()
obj.hello()
# with reflection
class_name = "Foo"
method = "hello"
obj = globals()[class_name]()
getattr(obj, method)()
# with eval
eval("Foo().hello()")
```

Perl

The following is an example in Perl:

```
# without reflection
$foo = new Foo();
$foo->hello();
# or
new Foo()->hello();
# with reflection
class_name = "Foo"
method = "hello"
*obj = *{"${class_name}::"};
&{ $obj{ $method} };
# or
&{ "${class_name}::${method}" };
# with eval
eval "new Foo()->hello;";
```

Java

The following is an example in Java:

```
// without reflection
Foo foo = new Foo();
foo.hello();
// with reflection
Object foo = Class.forName("complete.classpath.and.Foo").newInstance();
Method m = foo.getClass().getDeclaredMethod("hello", new Class<?>[0]);
m.invoke(foo);
```

Chroma key

Chroma key compositing, or chroma keying, is a special effects / post-production technique for compositing (layering) two images or video streams together based on colour hues (chroma range). The technique has been used heavily in many fields to remove a background from the subject of a photo or video – particularly the newscasting, motion picture and videogame industries. A colour range in the top layer is made transparent, revealing another image behind. The chroma keying technique is commonly used in video production and post-production. This technique is also referred to as colour keying, colour-separation overlay (CSO; primarily by the BBC), or by various terms for specific colour-related variants such as green screen, and blue screen – chroma keying can be done with backgrounds of any colour that are uniform and distinct, but green and blue backgrounds are more commonly used because they differ most distinctly in hue from most human skin colours. No part of the subject being filmed or photographed may duplicate a colour used in the background.

It is commonly used for weather forecast broadcasts, wherein a news presenter is usually seen standing in front of a large CGI map during live television newscasts, though in actuality it is a large blue or green background. When using a blue screen, different weather maps are added on the parts of the image where the colour is blue. If the news presenter wears blue clothes, his or her clothes will also be replaced with the background video. A complementary system is used for green screens. Chroma keying is also used in the entertainment industry for special effects in movies and videogames. The advanced state of the technology and much commercially available computer software, such as Autodesk Smoke, Final Cut Pro, Pinnacle Studio, Adobe After Effects, and dozens of other computer programmes, makes it possible and relatively easy for the average home computer user to create videos using the "chromakey" function with easily affordable green screen or blue screen kits.

Process

The principal subject is filmed or photographed against a background consisting of a single colour or a relatively narrow range of colours, usually blue or green because these colours are considered to be the furthest away from skin tone. The portions of the video which match the preselected colour are replaced by the alternate background video. This process is commonly known as "keying", "keying out" or simply a "key".

Processing a Green Backdrop

Green is currently used as a backdrop more than any other colour because image sensors in digital video cameras are most sensitive to green, due to the bayer pattern allocating more pixels to the green channel, mimicking the human eye's increased sensitivity to green light. Therefore, the green camera channel contains the least "noise" and can produce the cleanest key/matte/mask. Additionally, less light is needed to illuminate green, again because of the higher sensitivity to green in image sensors. Bright green has also become favoured since a blue background may match a subject's eye colour or common items of clothing, such as jeans, or a dark-navy suit.

Processing a Blue Backdrop

Blue was used as a backdrop before digital keying became commonplace because it was necessary for the optical process, but it needed more illumination than green. However, it is also further in the visual spectrum from red, the predominant colour in human skin.

Clothing

A chroma key subject must avoid wearing clothes which are similar in colour to the chroma key colour(s) (unless intentional e.g. wearing a green top to make it appear that the subject has no body), because the clothing may be replaced with the background video. An example of intentional use of this is when an actor wears a blue covering over a part of his body to make it invisible in the final shot. This technique can be used to achieve an effect similar to that used in the *Harry Potter* films to create the effect of an invisibility cloak. The actor can also be filmed against a chroma-key background and inserted into the background shot with a distortion effect, in order to create a cloak that is marginally detectable.

Difficulties emerge with bluescreen when a costume in an effects shot must be blue, such as Superman's traditional blue outfit. In the 2002 film *Spider-Man*, in scenes where both Spider-Man and the Green Goblin are in the air, Spider-Man had to be shot in front of the greenscreen and the Green Goblin had to be shot in front of a bluescreen. The colour difference is because Spider-Man wears a costume which is red and blue in colour and the goblin wears a costume which is entirely green in colour. If both were shot in front of the same screen, one character would be erased from the shot.

Background

Blue is generally used for both weather maps and special effects because it is complementary to human skin tone. The use of blue is also tied to the fact that the blue emulsion layer of film has the finest crystals and thus good detail and minimal grain (in comparison to the red and green layers of the emulsion.) In the digital world, however, green has become the favoured colour because digital cameras retain more detail in the green channel, and it requires less light than blue. Green not only has a higher luminance value than blue, but also in early digital formats, the green channel was sampled twice as often as the blue, making it easier to work with. The choice of colour is up to the effects artists and the needs of the specific shot. In the past decade, the use of green has become dominant in film special effects. Also, the green background is favoured over blue for outdoor filming where the blue sky might appear in the frame and could accidentally be replaced in the process. Although green and blue are the most common, any colour can be used. Red is usually avoided due to its prevalence in normal human skin pigments, but can be often used for objects and scenes which do not involve people. For example, in John Pizzarelli's song "Birthday Emotions" from the Sesame Street television series, painting backgrounds made by Gerri Brioso are used while the kids who are live-action are jumping through the air and celebrating a birthday.

Occasionally, a magenta background is used, as in some software applications where the magenta or fuchsia is sometimes referred to as "magic pink".

With other imaging and hardware, many companies avoid the confusion often experienced by weather presenters, who must otherwise watch themselves on a monitor to see the image shown behind them, by lightly projecting a copy of the background image onto the blue/ green screen. This allows the presenter to accurately point and look at the map without referring to monitors.

A newer technique is to use a retroreflective curtain in the background, along with a ring of bright LEDs around the camera lens. This requires no light to shine on the background other than the LEDs, which use an extremely small amount of power and space unlike big stage lights, and require no rigging. This advance was made possible by the invention of practical blue LEDs in the 1990s, which also allow for emerald green LEDs.

There is also a form of colour keying that uses light spectrum invisible to human eye. Called Thermo-Key, it uses infrared as the key colour, which would not be replaced by background image during postprocessing.

Diffraction

Diffraction refers to various phenomena which occur when a wave encounters an obstacle. In classical physics, the diffraction phenomenon is described as the apparent bending of waves around small obstacles and the spreading out of waves past small openings. Similar effects occur when a light wave travels through a medium with a varying refractive index, or a sound wave travels through one with varying acoustic impedance. Diffraction occurs with all waves, including sound waves, water waves, and electromagnetic waves such as visible light, X-rays and radio waves. As physical objects have wave-like properties (at the atomic level), diffraction also occurs with matter and can be studied according to the principles of quantum mechanics. Italian scientist Francesco Maria Grimaldi coined the word "diffraction" and was the first to record accurate observations of the phenomenon in 1665.

Richard Feynman Wrote

No-one has ever been able to define the difference between interference and diffraction satisfactorily. It is just a question of usage, and there is no specific, important physical difference between them.

He suggested that when there are only a few sources, say two, we call it interference, as in Young's slits, but with a large number of sources, the process is labelled diffraction.

While diffraction occurs whenever propagating waves encounter such changes, its effects are generally most pronounced for waves whose wavelength is roughly similar to the dimensions of the diffracting objects. If the obstructing object provides multiple, closely spaced openings, a complex pattern of varying intensity can result. This is due to the superposition, or interference, of different parts of a wave that travels to the observer by different paths.

The formalism of diffraction can also describe the way in which waves of finite extent propagate in free space. For example, the expanding profile of a laser beam, the beam shape of a radar antenna and the field of view of an ultrasonic transducer can all be analyzed using diffraction equations.

The effects of diffraction are often seen in everyday life. The most striking examples of diffraction are those involving light; for example, the closely spaced tracks on a CD or DVD act as a diffraction grating to form the familiar rainbow pattern seen when looking at a disk. This principle can be extended to engineer a grating with a structure such that it will produce any diffraction pattern desired; the hologram on a credit card is an example. Diffraction in the atmosphere by small particles can cause a bright ring to be visible around a bright light source like the sun or the moon. A shadow of a solid object, using light from a compact source, shows small fringes near its edges. The speckle pattern which is observed when laser light falls on an optically rough surface is also a diffraction phenomenon. When deli meat appears to be iridescent, that is diffraction off the meat fibres. All these effects are a consequence of the fact that light propagates as a wave.

Diffraction can occur with any kind of wave. Ocean waves diffract around jetties and other obstacles. Sound waves can diffract around objects, which is why one can still hear someone calling even when hiding behind a tree. Diffraction can also be a concern in some technical applications; it sets a fundamental limit to the resolution of a camera, telescope, or microscope.

History

The effects of diffraction of light were first carefully observed and characterized by Francesco Maria Grimaldi, who also coined the term *diffraction*, from the Latin *diffringere*, 'to break into pieces', referring to light breaking up into different directions. The results of Grimaldi's observations were published posthumously in 1665. Isaac Newton studied these effects and attributed them to *inflexion* of light rays. James Gregory (1638–1675) observed the diffraction patterns caused by a bird feather, which was effectively the first diffraction grating to be discovered. Thomas Young performed a celebrated experiment in 1803 demonstrating interference from two closely spaced slits. Explaining his results by interference of the waves emanating from the two different slits, he deduced that light must propagate as waves. Augustin-Jean Fresnel did more definitive studies and calculations of diffraction, made public in 1815 and 1818, and thereby gave great support to the wave theory of light that had been advanced by Christiaan Huygens and reinvigorated by Young, against Newton's particle theory.

Mechanism

Diffraction arises because of the way in which waves propagate; this is described by the Huygens–Fresnel principle and the principle of superposition of waves. The propagation of a wave can be visualized by considering every point on a wavefront as a point source for a secondary spherical wave. The wave displacement at any subsequent point is the sum of these secondary waves. When waves are added together, their sum is determined by the relative phases as well as the amplitudes of the individual waves so that the summed amplitude of the waves can have any value between zero and the sum of the individual amplitudes. Hence, diffraction patterns usually have a series of maxima and minima.

There are various analytical models which allow the diffracted field to be calculated, including the Kirchhoff-Fresnel diffraction equation which is derived from wave equation, the Fraunhofer diffraction approximation of the Kirchhoff equation which applies to the far field and the Fresnel diffraction approximation which applies to the near field. Most configurations cannot be solved analytically, but can yield numerical solutions through finite element and boundary element methods.

It is possible to obtain a qualitative understanding of many diffraction phenomena by considering how the relative phases of the individual secondary wave sources vary, and in particular, the conditions in which the phase difference equals half a cycle in which case waves will cancel one another out.

The simplest descriptions of diffraction are those in which the situation can be reduced to a two-dimensional problem. For water waves, this is already the case; water waves propagate only on the surface of the water. For light, we can often neglect one direction if the diffracting object extends in that direction over a distance far greater than the wavelength. In the case of light shining through small circular holes we will have to take into account the full three dimensional nature of the problem.

Diffraction of Light

Some examples of diffraction of light are considered below.

Single-slit Diffraction

A long slit of infinitesimal width which is illuminated by light diffracts the light into a series of circular waves and the wavefront which emerges from the slit is a cylindrical wave of uniform intensity.

A slit which is wider than a wavelength produces interference effects in the space downstream of the slit. These can be explained by assuming that the slit behaves as though it has a large number of point sources spaced evenly across the width of the slit. The analysis of this system is simplified if we consider light of a single wavelength. If the incident light is coherent, these sources all have the same phase. Light incident at a given point in the space downstream of the slit is made up of contributions from each of these point sources and if the relative phases of these contributions vary by 2∂ or more, we may expect to find minima and maxima in the diffracted light. Such phase differences are caused by differences in the path lengths over which contributing rays reach the point from the slit.

We can find the angle at which a first minimum is obtained in the diffracted light by the following reasoning. The light from a source located at the top edge of the slit interferes destructively with a source located at the middle of the slit, when the path difference between them is equal to $\lambda/2$. Similarly, the source just below the top of the slit will interfere destructively with the source located just below the middle of the slit at the same angle. We can continue this reasoning along the entire height of the slit to conclude that the condition for destructive interference for the entire slit is the same as the condition for destructive interference between two narrow slits a distance apart that is half the width of the slit. The path difference is given by $\frac{d\sin(\theta)}{2}$ so that the minimum intensity occurs at an angle θ_{min} given by

$$d\sin\theta_{min} = \lambda$$

where

- d is the width of the slit,
- θ_{min} is the angle of incidence at which the minimum intensity occurs, and
- $\lambda$is the wavelength of the light

A similar argument can be used to show that if we imagine the slit to be divided into four, six, eight parts, etc., minima are obtained at angles θ_n given by

$$d\sin\theta_n = n\lambda$$

where

- n is an integer other than zero.

There is no such simple argument to enable us to find the maxima of the diffraction pattern. The intensity profile can be calculated using the Fraunhofer diffraction equation as

$$I(\theta) = I_0 \operatorname{sinc}^2\left(\frac{d\pi}{\lambda}\sin\theta\right)$$

where

- $I(\theta)$ is the intensity at a given angle,
- I_0 is the original intensity, and
- the unnormalized sinc function above is given by sinc(x) = sin(x)/(x) if $x \neq 0$, and sinc(0) = 1

This analysis applies only to the far field, that is, at a distance much larger than the width of the slit.

Diffraction Grating

A diffraction grating is an optical component with a regular pattern. The form of the light diffracted by a grating depends on the structure of the elements and the number of elements present, but all gratings have intensity maxima at angles θ_m which are given by the grating equation

$$d\left(\sin\theta_m + \sin\theta_i\right) = m\lambda.$$

where

- θ_i is the angle at which the light is incident,
- d is the separation of grating elements, and
- m is an integer which can be positive or negative.

The light diffracted by a grating is found by summing the light diffracted from each of the elements, and is essentially a convolution of diffraction and interference patterns.

The figure shows the light diffracted by 2-element and 5-element gratings where the grating spacings are the same; it can be seen that the maxima are in the same position, but the detailed structures of the intensities are different.

Circular Aperture

The far-field diffraction of a plane wave incident on a circular aperture is often referred to as the Airy Disk. The variation in intensity with angle is given by

$$I(\theta) = I_0\left(\frac{2J_1(ka\sin\theta)}{ka\sin\theta}\right)^2,$$

where a is the radius of the circular aperture, k is equal to $2\pi/\lambda$ and J_1 is a Bessel function. The smaller the aperture, the larger the spot size at a given distance, and the greater the divergence of the diffracted beams.

General Aperture

The wave that emerges from a point source has amplitude ψ at location r that is given by the solution of the frequency domain wave equation for a point source (The Helmholtz Equation),

$$\nabla^2\psi + k^2\psi = \delta(\mathrm{r})$$

where $\delta(\mathrm{r})$ is the 3-dimensional delta function. The delta function has only radial dependence, so the Laplace operator (aka scalar Laplacian) in the spherical coordinate system simplifies to

$$\nabla^2\psi = \frac{1}{r}\frac{\partial^2}{\partial r^2}(r\psi)$$

By direct substitution, the solution to this equation can be readily shown to be the scalar Green's function, which in the spherical coordinate system (and using the physics time convention $e^{-i\omega t}$) is:

$$\psi(r) = \frac{e^{ikr}}{4\pi r}$$

This solution assumes that the delta function source is located at the origin. If the source is located at an arbitrary source point, denoted by the vector r' and the field point is located at the point r, then we may represent the scalar Green's function (for arbitrary source location) as:

$$\psi(\mathrm{r}\,|\,\mathrm{r}') = \frac{e^{ik|\mathrm{r}-\mathrm{r}'|}}{4\pi\,|\,\mathrm{r}-\mathrm{r}'\,|}$$

Therefore, if an electric field, $\mathrm{E}_{\mathrm{inc}}(x,y)$ is incident on the aperture, the field produced by this aperture distribution is given by the surface integral:

$$\Psi(r) \propto \iint_{\mathrm{aperture}} E_{inc}(x',y')\frac{e^{ik|\mathrm{r}-\mathrm{r}'|}}{4\pi\,|\,\mathrm{r}-\mathrm{r}'\,|}dx'dy',$$

where the source point in the aperture is given by the vector

$$\mathrm{r}' = x'\hat{\mathrm{x}} + y'\hat{\mathrm{y}}$$

In the far field, wherein the parallel rays approximation can be employed, the Green's function,

$$\psi(\mathrm{r}\,|\,\mathrm{r}') = \frac{e^{ik|\mathrm{r}-\mathrm{r}'|}}{4\pi\,|\,\mathrm{r}-\mathrm{r}'\,|}$$

simplifies to

$$\psi(\mathrm{r} \mid \mathrm{r}') = \frac{e^{ikr}}{4\pi r} e^{-ik(\mathrm{r}' \cdot \hat{\mathrm{r}})}$$

as can be seen in the figure to the right (click to enlarge).

The expression for the far-zone (Fraunhofer region) field becomes

$$\Psi(r) \propto \frac{e^{ikr}}{4\pi r} \iint_{\text{aperture}} E_{inc}(x', y') e^{-ik(\mathrm{r}' \cdot \hat{\mathrm{r}})} dx' dy',$$

Now, since

$$\mathrm{r}' = x'\hat{\mathrm{x}} + y'\hat{\mathrm{y}}$$

and

$$\hat{\mathrm{r}} = \sin\theta \cos\phi \hat{\mathrm{x}} + \sin\theta \sin\phi \hat{\mathrm{y}} + \cos\theta \hat{\mathrm{z}}$$

the expression for the Fraunhofer region field from a planar aperture now becomes,

$$\Psi(r) \propto \frac{e^{ikr}}{4\pi r} \iint_{\text{aperture}} E_{inc}(x', y') e^{-ik\sin\theta(\cos\phi x' + \sin\phi y')} dx' dy'$$

Letting,

$$k_x = k \sin\theta \cos\phi$$

and

$$k_y = k \sin\theta \sin\phi$$

the Fraunhofer region field of the planar aperture assumes the form of a Fourier transform

$$\Psi(r) \propto \frac{e^{ikr}}{4\pi r} \iint_{\text{aperture}} E_{inc}(x', y') e^{-i(k_x x' + k_y y')} dx' dy',$$

In the far-field / Fraunhofer region, this becomes the spatial Fourier transform of the aperture distribution. Huygens' principle when applied to an aperture simply says that the far-field diffraction pattern is the spatial Fourier transform of the aperture shape, and this is a direct by-product of using the parallel-rays approximation, which is identical to doing a plane wave decomposition of the aperture plane fields.

Propagation of a Laser Beam

The way in which the profile of a laser beam changes as it propagates is determined by diffraction. The output mirror of the laser is an aperture, and the subsequent beam shape is determined by that aperture. Hence, the smaller the output beam, the quicker it diverges.

Paradoxically, it is possible to reduce the divergence of a laser beam by first expanding it with one convex lens, and then collimating it with a second convex lens whose focal point is coincident with that of the first lens. The resulting beam has a larger aperture, and hence a lower divergence.

Diffraction-limited Imaging

The ability of an imaging system to resolve detail is ultimately limited by diffraction. This is because a plane wave incident on a circular lens or mirror is diffracted as described above. The light is not focused to a point but forms an Airy disk having a central spot in the focal plane with radius to first null of

$$d = 1.22\lambda N,$$

where λ is the wavelength of the light and N is the f-number (focal length divided by diameter) of the imaging optics. In object space, the corresponding angular resolution is

$$\sin\theta = 1.22\frac{\lambda}{D},$$

where D is the diameter of the entrance pupil of the imaging lens (e.g., of a telescope's main mirror).

Two point sources will each produce an Airy pattern – see the photo of a binary star. As the point sources move closer together, the patterns will start to overlap, and ultimately they will merge to form a single pattern, in which case the two point sources cannot be resolved in the image. The Rayleigh criterion specifies that two point sources can be considered to be resolvable if the separation of the two images is at least the radius of the Airy disk, i.e. if the first minimum of one coincides with the maximum of the other.

Thus, the larger the aperture of the lens, and the smaller the wavelength, the finer the resolution of an imaging system. This is why telescopes have very large lenses or mirrors, and why optical microscopes are limited in the detail which they can see.

Speckle Patterns

The speckle pattern which is seen when using a laser pointer is another diffraction phenomenon. It is a result of the superpostion of many waves with different phases, which are produced when a laser beam illuminates a rough surface. They add together to give a resultant wave whose amplitude, and therefore intensity varies randomly.

Patterns

Several qualitative observations can be made of diffraction in general:

- The angular spacing of the features in the diffraction pattern is inversely proportional to the dimensions of the object causing the diffraction. In other words: The smaller the diffracting object, the 'wider' the resulting diffraction pattern, and vice versa. (More precisely, this is true of the sines of the angles.)
- The diffraction angles are invariant under scaling; that is, they depend only on the ratio of the wavelength to the size of the diffracting object.
- When the diffracting object has a periodic structure, for example in a diffraction grating, the features generally become sharper. The third figure, for example, shows a comparison of a double-slit pattern with a pattern formed by five slits, both sets of slits having the same spacing, between the centre of one slit and the next.

Particle Diffraction

Quantum theory tells us that every particle exhibits wave properties. In particular, massive particles can interfere and therefore diffract. Diffraction of electrons and neutrons stood as one of the powerful arguments in favour of quantum mechanics. The wavelength associated with a particle is the de Broglie wavelength

$$\lambda = \frac{h}{p}$$

where h is Planck's constant and p is the momentum of the particle (mass × velocity for slow-moving particles).

For most macroscopic objects, this wavelength is so short that it is not meaningful to assign a wavelength to them. A sodium atom travelling at about 30,000 m/s would have a De Broglie wavelength of about 50 pico metres.

Because the wavelength for even the smallest of macroscopic objects is extremely small, diffraction of matter waves is only visible for small particles, like electrons, neutrons, atoms and small molecules. The short wavelength of these matter waves makes them ideally suited to study the atomic crystal structure of solids and large molecules like proteins.

Relatively larger molecules like buckyballs were also shown to diffract.

Bragg Diffraction

Diffraction from a three dimensional periodic structure such as atoms in a crystal is called Bragg diffraction. It is similar to what occurs when waves are scattered from a diffraction grating. Bragg diffraction is a consequence of interference between waves reflecting from different crystal planes. The condition of constructive interference is given by *Bragg's law*:

$$m\lambda = 2d \sin\theta$$

where

λ is the wavelength,

d is the distance between crystal planes,

θ is the angle of the diffracted wave.

and m is an integer known as the *order* of the diffracted beam.

Bragg diffraction may be carried out using either light of very short wavelength like X-rays or matter waves like neutrons (and electrons) whose wavelength is on the order of (or much smaller than) the atomic spacing. The pattern produced gives information of the separations of crystallographic planes d, allowing one to deduce the crystal structure. Diffraction contrast, in electron microscopes and x-topography devices in particular, is also a powerful tool for examining individual defects and local strain fields in crystals.

Coherence

The description of diffraction relies on the interference of waves emanating from the same source taking different paths to the same point on a screen. In this description, the difference in phase between waves that took different paths is only dependent on the effective path length. This does not take into account the fact that waves that arrive at the screen at the same time were emitted by the source at different times. The initial phase with which the source emits waves can change over time in an unpredictable way. This means that waves emitted by the source at times that are too far apart can no longer form a constant interference pattern since the relation between their phases is no longer time independent.

The length over which the phase in a beam of light is correlated, is called the coherence length. In order for interference to occur, the path length difference must be smaller than the coherence length. This is sometimes referred to as spectral coherence, as it is related to the presence of different frequency components in the wave. In the case of light emitted by an atomic transition, the coherence length is related to the lifetime of the excited state from which the atom made its transition.

If waves are emitted from an extended source, this can lead to incoherence in the transversal direction. When looking at a cross section of a beam of light, the length over which the phase is correlated is called the transverse coherence length. In the case of Young's double slit experiment, this would mean that if the transverse coherence length is smaller than the spacing between the two slits, the resulting pattern on a screen would look like two single slit diffraction patterns.

In the case of particles like electrons, neutrons and atoms, the coherence length is related to the spatial extent of the wave function that describes the particle.

Bitmap Image

In computing, a bitmap is a mapping from some domain (for example, a range of integers) to bits, that is, values which are zero or one. It is also called a bit array or bitmap index.

In computer graphics, when the domain is a rectangle (indexed by two coordinates), a bitmap gives a way to store a binary image, that is, an image in which each pixel is either black or white (or any two colours).

The more general term pixmap refers to a map of pixels, where each one may store more than two colours, thus using more than one bit per pixel. Often *bitmap* is used for this as well. In some contexts, the term *bitmap* implies one bit per pixel, while *pixmap* is used for images with multiple bits per pixel.

It is a type of memory organization or image file format used to store digital images. The term *bitmap* comes from the computer programming terminology, meaning just a *map of bits*, a spatially mapped array of bits. Now, along with *pixmap*, it commonly refers to the similar concept of a spatially mapped array of pixels. Raster images in general may be referred to as bitmaps or pixmaps, whether synthetic or photographic, in files or memory.

Many graphical user interfaces use bitmaps in their built-in graphics subsystems; for example, the Microsoft Windows and OS/2 platforms' GDI subsystem, where the specific format used is the *Windows and OS/2 bitmap file format*, usually named with the file extension of .BMP (or .DIB for *device-independent bitmap*). Besides BMP, other file formats that store literal bitmaps include InterLeaved Bitmap (ILBM), Portable Bitmap (PBM), X Bitmap (XBM), and Wireless Application Protocol Bitmap (WBMP). Similarly, most other image file formats, such as JPEG, TIFF, PNG, and GIF, also store bitmap images (as opposed to vector graphics), but they are not usually referred to as *bitmaps*, since they use compressed formats internally.

Pixel Storage

In typical uncompressed bitmaps, image pixels are generally stored with a colour depth of 1, 4, 8, 16, 24, 32, 48, or 64 bits per pixel. Pixels of 8 bits and fewer can represent either grayscale or indexed colour. An alpha channel (for transparency) may be stored in a separate bitmap, where it is similar to a grayscale bitmap, or in a fourth channel that, for example, converts 24-bit images to 32 bits per pixel.

The bits representing the bitmap pixels may be packed or unpacked (spaced out to byte or word boundaries), depending on the format or device requirements. Depending on the colour depth, a pixel in the picture will occupy at least n/8 bytes, where n is the bit depth.

For an uncompressed, packed within rows, bitmap, such as is stored in Microsoft DIB or BMP file format, or in uncompressed TIFF format, a lower bound on storage size for a n-bit-per-pixel (2^n colours) bitmap, in bytes, can be calculated as:

size = width • height • n/8, where height and width are given in pixels.

In the formula above, header size and colour palette size, if any, are not included. Due to effects of row padding to align each row start to a storage unit boundary such as a word, additional bytes may be needed.

Device-independent Bitmaps and BMP file Format

Microsoft has defined a particular representation of colour bitmaps of different colour depths, as an aid to exchanging bitmaps between devices and applications with a variety of internal representations. They called these device-independent bitmaps or DIBs, and the file format for them is called DIB file format or BMP file format. According to Microsoft support:

A device-independent bitmap (DIB) is a format used to define device-independent bitmaps in various colour resolutions. The main purpose of DIBs is to allow bitmaps to be moved from one device to another (hence, the device-independent part of the name). A DIB is an external format, in contrast to a device-dependent bitmap, which appears in the system as a bitmap object (created by an application...). A DIB is normally transported in metafiles (usually using the StretchDIBits() function), BMP files, and the Clipboard (CF_DIB data format).

Here, "device independent" refers to the format, or storage arrangement, and should not be confused with device-independent colour.

Other Bitmap File Formats

The X Window System uses a similar XBM format for black-and-white images, and XPM (*pixelmap*) for colour images. Numerous other uncompressed bitmap file formats are in use, though most not widely. For most purposes standardized compressed bitmap files such as GIF, PNG, TIFF, and JPEG are used; lossless compression in particular provides the same information as a bitmap in a smaller file size. TIFF and JPEG have various options. JPEG is usually lossy compression. TIFF is usually either uncompressed, or lossless Lempel-Ziv-Welch compressed like GIF. PNG uses deflate lossless compression, another Lempel-Ziv variant.

There are also a variety of "raw" image files, which store raw bitmaps with no other information; such raw files are just bitmaps in files, often with no header or size information (they are distinct from photographic raw image formats, which store raw unprocessed sensor data in a structured container such as TIFF format along with extensive image metadata).

Use of Dither in Textile Design

Dither is an intentionally applied form of noise used to randomize quantization error, preventing large-scale patterns such as colour banding in images. Dither is routinely used in processing of both digital audio and digital video data, and is often one of the last stages of audio production to compact disc.

A typical use of dither is: given an image in grey-scale, convert it to black and white, such that the density of black dots in the new image approximates the average level of grey in the original image.

The term "dither" was published in books on analog computation and hydraulically controlled guns shortly after the war. The concept of dithering to reduce quantization patterns was first applied by Lawrence G. Roberts in his 1961 MIT master's thesis and 1962 article though he did not use the term *dither*. By 1964 dither was being used in the modern sense described in this article.

In Digital Processing and Waveform Analysis

Dither is often used in digital audio and video processing, where it is applied to bit-depth transitions; it is utilized in many different fields where digital processing and analysis are used – especially waveform analysis. These uses include systems using digital signal processing, such as digital audio, digital video, digital photography, seismology, RADAR, weather forecasting systems and many more.

The premise is that quantization and re-quantization of digital data yields error. If that error is repeating and *correlated* to the signal, the error that results is repeating, cyclical, and mathematically determinable. In some fields, especially where the receptor is sensitive to such artifacts, cyclical errors yield undesirable artifacts. In these fields dither results in less determinable artifacts. The field of audio is a primary example of this. The human ear functions much like a Fourier transform, wherein it hears individual frequencies. The ear is therefore very sensitive to *distortion,* or additional frequency content that "colours" the sound differently, but far less sensitive to random noise at all frequencies.

Digital Audio

In audio, dither can be useful to break up periodic limit cycles, which are a common problem in digital filters. Random noise is typically less objectionable than the harmonic tones produced by limit cycles.

In a seminar paper published in the AES Journal, Lipshitz and Vanderkooy pointed out that different noise types, with different probability density functions (PDFs) behave differently when used as dither signals, and suggested optimal levels of dither signal for audio. Gaussian noise requires a higher level for full elimination of distortion than rectangular PDF or triangular PDF noise. Triangular PDF noise has the advantage of requiring a lower level of added noise to eliminate distortion and also minimizing 'noise modulation'. The latter refers to audible changes in the residual noise on low-level music that are found to draw attention to the noise.

In an analog system, the signal is *continuous*, but in a PCM digital system, the amplitude of the signal out of the digital system is limited to one of a set of fixed values or numbers. This process is called quantization. Each coded value is a discrete step... if a signal is quantized without using dither, there will be quantization distortion related to the original input signal... In order to prevent this, the signal is "dithered", a process that mathematically removes the harmonics or other highly undesirable distortions entirely, and that replaces it with a constant, fixed noise level.

The final version of audio that goes onto a compact disc contains only 16 bits per sample, but throughout the production process a greater number of bits are typically used to represent the sample. In the end, the digital data must be reduced to 16 bits for pressing onto a CD and distributing.

There are multiple ways to do this. One can, for example, simply discard the excess bits – called *truncation.* One can also *round* the excess bits to the nearest value. Each of these methods, however, results in predictable and determinable errors in the result. Take, for example, a waveform that consists of the following values:

1 2 3 4 5 6 7 8

If the waveform is reduced by, say, 20% then the following are the new values:

0.8 1.6 2.4 3.2 4.0 4.8 5.6 6.4

If these values are truncated it results in the following data:

0 1 2 3 4 4 5 6

If these values are rounded instead it results in the following data:

1 2 2 3 4 5 6 6

For any original waveform, the process of reducing the waveform amplitude by 20% results in regular errors. Take for example a sine wave that, for some portion, matches the values above. Every time the sine wave's value hit 3.2, the truncated result would be off by 0.2, as in the sample data above. Every time the sine wave's value hit 4.0, there would be no error since the truncated result would be off by 0.0, also shown above. The magnitude of this error changes regularly and repeatedly throughout the sine wave's cycle. It is precisely this error which manifests itself as distortion. What the ear hears as distortion is the additional content at discrete frequencies created by the regular and repeated quantization error.

A plausible solution would be to take the 2 digit number (say, 4.8) and round it one direction or the other. For example, it could be rounded to 5 one time and then 4 the next time. This would make the long-term average 4.5 instead of 4, so that over the long-term the value is closer to its actual value. This, on the other hand, still results in determinable (though more complicated) error. Every other time the value 4.8 comes up the result is an error of 0.2, and the other times it is "0.8. This still results in a repeating, quantifiable error.

Another plausible solution would be to take 4.8 and round it so that the first four times out of five it rounded up to 5, and the fifth time it rounded to 4. This would average out to exactly 4.8 over the long term. Unfortunately, however, it still results in repeatable and determinable errors, and those errors still manifest themselves as distortion to the ear (though oversampling can reduce this).

This leads to the *dither* solution. Rather than predictably rounding up or down in a repeating pattern, it is possible to round up or down in a random pattern. Dithering is a way to randomly toggle the results between 4 and 5 so that 80% of the time it ended up on 5 then it would average 4.8 over the long run but would have random, non-repeating error in the result.

If a series of random numbers between 0.0 and 0.9 (ex: 0.6, 0.1, 0.3, 0.6, 0.9, etc.) are calculated and we added to the results of the equation, two times out of ten the result will truncate back to 4 (if 0.0 or 0.1 are added to 4.8) and the rest of the times it will truncate to 5, but each given situation has a random 20% chance of rounding to 4 or 80% chance of rounding to 5. Over the long haul this will result in results that average to 4.8 and a quantization error that is random — or noise. This "noise" result is less offensive to the ear than the determinable distortion that would result otherwise.

Usage

Dither should be added to any low-amplitude or highly-periodic signal before any quantization or re-quantization process, in order to de-correlate the quantization noise from the input signal and to prevent non-linear behaviour (distortion); the lesser the bit depth, the greater the dither must be. The result of the process still yields distortion, but the distortion is of a random nature so the resulting noise is, effectively, de-correlated from the intended signal. Any bit-reduction process should add dither to the waveform before the reduction is performed.

Different Types

RPDF stands for "Rectangular Probability Density Function," equivalent to a roll of a die. Any number has the same random probability of surfacing.

TPDF stands for "Triangular Probability Density Function," equivalent to a roll of two dice (the sum of two independent samples of RPDF).

Gaussian PDF is equivalent to a roll of a large number of dice. The relationship of probabilities of results follows a bell-shaped, or Gaussian curve, typical of dither generated by analog sources such as microphone preamplifiers. If the bit depth of a recording is sufficiently great, that preamp noise will be sufficient to dither the recording.

Coloured Dither is sometimes mentioned as dither that has been filtered to be different from white noise. Some dither algorithms use noise that has more energy in the higher frequencies so as to lower the energy in the critical audio band.

Noise shaping is a filtering process that shapes the spectral energy of quantization error, typically to either de-emphasise frequencies to which the ear is most sensitive or separate the signal and noise bands completely. If dither is used, its final spectrum depends on whether it is added inside or outside the feedback loop of the noise shaper: if inside, the dither is treated as part of the error signal and shaped along with actual quantization error; if outside, the dither is treated as part of the original signal and linearises quantization without being shaped itself. In this case, the final noise floor is the sum of the flat dither spectrum and the shaped quantization noise. While real-world noise shaping usually includes in-loop dithering, it is also possible to use it without adding dither at all, in which case the usual harmonic-distortion effects still appear at low signal levels.

Which Types to Use

If the signal being dithered is to undergo further processing, then it should be processed with TPDF dither that has an amplitude of two quantization steps (so that the dither values computed range from, say, –1 to +1, or 0 to 2). This is the lowest power ideal dither, in that it does not introduce noise modulation (constant noise floor) and completely eliminates the harmonic distortion from *quantization*. If coloured dither is used at these intermediate processing stages then the frequency content can "bleed" into other, more noticeable frequency ranges and become distractingly audible.

If the signal being dithered is to undergo no further processing — it is being dithered to its final result for distribution — then coloured dither or noise shaping is appropriate, and can effectively lower the audible noise level by putting most of that noise in a frequency range where it is less critical.

Digital Photography and Image Processing

Dithering is a technique used in computer graphics to create the illusion of colour depth in images with a limited colour palette (colour quantization). In a dithered image, colours not available in the palette are approximated by a diffusion of coloured pixels from within the available palette. The human eye perceives the diffusion as a mixture of the colours within it. Dithered images, particularly those with relatively few colours, can often be distinguished by a characteristic graininess, or speckled appearance.

By its nature, dithering introduces a pattern into the image. The theory is that the image is supposed to be viewed from such a distance that the pattern is not discernible to the human eye. Unfortunately this is not typically the case and often the patterning is visible. In these circumstances it has been shown that a blue noise dither pattern is the least unsightly and distracting. The error diffusion techniques were some of the first methods to generate blue noise dithering patterns. However, other techniques, such as ordered dithering, can also generate blue noise dithering without the tendency to degenerate into areas with artifacts.

Examples

Reducing the colour depth of an image can often have significant visual side-effects. If the original image is a photograph, it is likely to have thousands, or even millions of distinct colours. The process of constraining the available colours to a specific *colour palette* effectively throws away a certain amount of colour information.

A number of factors can affect the resulting quality of a colour-reduced image. Perhaps most significant is the colour palette that will be used in the reduced image. For example, an original image may be reduced to the 216-colour "web-safe" colour palette. If the original pixel colours are simply translated into the closest available colour from the palette, no dithering occurs. Typically, this approach results in flat areas (contours) and a loss of detail, and may produce patches of colour that are significantly different from the original. Shaded or gradient areas may appear as *colour bands*, which may be distracting. The application of dithering can help to minimize such visual artifacts, and usually results in a better representation of the original. Dithering helps to reduce colour banding and flatness.

One of the problems associated with using a fixed colour palette is that many of the needed colours may not be available in the palette, and many of the available colours may not be needed; a fixed palette containing mostly shades of green would not be well-suited for images that do not contain many shades of green, for instance. The use of an optimized colour palette can be of benefit in such cases. An optimized colour palette is one in which the available colours are chosen based on how frequently they are used in the original source image. If the image is reduced based on an optimized palette, the result is often much closer to the original.

The number of colours available in the palette is also a contributing factor. If, for example, the palette is limited to only 16 colours, the resulting image could suffer from additional loss of detail, and even more pronounced problems with flatness and colour banding. Once again, dithering can help to minimize such artifacts.

Applications

Display hardware, including early computer video adapters and many modern LCDs used in mobile phones and inexpensive digital cameras, show a much smaller colour range than more advanced displays. One common application of dithering is to more accurately display graphics containing a greater range of colours than the hardware is capable of showing. For example, dithering might be used in order to display a photographic image containing millions of colours on video hardware that is only capable of showing 256 colours at a time. The 256 available colours would be used to generate a dithered approximation of the original image. Without dithering, the colours in the original image might simply be "rounded off" to the closest available colour, resulting in a new image that is a poor representation of the original. Dithering takes advantage of the human eye's tendency to "mix" two colours in close proximity to one another.

Some LCDs may use temporal dithering to achieve a similar effect. By alternating each pixel's colour value rapidly between two approximate colours in the panel's colour space (also known as Frame Rate Control), a display panel which natively supports 18-bit colour (6 bits per channel) can represent a 24-bit "true" colour image (8 bits per channel).

Dithering such as this, in which the computer's display hardware is the primary limitation on colour depth, is commonly employed in software such as web browsers. Since a web browser may be retrieving graphical elements from an external source, it may be necessary for the browser to perform dithering on images with too many colours for the available display. It was due to problems with dithering that a colour palette known as the "web-safe colour palette" was identified, for use in choosing colours that would not be dithered on displays with only 256 colours available.

But even when the total number of available colours in the display hardware is high enough when rendering full colour digital photographs, as those 15- and 16-bit RGB Hicolour 32,768/65,536 colour modes, banding can be evident to the eye, especially in large areas of smooth shade transitions (although the original image file has no banding at all). Dithering the 32 or 64 RGB levels will result in a pretty good "pseudo truecolour" display approximation, which the eye cannot resolve as *grainy*. Furthermore, images displayed on 24-bit RGB hardware (8 bits per RGB primary) can be dithered to simulate somewhat higher bit depth, and/or to minimize the loss of hues available after a gamma correction. High-end still image processing software commonly uses these techniques for improved display.

Another useful application of dithering is for situations in which the graphic file format is the limiting factor. In particular, the commonly-used GIF format is restricted to the use of 256 or fewer colours in many graphics editing programmes. Images in other file formats, such as PNG, may also have such a restriction imposed on them for the sake of a reduction in file size. Images such as these have a fixed colour palette defining all the colours that the image may use. For such situations, graphical editing software may be responsible for dithering images prior to saving them in such restrictive formats.

Dithering is analogous to the halftone technique used in printing. The recent widespread adoption of inkjet printers and their ability to print isolated dots has increased the use of dithering in printing. For this reason the term dithering is sometimes used interchangeably with the term halftone, particularly in association with digital printing.

A typical desktop inkjet printer can print just 15 colours (the combination of dot or no dot from cyan, magenta, yellow and black print heads), and some of these ink combinations are not useful because when the black ink is used it typically obscures any of the other colours. To reproduce a large range of colours, dithering is used. In densely printed areas, where the colour is dark the dithering is often not visible because the dots of ink merge producing a more uniform print. However, a close inspection of the light areas of a print where the dithering has placed dots much further apart reveals the tell-tale dots of dithering.

Algorithms

There are several algorithms designed to perform dithering. One of the earliest, and still one of the most popular, is the Floyd–Steinberg dithering algorithm, developed in 1975. One of the strengths of this algorithm is that it minimizes visual artifacts through an error-diffusion process; error-diffusion algorithms typically produce images that more closely represent the original than simpler dithering algorithms.

Dithering methods include:

- *Thresholding* (also average dithering): each pixel value is compared against a fixed threshold. This may be the simplest dithering algorithm there is, but it results in immense loss of detail and contouring.
- *Random dithering* was the first attempt (at least as early as 1951) to remedy the drawbacks of thresholding. Each pixel value is compared against a random threshold, resulting in a staticky image. Although this method doesn't generate patterned artifacts, the noise tends to swamp the detail of the image. It is analogous to the practice of mezzotinting.
- *Patterning* dithers using a fixed pattern. For each of the input values a fixed pattern is placed in the output image. The biggest disadvantage of this technique is that the output image is larger (by a factor of the fixed pattern size) than the input pattern.
- *Ordered dithering* dithers using a "dither matrix". For every pixel in the image the value of the pattern at the corresponding

location is used as a threshold. Neighbouring pixels do not affect each other, making this form of dithering suitable for use in animations. Different patterns can generate completely different dithering effects. Though simple to implement, this dithering algorithm is not easily changed to work with free-form, arbitrary palettes.

  - A *Halftone dithering* matrix produces a look similar to that of halftone screening in newspapers. This is a form of clustered dithering, in that dots tend to cluster together. This can help hide the adverse effects of blurry pixels found on some older output devices. The primary use for this method is in offset printing and laser printers, in both these devices the ink or toner prefers to clump together and will not form the isolated dots generated by the other dithering methods.
  - A *Bayer matrix* produces a very distinctive cross-hatch pattern.
  - A matrix tuned for *blue noise* (such as those generated by the void-and-cluster method) produces a look closer to that of an error diffusion dither method.

- *Error-diffusion dithering* is a feedback process that diffuses the quantization error to neighbouring pixels.
  - Floyd–Steinberg dithering only diffuses the error to neighbouring pixels. This results in very fine-grained dithering.
  - Jarvis, Judice, and Ninke dithering diffuses the error also to pixels one step further away. The dithering is coarser, but has fewer visual artifacts. It is slower than Floyd–Steinberg dithering because it distributes errors among 12 nearby pixels instead of 4 nearby pixels for Floyd–Steinberg.
  - Stucki dithering is based on the above, but is slightly faster. Its output tends to be clean and sharp.
  - Burkes dithering is a simplified form of Stucki dithering that is faster, but less clean than Stucki dithering.
- Error-diffusion dithering (continued):
  - Sierra dithering is based on Jarvis dithering, but it's faster while giving similar results.
  - Two-row Sierra is the above method modified by Sierra to improve its speed.

- Filter Lite is an algorithm by Sierra that is much simpler and faster than Floyd–Steinberg, while still yielding similar (according to Sierra, better) results.
- Atkinson dithering, developed by Apple programmer Bill Atkinson, resembles Jarvis dithering and Sierra dithering, but it's faster. Another difference is that it doesn't diffuse the entire quantization error, but only three quarters. It tends to preserve detail well, but very light and dark areas may appear blown out.

In Optical Fibre Systems

Stimulated Brillouin Scattering (SBS) is a nonlinear optical effect that limits the launched optical power in fibre optic systems. This power limit can be increased by dithering the transmit optical centre frequency, typically implemented by modulating the laser's bias input.

Applications in Electronics

An artificial jitter (dither) can be used in electronics for reducing quantization errors in A/D-Elements. Another common application is to get through EMC tests by smearing out single frequency peaks.

Bibliography

Adan, John McKay: *Encyclopedia of Textiles,* Prentice-Hall, Inc., Englewood Cliffs, N.J., 1972.

Alfred Jenks & Son: *Illustrated Catalogue of Machines Built by Alfred Jenks & Son, Manufacturers of Every Variety of Cotton and Wool Carding, Spinning, and Weaving Machinery, in All Its Departments*, Alfred Jenks & Son, Bridesburg, Pa., 1853.

Brill, T.: *Light: its Interaction with Art and Antiquities*, Plenum Press, New York, London, 1980.

Brouwer, J: *The Makers of the World, Caste, Craft and Mind of South India Artisans*, Oxford Press, Delhi, 1995.

Buhler, Alfred, and Eberhard Fischer: *Indian Tie-Dyed Fabrics,* Calico Museum, Ahhmedabad, 1980.

Burnard, J: *Chintz and Cotton: India's Textile Gift to the World,* Kangaroo Press, Kenthurst, NSW, 1994.

Cole, George S.: *A Complete Dictionary of Dry Goods*. W. B. Conkey Company, Chicago, 1892.

Comaraswamy, AK.: *The Indian Craftsman*, Munshiram Manogarlal Publishers, New Delhi, 1909.

Cooper, Ilay and John Gillow: *Arts and Crafts of India*, Thames and Hudson, 1996.

Dawson, T. L.: *Digital Image Design, Data Encoding and Formation of Printed Images,* University of Manchester, UK, 1998.

Denny, Elizabeth: *Textile Fabrics,* J.B. Lippincott Company, Philadelphia and London, 1928.

Diamond, A.S.: *Handbook of Imaging Materials*, Marcel Dekker, Inc., New York, 1991.

Dyer, Grace Goldena: *Fabrics and How to Know Them*, The Riverside Press, Cambridge, Mass, 1923.

Eldred, N.: *Chemistry for the Graphic Arts*, Hatcher Trade Press Inc., San Carlos, CA, 1992.

Espinasse, Francis: *Lancashire Worthies*, Simpkin, Marshall, & Co., London, 2010.

Geddes, Elisabeth and Moyra McNeill: *Blackwork Embroidery*, Dover, New York, 1976.

Hardingham, Martin: *The Fabric Catalog*, Pocket Books, New York, 1978.

Harmuth, Louis: *Dictionary of Textiles,* Fairchild Publishing Company, New York, 1920.

Hawkyard, C.: *Substrate Preparation for Ink-jet Printing*, University of Manchester, UK, 2001.

Hollen, Norma and Jane Saddler: *Modern Textiles*, Burgess Publishing Company, Minneapolis, 1952.

Humphries, Mary: *Fabric Reference,* Prentice Hall, Upper Saddle River, N.J., 2000.

Jayaker, P.: *A Neglected Group of Indian Ikat Fabrics*, Journal of Indian Textile History, Calico Museum of Textiles, Marg Publications, Ahmedabad, 1979.

Kadolph, Sara J. and Anna L. Langford: *Textiles,* Prentice Hall, Upper Saddle River, N.J., 2002.

Kleeberg, Irene Cumming: *The Butterick Fabric Handbook: A Consumer's Guide to Fabrics for Clothing and Home Furnishings*, Butterick Publishing, New York, 1975.

Meller, Susan and Joost Elffers: *Textile Designs: Two Hundred Years of European and American Patterns Organized by Motif, Style, Color, Layout, and Period*, Harry N. Abrams, New York, 2002.

Montgomery, Florence M.: *Textiles in America, 1650-1870*, W. W. Norton & Company, New York, 2007.

Parker, Julie: *All About Wool: A Fabric Dictionary and Swatchbook,* Rain City Publishing, Seattle, 1996.

Ramaswamy, V.: *Textiles and Weaver in Medieval S. India,* Oxford Press, Delhi, 1985.

Schaeffer, Claire: *Fabric Sewing Guide*, Krause Publications, Cincinnati, 2008.

Tortora, Phyllis G. and Robert S. Merkel: *Fairchild's Dictionary of Textiles,* Fairchild Publications, New York 1996.

Tozer, Jane and Sarah Levitt: *Fabric of Society: A Century of People and Their Clothes 1770-1870*, Laura Ashley Press, New York, 1998.

Tyler, D. J.: *Textile Digital Printing Technologies: Textile Progress*, Manchester Metropolitan University, UK, 1998.

Index

O

P

R

S

T

V

W

❑❑❑